ON THE ROAD TO **NIRVANA**

"Like nothing else I've read in the past decade, Gina Arnold's book brought back to me how it feels to be a fan, and to care desperately about rock 'n' roll."
Charles Shaar Murray

"Freewheeling, funny and deeply felt, *On the Road to Nirvana* is the frank diary of a seasoned critic and subterranean camp follower as she plumbs the murky aquifer that would feed mainstream rock 'n' roll in the eighties and nineties. Mirroring the common search for esprit in culture despoiled by corruption and social espionage, Gina Arnold's personal chronicle celebrates hard-core rock as candid self-definition and heartfelt destination."
Timothy White, editor-in-chief of *Billboard* and author of the award-winning *Rock Lives*

"... a wonderfully vivid guide to American independent rock of the last fifteen years."
Irish Times

"... a cohesive and valuable version of a largely untold story."
Independent on Sunday

At age four, Gina Arnold was taken by her parents to her first rock concert, the Grateful Dead at Palo Alto. She has hated the Dead ever since. She attended the University of California at Berkeley, where bands like X, the Go-Gos, and Faith No More played in the basement of her co-op. She has worked for the *San Jose Mercury News* and the *Los Angeles Times*, and currently freelances for publications including *Rolling Stone, L.A. Weekly, Elle* and *Entertainment Weekly*. She is a former NCAA champion swimmer and is also still a competitive member of the US Diving Association.

On the Road to Nirvana is Gina Arnold's first book. Her follow-up, *KISS THIS: Punk in the Present Tense*, is also published by Pan Books.

ON THE ROAD TO
NIRVANA

BY GINA ARNOLD

PAN BOOKS

First published 1993 by St. Martin's Press, Inc., New York

First published in Great Britain 1993 by Picador as *Route 666: On the Road to Nirvana*

This edition published 1998 by Pan Books
an imprint of Macmillan Publishers Ltd, 25 Eccleston Place, London SW1W 9NF and Basingstoke

Associated companies throughout the world

ISBN 0 330 34370 X

9 8 7 6 5 4

A CIP catalogue record for this book is available from the British Library.

Phototypeset by Intype London Ltd
Printed and bound in Great Britain by Mackays of Chatham

CONTENTS

ACKNOWLEDGMENTS

In America, this book was originally titled *Route 666*—a facetious, slangy term meaning, I'm now ashamed to say in the light of subsequent events, "the road to hell." It was first published in the summer of 1993, and barring these first two paragraphs, the entire text was finished on 14 December 1992—sixteen months before Kurt Cobain committed suicide, by a gun shot to his head. In retrospect I realize that this book is less about how it was, and more about how I wanted things to be. Certainly if I had written—or rewritten—any part of it after 8 April, 1994, it would be a darker and more negative story. It could even have been so at the time if I hadn't been so gravely blinded by naiveté and hope.

Nowadays I worry a lot about just where things went wrong. I wonder if there was anything I, personally, could have done differently to have made things not turn out how they did. I miss Kurt daily and I miss Nirvana more, but most of all I miss feeling how I felt about music back then: jubilant, and excited, and triumphant. But this book may at least serve as a document of how me and my tribe felt at the time these things were happening. I wrote it as a celebration of an era; I did not know it would turn out to be a tragic one.

When I started writing this book, a lot of people who were getting involved expressed their dismay at the apparent one-sidedness of each chapter. They felt that the description of their own scene was being left solely in the hands of one or at most two different people whom I relied on for my information, especially in the cities—such as Minneapolis and D.C.—where I've never been myself (because I was always kind of everywhere and nowhere, watching and imagining it all from alone in my room). They felt that too many people's names were being left out of the telling, and certainly there is a lot of truth in that accusation: in every city I mention here, hundreds of people contributed as much or more than the bands that are written about. Record store owners, club bookers, college radio deejays, and us plain fans have all, over the years, created this incredible network, this rich underground life, and respect is thoroughly due.

The sad fact is, given the time that I had at my disposal (like none) and the time period—twelve years—I was covering, it wouldn't have been possible to do the exhaustive interviewing of everyone involved. Besides, after years of writing abbreviated twelve-hundred-word stories in newspapers and magazines, I really wanted to give certain people a good long stretch to tell their tale in. So I settled on doing a few extremely broad overviews, making my story into a mythic, rather than specific, look at this life. It's clear to me that I could have interviewed anyone who worked in college radio, anyone who ran a record label, or wrote a fanzine or opened a club, any band member, any fan—anyone who was there at the time, in Minneapolis, or Boston, or Athens, or Seattle—and gotten as good or better of an overview of this life. Another author might have focused on Sonic Youth in place of Jane's Addiction, or interviewed Bob Mould instead of Paul Westerberg, or Candice instead of Calvin, or Henry Rollins instead of Mike Watt; made any number of like substitutions, but it would all have turned into the very same tale. The stories they told might have been entirely different, but the book itself would have been essentially the same. Each place I wrote about deserves a book of its own—preferably one written by someone who was there all along.

I still must apologize to the hundreds of people whose points of view were left out of this particular telling, but I look forward to reading their comments somewhere else, somewhere soon. This book, however, could not have been written without the willing participation of everyone mentioned herein and tons of other people as well. But particular thanks must be given to my family for services rendered: my sister Vivien for fetch-and-carriage, entertainment, sympathy, and patience, and my brother Corry for similar services.

Thanks must be given also to my parents and, of course, my long-suffering friend Isabelle for putting up with all my bullshit and never once complaining: without her constant help and encouragement, this book would never have happened. She also got me started by thinking up the sentence "I grew up thinking that everything had already happened," as I sat in front of the computer one day, stumped for an opening line.

Greil Marcus is the person most responsible for getting me started on this book. Additionally, his moral support and his inspiring work together have united in keeping me writing at times when I might otherwise have quit.

Additionally, Ms. Kelly Horan was my invaluable computer expert. Glenn Morrow provided tons of background information and more moral support. John Silva and Gold Mountain Management were never less than accommodating. Scott Becker, Mark Kemp, and Lisa Fancher kept on faxing me stuff at a moment's notice, ever without complaint. Jason Cohen's M.A. thesis came in handy in the end-crunch. Fugazi's mere existence kept my spirits up throughout this entire journey, and thoughtfully provided me with tapes of the shows mentioned herein.

To its individual members: Kurt Cobain and Courtney Love were accessible and helpful throughout the writing of this tale. Eddie Vedder, Dave Grohl, and Shelli and Krist Novoselic were also totally cool. Ted Mico's invaluable help made all the difference to the Lollapalooza chapters. Debbie Fox has been (and is) a generous and funny friend, and also inadvertently saved me from certain death in Berlin by introducing me to Mata Hoffmann, who was another total sweetheart. The Young Fresh Fellows' extreme good nature in letting me tag along on their tour of Europe last April still stands as a career highlight. Best love to everyone who attended any of those shows.

Thanks must also be given to everyone at the IPU Convention, everyone at Sub Pop Records, everyone who contributed fliers, particularly Jill Fonaas in New York, Dave Clingan in Portland, Clea Hantman in San Diego, Debbie Shane in San Francisco, Kim Warnick in Seattle, and everyone at BGP. Story ideas that were funded and/or initiated by the *San Diego Reader* and *Option* magazine generated much of the stuff herein, and some of those stories were suggested by the ever-resourceful Ms. Julie Lovering, née Farman. Portions of Chapters 9, 13, and 15 first appeared in *Option* magazine. Portions of Chapter 17 appeared in the *L.A. Weekly.* Chapter 16 appeared in the *San Diego Reader.* Chapter 2 was rejected in its entirety by *Image* magazine in San Francisco. This book is dedicated to Frances Bean Cobain, Gina Van Italie Morrow, Hannah Henrietta Kaye, and all the other baby riot grrrls whose time is still to come.

INTRODUCTION
BEGIN THE BEGIN

Music does my wishing for me.
– Exene Cervenka, 1984

HONOLULU: "I hope you have good health insurance," Debbie says anxiously. We're standing in a back alley in Honolulu, getting ready to go into the Nirvana show at Pink's Garage. All around us the surfer boys are standing by their cars, changing their karate slippers for Mexican army boots. The two of us look down at our legs apprehensively. Two minutes later we are jammed into the club so tight we can't even sway. There's water coming off the walls—wood sweats, don't you know—and as for our faces, they've just poured out every ounce of moisture in our bodies and then dried off immediately from the heat. I catch a glimpse of my forearm, on which, earlier in the day, I'd drawn the K shield symbol in indelible ink on the same spot as Kurt Cobain's tattoo: now both it and the club's stamp have completely disappeared from my flesh. I feel like I'm on the planet in *Dune*.

Then the room roars. Nirvana is onstage. I can just see the tippy tops of their pointed little heads. They begin with the song "Aneurysm," there's a quick lurch left, and I'm lifted off my feet, carried forward on an exoskeletal tide, as the entire room starts shrieking and stomping martially in unison along with the band. The beat slows down, and Kurt approaches the mike, by which time, along with everyone else, I think I'm actually holding my breath. *Come on over and do the twist.* He cracks the hard *t* like a bullet—ping!—and the audience moans. "Aaaahhh-ow!" *Overdo it and have a fit!*

"Aaaaah-ow."

Love you so much, it makes me sick . . .

"Aaaaah-ow."

Come on over and shoot the shit . . .

"Aaaah-ow . . ." And this time the whole room pauses, as if with the beat. There's a palpable gasp as our lungs expand with his. Then: *"Beat me out of it!"* we bellow all together. *"Beat me out of it."* For the tiniest second, we stand rock still, catching what breath we have. Then BOOM; BOOM! The band begins the verse, and we leap heavenward again. My feet don't find the ground for a full minute and a half, and by the time they do I've been carried away on a tide of flesh. Everyone's bumping heedlessly into one another, skin slapping sinew and then—schwack!—sticking. And yet our bodies have suddenly lost all sexual properties and have become mere tissue. It has happened at last. We are finally free of suggestion.

An hour later we burst out on the pavement, sopping wet. Nirvana fans were pouring out all around us. The alley was full of hefty boys in backward ball caps, all shirtless, their faces glowing red with the mysterious exertions inside. Many of them had no shoes on; my own legs were mud-spattered, and my green frock had somehow acquired a big hole nowhere near a seam. We milled about dazedly in the warm Hawaiian night—almost satiated, almost postcoital. Quickly, Debbie and I ran across the bigger boulevards to the ocean, where we plunged into the surf.

And then, I remember—I will always remember—looking up at the lights of the high-rise Hilton Hawaiian Village and thinking: Somewhere behind one of those cubelike balconies, Kurt and Courtney were anticipating their imminent wedding, while all around them, surrounded and confusing, Middle America in its rawest, ugliest, newlywed state slept peacefully, entirely unaware of the monster in its midst. I looked up at that hotel that night from my secret offshore vantage point and thought blissfully of kings and queens and conquering heroes, of the Trojan Horse and the French Revolution and that part of the Bible where it says that the meek shall inherit the earth. I floated on my back and stared at the shoreline, and as I did so my mind turned idly on the thought of nearby Pearl Harbor. I felt like an explosion had gone off a long, long way away and now we were bathing placidly in the warmth of its rays. If war were cathartic, if war were a happy thing, if war were like the Special Olympics and everyone went home the winner, then this is what it would be like when it was over. You know how the Eskimos have three hundred words for snow because it's the most important facet of their life? In America, there should be more synonyms for violence, including one that does not imply either injury or rage. There should be more words for success.

ONE

BLEW

ONE
GOOD TO GO

Don't doubt yourself.
– Madonna

I grew up thinking that everything had already happened. The Beatles, the Beach Boys, Beethoven, Bread. That Elvis Presley crushed McCarthyism in America, the Beatles elected JFK, and the Rolling Stones were responsible for the rise and fall of Robert Kennedy. After which the Doors singlehandedly ended the war in Vietnam. I grew up thinking that rock music mattered, but that everything worth hearing had already been laid down on vinyl, that the glorious days were long since passed. Clad in bulky bad clothing of beige and baby blue, my fat generation would be allowed—if we were very good and very lucky—to chronicle its history. We'd be worshipful little sisters and brothers, timid imitations of our older, better forebears, our minds made by force of circumstance—read: classic rock radio—into some kind of collective Homer, passing down the fucking lyrics of "Teach Your Children" from generation to generation. In short, I grew up thinking I was born too late.

And then one night I went to see the Sex Pistols, and from then on I knew that I'd been completely wrong. I hadn't been born late at all. It was just that everybody else had been entirely premature, doomed to incubate things for better days to come. I was just a child then, a tubby and insecure white suburban high schooler, but when I saw the Sex Pistols, I went totally ballistic. A great chasm of possibility immediately yawned open, a canyon of hope that simply hadn't been there before. And I leapt into its breach, my friends. I dove on in.

Punk meant a lot of things to me—it meant freedom and

violence and announcing your discontent with society as it was; it meant being able to recognize your utter alienation while simultaneously entering a whole new and more satisfying community of outcasts—a sort of "Island of Misfit Toys" for human beings. But one thing it never seemed to promise was mainstream success. Hearing "Because the Night" and "Psycho Killer" on AM radio in the late seventies was all very well, but for punk rock to have really succeeded on its own bloody terms, I knew it would have to change the entire economic structure of the industry. It would have to create, say, an entirely new network of finance and reward: a system of labels and artists and entrepreneurs, a chain of new radio stations and record stores and nightclubs, catering to a new community, all systems go, to a world full of busy workers.

Then and only then, maybe, one day, when those people had striven hard enough, the rest of the world would wake up.

And one day it did. I get angry when I hear people say that Nirvana's music is a rehash of negativity, that it's depressing and sloppy: those same people don't question the impact of the Beatles, or the sheerly evocative pleasures of anything on Motown. Nirvana's music—grunge music—reflects a time, my time. And my time has its own history, its own leaders, its own rules. It's not merely that I'd rather hear good music on the radio than bad: it's that I think people liking good music is indicative of better things. It's like having a good President rather than a bad one. It's not that everything will change all at once, it's that at least the people have voted for better principles. Nirvana's being on the radio means my own values are winning: I'm no longer in the opposition.

I knew this the moment I saw Nirvana play in Hawaii that night, its members leaping, guitars and all, onto a surface of human bodies that roiled beneath them as furiously as the ocean at Haleiwa. I knew it two months earlier, when Nirvana played to sixteen thousand screaming fans at the Cow Palace of San Francisco on New Year's Eve: *Nevermind* had reached number one on the Billboard charts that very week, and Nirvana's manager was yelling at someone backstage for taking too many beers. I looked at him unbelievingly: "But John! You guys are millionaires now!" and he struck his forehead with his fist.

At that time, Nirvana had been touring nonstop since June (including a slot on the Reading Festival lineup, which they'd headline next year) then in the United States, then in Australia and Japan, and now, two last gigs in Honolulu before heading home for a four-month rest. It was almost exactly a year since they'd finished recording *Nevermind,* ten months since I first met them, eight since they'd been so broke that they'd had to pawn their amps to buy tickets back to Seattle for a weekend visit.

In that time, Kurt had met Courtney Love, whom he'd marry the day after the Honolulu show. He'd alienated everyone from his band members to *Rolling Stone* readers to Weird Al Yankovic. (*"The lyrics sheet's so hard to find, what are the words, oh nevermind, don't know, don't know, don't know, don't know . . ."*) He had achieved, as they say in the record business, "world domination": meaning that when I went to Europe a couple of weeks after the Hawaii show, every alleyway and construction site from Copenhagen to Madrid was sporting *Nevermind* posters. You couldn't walk round a corner without spotting Kurt, Krist, and Dave floating jubilantly in blue liquid.

Between its September release and New Year's Eve of 1991, 3.5 million people bought *Nevermind.* They did so in part because MTV played the shit out of the video for "Smells Like Teen Spirit"—a sepia-toned art flick that portrays high school as a dusty, brown sea of misery liberated only by anger. But, though MTV and Nirvana's record company, Geffen, like to claim that they "created" *Nevermind,* in fact the album sold genuinely well from the second it was released, entirely on merit. Its expression of early-nineties zeitgeist was so strong that it leapt out of stores seemingly of its own accord, reflecting the public's true will and not just that of radio and the record industry. Its essence reminded listeners that even life in beige mini-malls could be a dangerous and suggestive thing, that apathy and dumbness were a form of surrender that didn't need to occur just yet.

But more than merely instigating a campaign of name recognition and superhype, Cobain's songs had inspired a kind of defiance of the norm that augured strangely for the year—an election year—to come. When I heard that *Nevermind,* an album whose first line is "Load up on drugs and bring your friends," had gone to number one the first week of 1992, my first thought was, "Bush will not be reelected."

And when the notes of *Nevermind* faded briefly from America's minds, main man Cobain's scraggly, pinwheel-eyed presence then reared up in the media—wearing a yellow ball gown on "Headbanger's Ball," wearing a holey sweater and a Flipper shirt on "Saturday Night Live," wearing a hand-lettered T-shirt that said "Corporate Magazines Still Suck" on the cover of *Rolling Stone*—thus personally negating once and for all that scariest of all scenarios that we as adults have so often feared: the possibility that life might always be like high school, with the same percentage of popular people always snubbing everyone else at the lunch tables.

Of course, when Nirvana refuted that theory and subsequently went to number one, the popular people went berserk. "Marketing strategy or fluke?" asked *The New York Times,* aghast. *Rolling Stone* assigned a reporter to go out to Aberdeen, Washington, where Kurt Cobain was raised, and hang out in bars with rednecks, to see what they had wrought. Then the underground began to carp, and finally, the mainstream press, titillated as usual by rumors of heroin use and worse, began an all-out campaign to turn Nirvana into a national cartoon.

In fact, all these people had missed the point entirely. The only person who really got it down on paper was Blake Babies singer Juliana Hatfield. She put it in a song. *"Here comes the song I love so much, makes me wanna go and fuck shit up. Now I've got Nirvana in my head, I'm so glad I'm not dead . . ."*

The thing is, lots of shit albums go to number one—Mariah Carey, Def Leppard, Skid Row. And a bunch of other bands you'll never hear or care about again often sell in the millions.

But Nirvana's arrival at the top of the heap is different, because Nirvana comes from a different place altogether. They came from my world, the world of the underground, where, Robert Christgau once said, "bohemian dreams still burn vividly."

My bohemian dreams began so long ago that I can't trace their birth. It may have been as far back as when I read *Vile Bodies* and *On the Road*, books about people who had drawn fierce borders between themselves and society, lines that they subsequently forced the rest of the world to cross. Or perhaps it was a little later, in the pages of *Creem* magazine, where writers like Jaan Uhelszki and Lester Bangs created in my mind a strange portrait of a tiny world where everybody dressed cool, made witty remarks, and was in possession of great record collections.

That, after all, is my poor generation's symbol of a roving mind: great record collections in cardboard boxes, kept the way monks hoarded literature from marauding pagan masses. Piled up against the walls of the bedrooms of long-suffering—"Honey, can't you get rid of some of the stuff in the basement?" (*absolutely not*)—moms. Record collections that signified the soul. Instead of knowing charming and witty men, instead of knowing Neal Cassady or Dennis Hopper, I was going to be stuck in the late twentieth century eating fro-yo and Doritos with a bunch of dorks in dorm rooms, poring over old copies of New York Dolls albums and *Rolling Stones*, discussing the merits and demerits of *Metal Machine Music*, pretending I liked David Bowie a lot more than I actually do.

This, I knew, would be a pretty pathetic substitute for life in swingin' London circa 1965 or downtown New York or western Hollywood circa 1969. But, looking around my vanilla suburb, I saw that I had no other hope. Aesthetically my life was so unpleasing. In California in the seventies, popular art—what one saw of it—was by Patrick Nagel and Peter Max, and even Roy Lichtensteins or Wayne Thiebauds are hardly things of great beauty. Fashions were at their most hideous: my friends and I wore shapeless painter's pants and overalls and work shirts, brown platform shoes, wide-lapelled jackets in dueling neutrals, and on occasion, haltertops that showed off our indifferent figures. The buildings in my community were gray and square, while the radio blared out cheesy disco songs unendingly for the entire continuum of my first twenty years. Driving to swim practice every morning at six A.M. this was me: internally screaming, "Change the station, change the station!" while all around me the team sings along. "Burn baby burn, burn! Disco Inferno; burn baby burn, burn!" Ugly, ugly, ugliness, that was all I knew.

But I also knew I ought not to complain. Economically speaking, my brother and my sister and I had been born into the richest era and richest circumstances and the richest area that the middle classes would ever see. Externally, our lives were of the grimmest suburban excess, all wide green streets and big beige shopping malls and three square meals a day, plus lots of loose change for after-school snacks as long as you remembered to strap on your bike light before you rode home from swim practice, in which case your mom would kill you and that would be the end of your so-called happy life.

As my brother used to put it, we suffered a tragically happy childhood.

That's where I came from externally. But internally, I longed to find a place of glamour and romance, where smart people stayed up all night and shocked the bourgeoisie, and the more I thought about it, the less hope I had. Not only were history and economics not on my side, neither was my gender.

I remember when I realized that white girls from the suburbs get no respect. It was at a Bruce Springsteen concert in 1978. My friend Megan and I were sitting in the balcony at Winterland, listening all rapt to "Racing in the Streets." At the time, I swear to you, I thought the song was all about me and Megan, cruising up El Camino Real in her next-door neighbors' two-door Fiat, which we were allowed to borrow sometimes to make ourselves feel cool, because we had the kind of parents who understood that Hondas really didn't cut it. That, I thought, was the American experience. That, I thought, if I thought at all, was a sign of Bruce's true greatness, that he could write a song that was ostensibly about the East Coast blue-collar working class, but was actually about two suburban white girls in a middle-class suburb of California.

And then one day a few years later, I suddenly thought, "But that's absurd!" Lying out by the neighbors' pools in our bikinis, Tabs in hand, idly paging through *Vogue,* listening to Bruce, gabbing about guys . . . I realized: that's not what Bruce was talking about at all! That's not what anybody's talking about in art, except derogatorily, as a big huge burn on the girls themselves, like in *Desperately Seeking Susan* or "Beverly Hills 90210." It is not a positive experience, according to high-brow art and literature and music, it is a negative one. Because nobody respects middle-class white girls from the suburbs, not even middle-class white girls from the suburbs themselves. Black women from the inner city, yes. They're respected in pop culture. Men of all colors and nationalities, whatever their experience: rural, working-class, rich white dudes fishing in Idaho or climbing mountains or seeking solitude in New Mexico, yes. Older guys with graying temples musing about their divorces in New England, sure. Gay men in groovy outfits, speaking out passionately about homophobia and AIDS, are given great gobs of credence by the glitterati of Hollywood. But where do you see the middle-class white girl, except portrayed as neurotic or crazy or a bitch? The serious women, the politicians, the activists, the doctors—even Madonna is reviled by most people, for her canniness, for supposedly using people, for everything she stands for.

Of course, they've brought it on themselves, the rich white girls from the suburbs. They've been spoiled and brainless and jealous of one another, they've sought after the shallowest of goals, they've been taught to loathe or reject all the things that could make life worthwhile. But how could they not? What, after all, was going to make life worthwhile? We didn't know. Oh, I see myself back then, at an after-school cookout at Pescadero Beach, nodding and smiling eagerly as one of the popular boys told me how great *A Trick of the Trail* by Genesis was, even though I hated that album more than almost any other ever recorded. If only, I used to wish, I was like my girlfriends, and could simply not care about these things! Because it doesn't do to care about things; it's so inelegant, so frightening, so complicated. And when it involves lying, you wind up feeling less dignified, more alienated, than ever. You sell yourself out, and for what?

Years later, in the midst of explaining to me why it was that he didn't feel alienated, Henry Rollins said, "Alienation means you want in, and I don't want in. I'm not outside knocking; I don't even want to go to the dance."

"Ah, but Henry," said I, sadly, "that's easier said than done!" Secretly, I felt, though I'd never have dared tell him so, it would be a lot easier to reject society the way Henry's done if you were bald and built and covered in tattoos. Search and destroy: easy for him to say. What if you were always just the powerless girl, sitting at the back of the room?

Laughing wryly, Henry said he'd be glad to be the background to my personal apocalypse. Fortunately or unfortunately, by that time, I no longer needed one.

Fortunately/unfortunately—that's a game my mother used to play with me. "Fortunately, we're having fresh peas for dinner. Unfortunately, you have to shell them." Fortunately, I did eventually find out about punk rock. Unfortunately, it took me ages to stop knocking; to stop wanting to knock, even though all around me society disintegrated and legions of my peers became obnoxiously well-off yuppies. As the seventies drew to a close and the eighties began, I still lifted my paw up eagerly—dressed in Calvin Klein jeans with a perfect crease ironed down the middle, three-inch-high candies, and my Vidal Sassoon haircut—still pounded away at that dumb door all anxious to be admitted. But finally one day my paw dropped; it fell to my side. *Quietus.*

*

Punk rock changed my world, and thanks to Nirvana, it's now changed a lot of *other* people's too. It lost its way a lot of times, doubling back into byways we once knew were corrupt and lonely, then rearing out again from the very belly of the beast. Punk took a twisted route—Route 666—and it often got mangled in translation: few styles and fashions have been more misrepresented by the press, few have stayed underground for quite as long. It began so far back that I barely remember it—in New York with the Ramones, in Detroit with the Stooges—then wafted across the Great Plains in strange gusts and eddies, like a cloud of sonic dust, settling first here, then there, leaving each community it landed in with a poisonous residue of doubt and hope and flagrant behavior, leaving me and those like me with a mind full of memories of magical moments when the world went white with light and sound and the days lasted longer and the air smelled like glue.

Bohemia sheltered us all from harm, and bohemia has always been forgiving of both class and gender. Now that there's no honor conferred upon the starving artist, bohemia's generosity of spirit is its only attraction. I understand perfectly how rappers from the ghetto, newly made superstars, don't find any romance in starving-artisthood; how they long to buy in rather than sell out; accumulate as much wealth and power as possible. But I wonder sometimes if what they buy into ever seems worth it. For those from my background, rejection of a world where the standard is merely money or beauty is the only route possible. Art has always been the only escape.

But what, to a person brought up in a twentieth-century suburb, is art? Movies, painting, sculpture, dance, these things were as closed and as white and as ultimately monied as, oh, opera, or polo, or debutante parties—and for that reason, just as boring. The sciences? Coming, as I did, from Silicon Valley, I saw legions of intelligent kids with no social graces—the computer nerds and plastic surgeons who subsequently became rich and greedy—as almost more destructive to my peace of mind than even the dumb hordes of squares in marketing they conquered. Rock 'n' roll? Rendered visually horrible to young people like me by the supremely sluggish beat of the Eagles ("You've . . . gooot . . . the . . . best of . . . . mah . . . . love . . . . zzzzzz") and the unpleasant imagery of a ruling class made up of cretinous old British farts with muttonchops and mustaches. Not to mention hippies.

One was lost.

Until suddenly, while standing in the kitchen baking cookies for the next day's swim meet, I heard it on the radio, on KSAN, the local prog rock station. Or maybe I was in my room, cutting pictures out of magazines, or hanging around the house of a morning, having cut school for the zillionth time ("Dear office, Gina can't come to school today as she had an asthma attack last night and needs to rest. Signed Mrs. A"). However it was I heard it first, it immediately erased the stale sound of Rod Stewart and Leo Sayer and the Bee Gees and Crystal Gayle in an instant. There it was, booming out of the speakers, blaring into my heart, plonking my imagination down right where it wanted to be, in London and New York, with a very short haircut, wearing flattering peg-leg jeans: "*Romeo was restless he was ready to kill/he jumped out the window 'cause he couldn't sit still/Juliet was waiting with a safety net/she said, 'Don't bury me 'cause I'm not dead yet.'* " There it was: the road to nirvana, yawning wide open; totally obvious; paved in gold. My brain sat bolt upright. Say what? "*Why don't you show me 'bout the mystery dance? I want to know about the mystery dance. I want to do it 'cause I've tried and I've tried and I'm still mystified, I can't do it anymore and I'm not satisfied . . .*" Sharp, angry, fast, mean-spirited: wide awake, defiant—everything my world was not. The Ramones, Elvis Costello, the Police, Blondie, the Talking Heads, and the Clash . . . there was no question at all as to what it was the sound of. *Jailbreak*. Out of here. Real, real, real gone.

After all, you can't escape from anything until there's somewhere good to go.

TWO

BRIAN JONESTOWN

You know what I hate about rock? I hate tie-dyed T-shirts. I wouldn't wear a tie-dyed T-shirt unless it was dyed with the urine of Phil Collins and the blood of Jerry Garcia.

– Kurt Cobain, 1992

I once met a girl who'd been to see the Beatles at Candlestick Park. She remembered every moment of that evening, from the exact time her ride was supposed to pick her up to the amount she'd given up in babysitting fees for the privilege of attending. That's how the Sex Pistols' last show in San Francisco is for me. I remember everything, from the rain storm that dogged the day, to the type of pizza (olive and mushroom, BBQ sauce) my friends Kelly and Megan and I picked up at Jose's Famous Pizza in Palo Alto to eat on the way. I remember standing in the line outside Winterland and striking up a conversation with a scary-looking punk rocker named Les who told me he used to play bass in the opening act, the Nuns. He asked me where I was from and I stole a line from *A Chorus Line* in reply: "I don't know, I've blocked it out." "Ah, Walnut Creek!" crowed Les.

Inside the club, I lost Kel and Meg, pushing my way up to the stage, where I stood alone in awestruck silence. I remember Jennifer Miro pretending to hang herself during the song "Suicide Child." I remember Penelope Houston's salt-and-pepper buzzsaw haircut (my own had Farrah Fawcett wings). I remember the Sex Pistols' entire set as one Joan of Arc-like vision, the thick rock of the bass lines, the screech of guitar. I remember Kelly and Megan grabbing me by the elbows, dragging me backward through the crowd and out to the car, as the strains of "No Fun" came through the auditorium walls. I remember that the song "I Go Crazy' by Paul Davis was playing on KFRC when we got back into the car and drove off grimly into the San Francisco night. Kelly and Meg hated every minute of it. They were mad at me for weeks.

But after that, all things punk were good things. Mirrored sunglasses. The color turquoise. Geometric shapes. Zippers. Japan (the country, not the rock band). Fifties toasters. Fake fur and warm leatherette. Gas-guzzling Chevy Impalas. Vinyl anything. Black boots in girls' sizes. Red pumps. Mickey Mouse T-shirts. See-through plastic raincoats and jelly shoes. Lamé socks. Tacky postcards. "Leave It to Beaver" reruns. Linda Blair. Tom Petty and the Heartbreakers. Peg-leg jeans, which were, incidentally, once almost impossible to find west of Canal Street in Manhattan.

All of these items are things we take for granted now, because you can find reasonable facsimiles of them in Woolworth's or Macy's or the Gap. But there once was a time when those things were hard to find. There was a rush of discovery in every single piece of junk culled from Quality Marts and thrift stores, a sense of real achievement in wearing any outfit that defied the baby blue and fluffy-haired conventions of 1976. There was a time when it made me incredibly happy just to see someone dressed like a punk walking down Columbus Avenue.

And then, very briefly, there was a time when it was "Hail fellow, well met" almost every step of the way.

If there were ever a machine invented that could telescope back in time, I'd like to see a picture of myself watching the Talking Heads' free show at Sproul Plaza in September 1978. Alone as I felt at the time—OK, so my dad was there, looming away in the background, having kindly driven me up to the gig—I'm certain that I was actually sandwiched between some of my greatest friends of the future, all of whom I now know were standing there beside me. It's as if fate had decided to group together all the people who'd meet up later on the road of life in one brief pre-party get-together.

But instead of getting together, instead of smiling on each other, the whole thing ended up being exactly like the party I'd been to a few months before introducing all Yale acceptees. Full of shy snobs, noses twitching with excitement, eager but silent: too wrapped up in our own worldview to figure out how to make contact with one another.

By this time of course the Sex Pistols had already broken up, and unbeknownst to me, Black Flag—later dubbed the first of the post-punks—had already formed. Meanwhile, while I was still moldering namby-pambily in high school, other people were creating the scene I'd eventually step into. Thinking back to that time, V. Vale, the former editor and publisher of *Search and Destroy* magazine and one of San Francisco's earliest punk rock devotees, recalls: "Punk rock didn't even have a name yet. People who wanted to call you something from out of the window of their car would just yell 'Fag!' The big shift in public consciousness came when people started yelling 'Devo!' "

Vale first heard of "it," as punk was then known, by means of the *New Musical Express*, which did a big spread on New York's CBGB's scene (as yet unnamed), which he pinned to his refrigerator for an entire summer in lieu of actually going there. The article talked about bands like the Ramones and Talking Heads and Blondie, in addition to the English version, the Sex Pistols, all of whom were highly influenced by the then-defunct band the New York Dolls (whom, coincidentally, Pistols impresario Malcolm McLaren had managed for a time back in 1975).

Vale claims that the first pre-punk event in San Francisco was Iggy Pop's appearance at Bimbo's in 1975, where he stripped down entirely, and, according to legend and *Chronicle* pop critic Joel Selvin, had oral sex performed on him by a member of the audience. The first real punk event, however, was the

Ramones' appearance at the Savoy Tivoli, in August 1976. Vale, who was there, estimates the audience "at around thirty people. Nobody there looked punk at all, it not having a name yet. The people sitting behind me later formed the Nuns, and they were dressed kind of glam, like the Dolls."

In December 1976 the Mabuhay Gardens, a Filipino restaurant on Broadway, started hosting punk nights. By then, several S.F. punk bands had been born in the practice spaces, warehouses, and tiny nightclubs of North Beach, where members of bands like the Nuns, Mary Monday, and Crime first attempted to transplant to western shores the attitude and ideals of bands like the New York Dolls and the Ramones—seen only, in those foggy pre-MTV days, in fuzzy black-and-white photos in tattered copies of *New York Rocker* and *New Musical Express*.

Like many great art movements, punk boiled up spontaneously, not just on the King's Road in London, but in various spots all around the world. The Lower East Side. Sydney, Australia. And San Francisco, which for many reasons was the perfect place for American punk rock to prosper. First, there's a long tradition of rebelliousness, ranging from the Communists of the thirties and forties through the beats of the fifties and hippies of the sixties. Psychologically, San Francisco was ripe.

But punk rock was always first and foremost strongly anti-hippie, and in 1976 the Bay Area was just as much the hotbed of diehard hippiedom that it is now.

"We were fed up with all the crap of the seventies, with disco, with country rock, with posy glam bands and people like Jeff Lynne of ELO saying he looked forward to the day when they could send holograms of themselves to arenas to 'play' all over the world," adds Jello Biafra, then of Dead Kennedys. "And it wasn't just in San Francisco. My hometown, Boulder, Colorado, was one of the country rock meccas of the seventies. Firefall lived there, and they were considerably worse than Journey! Something drastic needed to be done about these people, and punk was it."

In the Bay Area, where seventies rock dinosaurs flourished, this basic discontent with the ugly aesthetics of the seventies culture was aggravated by irritating daily contact with the big beast of hippiedom (a mastodon that blunders around there even to this day, in the guise of the exact same hippies who pissed us all so bad in 1977, such as Steve Miller, the Starship, and especially the Grateful Dead). Everyone knows what familiarity breeds, and in the beginning punk rock was a vast celebration of utter contemptuousness.

In those days, I used to take the SP train up to the city on Fridays and my sister and I would go hang out at the Mabuhay, wishing we knew all the cool-looking people there. We found a sympathetic hairdresser who cropped us and then taught us how to spike our hair with gelatin. We bought paper jumpsuits at the hardware store and wore them to the Larkin Street Cinema, where we watched the Devo shorts and some boring movie with one shot of Debbie Harry in it all afternoon. (There was a guy in the audience whom I've never forgotten. He had his cheek pierced, and attached to it was a dog chain leading to his ear hole.) We saw Patti Smith at Winterland on the hottest day of the year. I remember her singing Debby Boone's "You Light Up My Life." And once I wrote a letter to Joel Selvin complaining that he didn't understand the worth of the Sex Pistols and he published it in the *Chronicle*'s Pink Section, thus branding me a pariah at my high school for the entire last five months of the school year.

One place I didn't go, but where the germ was being incubated at incredible speed, was in the halls of the San Francisco Art Institute on Chestnut Street. It was there that a nineteen-year-old Seattle native, Penny Houston, joined up with Danny Furious and Greg Ingraham, a.k.a. Greg Sears, to form the Avengers (Jimmy Calvin Wilsey joined two months later). At their first gig, the band played only covers, and Penelope wore a black leotard, fishnets, a man's shirt over it all, and a tie around her neck.

"I was actually the most punk rock person in the band," Penelope recalls now. "When I was in college in Bellingham,

Washington, in 1976, people used to call me Penelope Punk, because I'd put my hair in pigtails that stood straight up on end and I wore a black vinyl jacket. Then a friend of mine told me there were these punks in England who ripped up their clothes and pinned them back together and things. You know what it's like when you start thinking about doing something, mulling it over in your mind, and then it turns out there's a whole lot of people actually doing it somewhere else? It was like that. That very night I think I safety-pinned a flyer to my jacket and wore it around town."

Similarly, Jean Caffeine was a seventeen-year-old junior at George Washington High School in 1976 when she started seeing flyers for a show at the Mab featuring Crime and the Nuns pinned up all over town. The day of the show, she went over to the club, banged on the door, and begged to be let in for free. After that, she was hooked. "I started hanging out all the time, not going to school or only going after all-night parties at places like the *Search and Destroy* office, or at KSAN, or at a guy called Super Joel's house . . . I had this hideous blue-and-purple hair—we all got cut for free at Vidal Sassoon, and they'd convince us to do these terrible things to it."

Caffeine soon took the proficiency exam to get out of high school. She moved out of her parents' house and into an apartment in the Fillmore with the infamous Will Shatter of Negative Trend (and later Flipper) and a friend of hers called Michael Kowalski, whom Vale now calls "the punk archetype, very influential, the Wild One incarnate." They bought the Damned's *Damned, Damned, Damned* record and the self-titled Clash debut record, as well as the singles by the Sex Pistols. (*Never Mind the Bollocks, Here's the Sex Pistols* wasn't released until late 1977, only weeks before the band's demise.)

By the time Jean Caffeine was fully entrenched in the punk rock scene, the Avengers had written a lot of originals, including "The American in Me" and "We Are the One." They were already a popular act at early punk clubs like the Mabuhay on Broadway, Club Foote, the Deaf Club, 330 Grove Street (the Gay Community Center), and the Valencia Tool and Die. By then there were other bands in the area who drew a core audience of up to two hundred: the Offs, U.X.A., the Sleepers, the Mutants, and the Dils, to name but a few. The audiences of most shows were made up of members of other bands, who would stay long after the sets were over to hang out, or pick up a burger at Clown Alley on Columbus, or drive to the beach to drink. When bands came from out of town—Circle Jerks or X from L.A., or D.O.A. from Vancouver— they all stayed at one another's houses. With no one ever having the hope of being offered a record contract, there was a lot more camaraderie than competition.

"Oh yeah, we were very much of a community," Vale says now. "It was the last pre-postmodern community founded on art. It was pre-self-conscious," he adds. "It hadn't been codified, and it was untouched by commercial aspects—it was pure. Media coverage makes people self-conscious, and the press didn't cover us back then. And I don't think it can happen again. That's why I think everyone who was there then has gone through a period of mourning over the loss of it."

Vale had started *Search and Destroy* in order to document the scene. He modeled it somewhat after Andy Warhol's *Interview,* which had, he recalls, already run a piece on the Ramones. The first issue came out in May 1977, and soon *S & D* was a sort of clearinghouse for punk rock fans. At the time, Vale remembers, his rent in North Beach was $37.50 a month.

By that time, San Francisco's reputation as a punk mecca was confirmed. "L.A.'s punk scene was always more glitzy," Houston recalls. "There weren't so many people who got into it who'd been doing weird things before punk came along and just did punk as part of that thing. The ones from the suburbs were younger and angrier and wanted to annoy their parents more. In L.A., punk really wasn't as arty—or as politically correct."

It was the political angle of punk that drew Eric Boucher here. As a freshman at U.C. Santa Cruz in 1977, he recalls blasting the Sex Pistols' first single one night and immediately cutting off his hippie hair, putting it inside a Ziploc bag, and nailing it to the door of his dorm room. He dropped out his first semester, moved back to Boulder, Colorado, and then worked long hours in a nursing home laundry to earn the money to move back to San Francisco, enroll at a school of drama on Powell Street, and form his own band. The day he drove to S.F., in February 1978, he went straight to the Mabuhay Gardens after a day's drive that began in Utah at five A.M. He got there just in time to catch the Nuns and Negative Trend. He was nineteen years old.

"When I moved here," says Boucher, now known to most people as Jello Biafra, "my feeling was, 'If I do this right now, I'll be able to tell my grandchildren that I saw the Dils play a tiny club in San Francisco in the winter of '78.' "

These days Biafra is a speaker, poet, and the owner of a record label, Alternative Tentacles; he also sports a pointy beard. Sitting on the couch of Hyde Street Studios late one night between mixes of a song for his new LP with a new group called Tumor Circus, he holds forth on the merits of days of old. This is how he talks: "There seems to be an organized campaign by a growing number of people, particularly in *Spin*, who are claiming that punk ruined music and got people against making technical-trained-musician perfect music, and that a whole generation of musicians went down the drain. Even Frank Zappa has said this. But I have to disagree with that pretty emphatically. Punk was an outbreak of new talent that happened all over the world and opened the door to a whole new generation of people who had ideas to replace the bankrupt swill that was being regurgitated [by people] who blew a lot of their talent and shot their wads in the sixties, but who maintained a stranglehold on the airwaves in the seventies by churning out repetitive pabulum and whatnot. [Punk] was just like '63, '64, '65, a whole new generation of people who would define music as we know it. And up till now, up till rap happened, most of the people who have any impact whatsoever today you can trace back to the punk scene."

Biafra's bid for impact came pretty suddenly, after he answered an ad on the bulletin board of Aquarius Records put there by the soon-to-be Dead Kennedys' East Bay Ray. By mid-July the DKs were playing live. "It was such a stupid and naive thing to do," Biafra says now. " 'Bye mom, bye dad, I'm dropping out of school so I can go immerse myself on the S.F. punk scene and start a band!' And I'd never written a lyric in my life! I just wanted to be as good as the people I liked. I was driven by that—wanting to be Jim Morrison one day and Iggy the next, and the lyrics to be as cruelly barbed and as intricate as Ron Mael from Sparks."

It's open to question whether Biafra ever achieved those goals. But one thing is certain, by the winter of 1978—ten months after the Pistols broke up—the third and last wave of S.F. punk rockers, led by Dead Kennedys, had begun their reign. By that time punk had hit the suburbs. In Moraga, for example, two Campo Linda High School students dusted off an unused Whittler's Club in order to sponsor a school dance, at which they booked Dead Kennedys (called, for the purpose of approval by the PTA, the Creme-sicles). And in 1979 Biafra ran for mayor, coming in a very respectable fourth. (Afterward, Quentin Kopp made it a law that people could only run for office using their real names.) Thanks to him, the punk rock scene in San Francisco had finally attracted media notice. From then on, it was a downhill slide.

Not that it was Biafra's fault: a lot of things combined to make punk rock's end inevitable. One such factor was violence: kids coming in from the suburbs to take part in a scene that the media had vastly distorted. Penelope recalls that when her band, the Avengers, opened for the Sex Pistols at Winterland, hordes of strangers in the audience stood there yelling, "Fuck you, fuck you!" and spitting, because that's what they thought punks did. "I was, like, 'Wha?' " recalls Houston.

Later on, the violence escalated. "Some of us had talked for years about how great it would be for us to get our music to younger kids and how once they saw the energy they'd automatically like it," Biafra explains. "But what we didn't realize is that they might not like it on our terms. So when younger people did start coming to shows in droves, they brought the arena rock mentality with them, including fights, jumping off the stage just to see if you could hit people . . . In my case there were physical attacks on the band, on me in particular."

Some people blame drugs for the demise of the scene, but that may be too simplistic an answer: "In the beginning," Vale claims, "a lot of punks wouldn't smoke pot or drop acid because that was seen as hippie-ish."

Biafra adds, "The pioneers of any scene, the people who have an appetite for creative danger, are always going to play around with that. I am very bitter toward the drug scene for ruining or killing so many of my friends. When you're an artist with something dangerous to say, drugs are the cops' best friend."

A more potent enemy than drugs, however, was disillusionment, born in part of industry indifference. Biafra believes that there was a conspiracy among major labels to shut out punk rock bands from signing labels, and indeed, the only California band signed to a label during those vital years before 1980 was the Dickies, and rumor had it that was because one band member had an uncle at A&M. (Ironically, Jello's label, Alternative Tentacles, is discussing plans to put out a Dickies single in 1993.)

"In the early days there was a feeling that 'We are the new vanguard, we are going to take over the airwaves, take over this, take over that, because this is the time that will define the next decade,' " Biafra says now. "There was such songwriting talent, such great visually dynamic bands. But it became obvious by mid-'78 that *none* of these bands were ever going to be let in the door. I remember once I was in Aquarius Records and Penelope was in there and some woman came up to her and said, 'Hey, when are you guys going to make an album?' and Penelope burst into tears!"

After doing one Dangerhouse single, the Avengers did eventually release a record, a four-song EP on the White Noise label, a few months after they disbanded in 1979. (Ironically,

Peter Paterno, the man responsible for releasing it, now runs Hollywood Records.) Dead Kennedys' "California über Alles" was first released on their own Alternative Tentacles label in June 1979 and then was reissued by Fast Records in 1980 in England and sold 20,000 copies, a fact that rocketed DKs to a viable European career. Subsequently, the band released an album, *Fresh Fruit for Rotting Vegetables*, on IRS Records. (Subsequent Dead Kennedys records have all been released on Biafra's own Alternative Tentacles label.)

But by that time, the original scene in San Francisco was entirely over and done with. Penelope had moved to L.A. to pursue a film career. Jean Caffeine moved to New York, where she became a member of a notorious seven-woman outfit known as Pulsallama, which also featured the actress and performance artist Ann Magnuson. The Mutants, the Offs, Crime, and almost every other punk band broke up. Michael Kowalski and Flipper's Will Shatter both died of drug o.d.'s several years later. Jello's band continued to flourish here until 1986, when creative differences brought it to an end.

Since that time, a whole new generation of hardcore and thrash and rap alternative bands have come of age in the Bay Area. Many of them are quite good, and most of them have done better than their direct forebears, getting label deals and enormous followings, as well as fulfilling careers and critical acclaim. But everything's a lot different now. These scenes all exist separately, and everyone in them has, as Jean Caffeine says, "such obvious lineage. Everything's so co-opted. It's like peg-leg jeans. They used to be our treasured possessions, and now you can get them in every possible color at the Gap. It's a lot harder to be individual now . . . But on the other hand, it's nice to be able to get 'em when you want 'em."

"I do think," Biafra adds, "that it's good that there's so many people doing bands. It used to be you did Pop Warner football or high school athletics, or you didn't achieve. And now there's this whole generation of kids picking up guitars instead of baseball bats. I think that's pretty damn healthy."

So, even though no one from the S.F. punk rock scene ever

really made it big, the world owes a big debt to its existence anyway. Without punk rock, we'd still be stuck wearing baby-blue work shirts and wide-legged jeans. Without punk rock there'd be no college radio, no SST Records, no Cure. Madonna couldn't be going around in her bustier, and Sonic Youth wouldn't be on Geffen. There'd be no Replacements without punk rock, and certainly no Lollapalooza Tour. Punk rock was a Gallipoli of sorts, losing the battle, killing all the foot soldiers, and yet ultimately winning the war.

"I think in the end, the punk rock scene was just like the dope that killed our friends that was too strong," concludes Caffeine. "It couldn't have succeeded in its full-strength version. It was way too dangerous."

And yet it's hard not to yearn for those innocent days, forgotten or distorted by the public at large. Even as it happened, Penelope remembers thinking it was like the Beat thing, or Paris in the 1920s. "It had that quality of happening now, of being created as we spoke," she explains. "A lot has been written about that time, and it's either this huge overview, or it's about how sordid it all was. And that's not what it was like. The other day this thing happened that reminded me of that time. It was the first night of summer, it was really hot out, though the sun had gone down, and we went to the Mission to meet up with the Mekons, and all these people were walking down the street that I knew. It was a really neighborhoodly, happy feeling, and it reminded me of what it was like to be in a band back then. That's how North Beach used to be all the time."

Jean Caffeine concurs with that view entirely. "At the time, I thought 1977 was my sixties. We talked a lot about how it was our Summer of Hate. It really seemed like living in a point in history. But in retrospect, I guess it was a pretty small point."

I'm not so sure about that, though. When Kurt Cobain was in high school in 1987, his favorite bands were Dead Kennedys and Flipper. Jello: "It was such a big thing for me to see the Ramones, in January of 1977, horrifying the country-rock glitterati of Denver at a club called Ebbets Field. They went out of their way to make it seem simpler than it was, so you thought, 'Let's go start a fuckin' band!' That moment rekindled my interest in life itself. If it weren't for that . . . I cannot see myself pushing papers, or going the route some people in Boulder did, going on listening to ELP and smoking pot for the rest of my life. In all honesty, without punk rock, I would be dead. I swear I would be dead."

THREE

LEFT OF THE DIAL

A lot of great bands over the years have been lost to higher education. That's why I hope tuitions just keep going up and up.
– Gerard Cosloy

Once upon a time, radio was a sound salvation. It played all the time, in the kitchen, in the bedroom, on the pool deck, in the car. The tinny pop chug-a-lug wired the air around it with bright-minded echoes of retro romance and fakey fun, filling up the empty blue space that envelops all suburbia with the simplest of all possible remedies for boredom: a beat. You had your little radio on all the time, night and day, and it brought you something rich and nimble: dumb ideas and wacky fantasies, pretty pieces of movable furniture for your headroom, private and possibly ridiculous visions of a lovesexy life. I even used to like the way songs were repeated over and over all week long in high rotation: they changed so gradually, like the seasons, till suddenly, months later, you noticed you never heard your favorite anymore. Oh, when television was static and unreal and movies so hard to belong to, there was always the radio to light up your inner life. Inside its plastic confines, song followed sweet song, day in and day out. You turned each other on.

But one day the radio died. Disco killed it. In Frederic Dannen's book *Hitmen*, he describes the complex record company machinations that led to a monetarily based system of radio formatting so constipated and corrupt that any new record of merit or imagination without a large budget behind it would have no way of being played.

Add to that the mechanization that developed in the late seventies and early eighties: autoprogramming, which eliminated the fine art of disc jockeying. Then there was a simultaneously disturbing rise of personality radio, plus the demographic polarization of the charts into the separate worlds of Black (Urban), AOR (Album-Oriented Rock, or seemingly, Always on the Radio), and CHR (Contemporary Hit Radio). Rock 'n' roll radio was ruined. To quote Abba, who shut down around the same time, no more carefree laughter. Silence ever after.

Throughout the seventies my brother and sister and I listened to two stations: KFRC-AM, the trashy top-forty station that was the only one we could get in our mother's dumb Barracuda, and KSAN-FM, the ground-breaking free-form AOR station that had, once upon a time, led American radio out of a thicket of quick hits and, in 1977, jerked our attention toward punk rock.

We loved KSAN so much. Its deejays (Bonnie Simmons, Tony Kilbert, Beverly Wilshire), its music (from Bruce Springsteen to Bob Marley to the Clash to the Talking Heads), its spirit, its live broadcasts from the Savoy Tivoli and Winterland, and its unspoken conviction that rock 'n' roll music still had meaning in this world, in spite of the marketplace. It was the soundtrack to San Francisco: to Armistead Maupin's *Tales of the City,* which we read serialized in the *Chron* every morning, to the free Pearl Harbor and Tubes shows we'd periodically see at Embarcadero Center, to tooling up Columbus Avenue after an afternoon spent browsing at Tower Records on Bay.

Always, my favorite deejay—my whole family's favorite deejay—was Richard Gossett. Vocally, he was almost a stereotype of the laid-back FM deejay made fun of on "Saturday Night Live" and the movie *FM*: a low, even boy's voice, muttering into the night. He was funny, in a dry sort of way, and often sounded stoned (or so my brother, who knew about such things, postulated gleefully). But what I liked best about Richard was his music. It was on his show—weeknights, six to ten—that I first heard Elvis Costello, the Jam, the Police,

Television, Talking Heads, and the Clash. He played a lot of Michael Jackson, Graham Parker, and Toots and the Maytals. And there was a long time when his favorite song was "You're the One That I Want," by John Travolta and Olivia Newton-John. He used to segue it into "Rockaway Beach" by the Ramones all the time, thus unwittingly teaching me everything I needed to know about the magic art of radio programming. Rule number one: there are no real borders between genres and artists, only pretend ones, born of stupid snobbery and fashion. Rule number two: act on that principle alone, and you'll be all right.

When I went away to college in Los Angeles, I used to irritate my entire dorm by talking incessantly about how great KSAN was: how much better was its musical taste, how superior were its deejays, how much more fun it was to listen to in general than the bland white sound of L.A.'s monster rock stations. I couldn't walk into a room that had KMET or KLOS on its dial (inevitably playing tracks from Supertramp's *Breakfast in America*, an LP I can't hear without thinking of that time) without starting in on my long sad story: KSAN this, KSAN that, and how in San Francisco the Ramones play for free in Embarcadero Center . . . information to which everyone at UCLA's unanimous response was, *So?*

But by the time I came home, KSAN sounded different from what I remembered: more staid, less adventuresome, filled with a new, oppressive atmosphere that permeated its offices and came right through the receiver. It seemed that while I'd been away, they'd been sold to an entertainment conglomerate, Metromedia, Inc., which had instituted a number of changes, including a stiff playlist. Rumor had it that Richard Gossett was fired for not adhering to it: one day, in defiance of it, he played the Clash's "Complete Control," and that was the end of that. (If this rumor's not true, please don't ever tell me.) You know, it's right what they say about how you can't go home again.

KSAN struggled on as a corporate giant for a couple of years before turning into a country-and-western station.

Richard Gossett got various shifts in one or two other places, but wound up getting a job at the Anchor Steam Brewery. And instead of sticking to the stiff new formats that were emanating from the corporate ogre, I, like so many other people in those fateful years, turned to the left of the dial.

College radio stations had, of course, always existed in some form or another—as a training ground for electrical engineers and as an extracurricular activity for campusbound newsies, sportifs, and queers. By the mid-seventies, following the trend of the post-hippie music world, many such stations boasted late-night radio shows hosted by collegiate music fiends who delighted in playing the longest tracks off albums by obscure British art bands: Pink Floyd, Gentle Giant, Caravan. But when mainstream radio lost its grip on music, then the long-dormant airwaves of the college radio stations (reserved for years for *um*-ridden play-by-plays of intercollegiate football games) at schools ranging from the University of Texas and the University of Kansas to Upsala College in Orange, New Jersey, and to the University of San Francisco and U.C. Berkeley, where I was, began simultaneously to create new music programs that dealt more competently with the rest of radio's insufficiencies.

And suddenly—not gradually at all, but quite suddenly—those stations became an invaluable American network, linking the nascent punk rockers of each city to one another, and providing all the bands within a community with a way in which to prosper. Years later, while dining at an industry conclave with R.E.M. and a bunch of record company VIPs, Peter Buck asked the collected party how many had worked in college radio. Every single person present at the table—twenty-five or so, ranging from journalists and mainstream deejays to industry execs, record store clerks, and musicians, including a couple of Buck's own friends—raised a hand.

In some ways, the story of college radio has been like a fairy tale come true—or, at the very least, a made-for-TV movie: the geekiest, most unpopular nerds at the college decide to barricade themselves into a closet and start a gonzo radio station, alienating their more popular peers and professors by blaring out noisome, underproduced garage rock featuring the F word and worse. But the radio station struggles on, the geeks grow up and prosper, and *voilà!*, the records they've been playing—by U2, the Cure, R.E.M.—go platinum! The deejays get hired to positions of influence by major record companies! The airwaves have been won back by the righteous, and rock 'n' roll will rule again.

Oddly enough, that's almost exactly how it happened. For a while there in the early eighties, college radio really was our sound salvation. It, after all, still played free-form radio, nipping expertly from James Brown to James Chance, from Fairport Convention to the Slits, soundtracking not just the hits of the moment but the history of rock, giving it some context, teaching its listeners its secrets, creating an interior world of newfound glamour and romance and escape. And they provided an outlet for all the record nerds and frustrated musicians to meet each other, enabling them to form a community of misfits, maybe twenty people per town, generally just enough people to tempt bands to the area, to play whichever VFW hall or old-man bar was willing to allow them on the premises. And lastly, the stations, such as they were, became the inevitable conduit for all the independently released records to be given their due. They played the unheard music.

The college radio effect happened at the same time in obscure tiny towns all over America—at Oberlin in Ohio, at Florida State, at Evergreen in Olympia, Washington . . . anyplace where there was a bunch of bored and frustrated white kids with large record collections, and one kid in particular with the will to make things happen. But Boston was the city where this all happened in the most concentrated manner, and where the significance of college radio began to take on a larger meaning. Thanks to a predominance of colleges—some, like Harvard and MIT, containing far more than their share of record geeks and electrical whizzes—plus a proximity to New York City, it became a hotbed of punk rock early on. As early as 1976, WTBS (later called WMBR) at MIT had begun running the first punk rock show in America. And then, not surprisingly, since Boston is a city overrun with hypercompetitive overachieving white kids, Harvard's college station, WHRB, followed suit. Pretty soon, every significant college station in Boston—Harvard, MIT, Emerson, and Boston College—had its own resident punk rock show.

Scott Becker was a freshman at Tufts University in Boston when he tuned in to "Shakin' Street," the late-night proto-punk program on Harvard's WHRB, in 1977. "I remember I heard the New York Dolls, and then the Ramones, for the very first time on the radio, and it shocked the hell out of me. That guy got the Pistols' import 45's first of everybody. Shortly after that, Oedipus, who back then had pink hair and a 45 adaptor tattooed on his shoulder, started doing a punk rock show on MIT's station, and pretty soon, every college in Boston had a punk rock show on their station.

"Before, that, when I was in high school in Connecticut in the mid-seventies, the AOR station seemed so hip," recalls Becker. "But then suddenly it started to dawn on me that it wasn't that hip at all. It was punk rock that did it. It was just clear that there was the whole new scene and all these new labels and exciting new records, and commercial radio just rejected it, totally."

Becker describes himself as a high school recluse. "I just loved radio, way more than TV. I don't know what other kids did after school, maybe played football or smoked pot, but I ran home and listened to the radio for hours and hours and hours." When he applied to Tufts, one of his main concerns was the on-campus station, WMFO. But as a freshman, he found himself too shy to volunteer. "I went to a couple station meetings, but everybody knew each other and I was too out of it."

Happily, as a sophomore, his next-door neighbors were involved. By the end of the year, he was music director and, he recalls laughingly, part of an embattled cabal, immediately tied up in a serious intrigue. His first priority at the station was to emphasize and add records such as those from the nearby Rounder Records label—a specialty label featuring bluegrass, blues, and a new record by George Thorogood and the Destroyers—to the playlist. "We were ten watts, no guidance, no faculty advisor, no money, and no one got paid, and whenever we asked the student council for money, they'd go, 'Well, don't you get free records?' For us to just be on the air was really an accomplishment. We went from trying to imitate an AOR station to making our own."

Tufts's station wasn't as punked out as larger Boston college stations (though, Becker recalls, there was a gradual shift: " 'Less Dead—more Ultravox' was our rallying cry"). Instead, its main concern, Becker recalls, was remaining free-form. "That didn't mean a person could play anything they wanted," he notes, "it meant playing a broad mix of different kinds of music. That was the ongoing philosophical debate of the era. We'd get into these big arguments with the student body 'cause they thought the music we played was weird. There was always a lot of politicking and intrigue around the station management. Someone was always trying to boot the general manager and put someone else in his place. But our main point of argument was specialty programming. We had an all-Portuguese hour, which served a really large local Portuguese-speaking community, and the student body was always going, 'But no one here speaks Portuguese!' And we had an R & B show that was real alien to white middle-class kids, that played the worst kind of disco and 'quiet storm' stuff."

These kinds of debates are still going on at college stations around the country, though in these trying times, merely getting funding for something as anachronistic as radio is difficult enough without adding in the trials of keeping programming consistent.

And then there's the all-volunteer effect, whereby the unpaid deejays feel their labor gives them the right to do what they want. Some stations had to actively discourage putative deejays who wanted to play bad commercial stuff. "At 'MFO," says Becker, "that wasn't a problem: we had a totally completist attitude toward the record library. Playing indies was important while I was at WMFO, but it's important to remember there were a lot fewer indies in 1977, when I got there, than there were in 1981, when I left."

Though labels like Dangerhouse and Berserkley and Rounder were forerunners of the coming game, the American independent label network began establishing itself on firmly punk rock grounds only around 1980. By the time Geoff Weiss got to Harvard's WHRB in 1981, the process was in full swing, and as music director of 'HRB, he was in a perfect position to help consolidate its gains.

Unlike most college radio stations, WHRB is a fifty-thousand-watt commercial station—95.5—that the university had purchased years before, when radio licenses were less valuable. In addition to rock shows, it has ambitious classical, country, and news programming. In 1981, Weiss recalls, "I felt like it was following more than leading. Musically, it was not as ambitious as it could be. There were quality deejays on it, but no real music fiends."

Weiss had become a punk rock aficionado at age fourteen. Living twenty miles from a town on the edge of a dirt road in the backcountry of Vermont, he used to go, he remembers, into town with his doctor father for the evening to pass the time while his dad made his medical rounds. He passed it by reading every word of every magazine on the newsrack outside the train station: *Guns and Ammo, Soldier of Fortune,* and his favorite of all, *Creem,* which at the time was raving about the Ramones, Blondie, and the Dictators.

Weiss, who seems to have had a natural collecting bent from birth, immediately went nuts. He started collecting everything punk he could get his hands on. "Some of it I could buy at Britt's Department Store. I got the Ramones' second single there, and some English stuff on major labels that hadn't gotten axed. And I'd get my grandma in New York City—who was eighty, mind you—to go to the Bleecker Bazaar and get me things. I'd give lists to people who were going to a city—any city—to get stuff for me. My parents went to London and brought me home box loads. I took the bus to Boston to see the Ramones and the Clash."

When Weiss began at Harvard in 1981, he, along with his friend Jim Barber, gradually managed to lasso the helm of the station for their own use. One of the things they worked at changing was the playlists' former emphasis on English music. Like characters in a Neil Diamond song, they began to look toward America. WZBC (at Boston College), he recalls, was interested in the newest, most radical English dance stuff, while he and Barber preferred to emphasize new American bands, as well as those of Swedish, Dutch, Australian origin—anything, as long as it was good and rare.

But there was a good reason, Weiss adds, why most stations before that time were fixated on English output: "The English made more records. There were labels like Stiff and Chiswick and Factory, all putting out great punk rock records. But all the great American punk rock bands—the Dils and the Avengers and the Heartbreakers—didn't even get to make records. The Heartbreakers you had to buy on import! It wasn't even until 1980—till Dead Kennedys and the Misfits came out—that American punk bands started to get stuff on vinyl, and by then a bunch had already broken up. I remember that was the year I went to D.C. for the weekend and into Yesterday and Today Records and I found out about Dischord Records: the Bad Brains, Minor Threat, SOA—all these seven-inches were coming out, and suddenly you could get them at Newbury Comix! It became available to people who were willing to look."

After that, he remembers, in his capacity as music director, "Dischord and Black Flag were our priority records. And we sought out the newest, strangest, extremest American stuff. We were hardcore record collectors and we got tons of demo tapes from all over the world. We weren't just reading *New York Rocker*; we were going out and getting records no one else could get."

Weiss's practice gleaning records as a kid now came in handy. Once again he found himself giving record wish lists to people on their way to Europe. He worked weekend swap meets, buying punk records for a quarter each, and combing the racks of record stores in New England, upstate New York, D.C., and Florida, where his grandparents lived. Obsession with vinyl, with music, with noise: this was a unifying hallmark of the exhilaration of the times.

All this time—at least in part because of college radio's intensity of support—Boston was turning into one of the most exciting cities for local bands in America. There were all these great bands—Mission of Burma, the Young Snakes, the Del Fuegos, Human Sexual Response, the Neats—and they played all the time. 'HRB or 'MBR would announce some loft show in the morning, and in the evening it'd be packed. Those were the days.

Julie Farman Lovering was seventeen years old when she moved to Boston from a Massachusetts suburb. At that time her favorite band was Cheap Trick, and she remembers the cool "punk rock" outfit she wore to her first show: black spandex pants tucked into brown cowboy boots, a man's purple shirt with gray pinstriped tie and pink wraparound sunglasses: "I thought it was so bitchin', and the fact that everyone was staring at me weird just proved it!"

Luckily for Julie's nascent fashion sense, she found a place to live by means of the ad column in the *Boston Phoenix*, and her first two roommates were members of the local art rock bands, the Girls and the CCCP-TV. "Of course I instantly realized I was totally uncool and adopted their lifestyle, their musical tastes, and their radio station," remembers Julie.

That station was WMBR, the MIT station. A lifetime later, caught by chance in the middle of a harried afternoon meeting about Stevie Ray Vaughan's new LP in her third-floor, ocean-view office in Santa Monica, Julie can still recite the lineup of 'MBR's Late Riser's Show, which aired Monday through Friday, ten to twelve. "Monday was Albert, Tuesday was Greg, Wednesday was Tammy, Thursday was David. Greg would say really obnoxious things about local personalities . . . and Albert did this thing, 'Jim Bob at the Movies,' and everybody would be talking about what they'd heard on 'MBR all day."

Julie got a job as a waitress at a bar called the Rat, a divey little club near Kenmore Square. The Del Fuegos were the dishwashers. "I loved it 'cause I could go to work at eight P.M. and dress as obnoxiously as I wanted." There she was subjected to the process of hearing four bands a night, six nights a week, honing her own ideas of what ruled and what sucked. ("They almost all sucked.") Presently, Julie became the Rat's talent booker, helping to host all the top independent bands: R.E.M., the Replacements, the Dream Syndicate. "All my inspiration for booking came from 'MBR's playlist," she recalls. "Because we didn't advertise anywhere except there. We'd do ticket giveaways with them, co-presents. They'd list it on their concert report at eleven-thirty every morning and that was enough. They'd jam the hell out of a band and that night the club would be packed. The student population was humongous, and everyone there listened to their own college station out of some weird sense of patrician duty or something. I mean, I highly doubt that people in L.A. listen to KXLU just because they happened to go to Loyola Marymount, but MIT and Harvard are like that."

Later on, in her role as manager for the bands the Neats and the Lyres, Julie saw the college radio system in action all over America. "But Boston radio was great, the people running it were so great; the music was always great. I remember hearing 'The Message' on 'MBR, the first rap song I ever heard sandwiched between all this indie rock. It ['MBR] was so totally adventurous, but it wasn't just that . . . it was that it was accessible, too. You could call up the deejay, or a band on tour would be doing an interview there. You could just call 'em up at the studio and invite them over to your house."

If Boston's scene had a drawback in those days, Julie says, it was that it was drug-driven. "For me, being into punk rock was all about freedom and doing what I wanted to do and having my own apartment and knowing the bands, but a lot of the time I think we were following the drugs, not the bands. Sadly, I think for a long time the really exciting part about the 'mats coming to town was more the scene than the show.... It was going into the bathrooms with the girls and the band and bonding and doing blow."

Julie adds that Boston's scene was monumentally clique-oriented, eventually becoming overly dependent on who knew who at what station and who managed the band. "The Pixies started to happen right before I left Boston," she comments, "and they did not have our blessing. They didn't come up through the appropriate ranks, didn't have the right friends or manager, didn't play the right clubs; they were on some farty English label.... We were all, like, 'How dare they *have* a label!' Before I left Boston, I had never heard one note of the Pixies and I just hated them ... *hated* them!" Ironically, Julie is now married to ex-founding Pixie David Lovering.

Meanwhile, over at 'HRB, Weiss and his cronies—the Allston Art Rock Mafia, he refers to them now—also fostered strong relationships with local bands. Mission of Burma was their house band, while others—the Lyres, Dumptruck, Christmas, Volcano Suns, and later Big Dipper—were forging a community of bands that, like the communities to follow, actually started drawing would-be musicians and writers and radio deejays to the city. Boston was the home base for a number of crucial fanzines, including *Conflict*, the photocopied bully pulpit of the future label owner and tastemaker Gerard Cosloy, the Murray the K of Sonic Youth. Obscurity for obscurity's sake was almost a byword of their reign there. Weiss's copy of his favorite record of that era, an independently pressed 45 called "Communiqué" by a Cincinnati-based band called Lucky Pierre, which he played on his program every week, was the only copy in existence, making it literally unique: the perfect single, the rarest of all possible breeds.

In fact, Weiss and company may have carried their obsession with obscure records a bit too far: at least, that's how it seems in retrospect, especially now that the same stance, grown impracticable and anachronistic, still trickles weakly through the pages of *Spin* and on the airwaves of the leading college radio stations, which tout new bands as Godhead with little or no provocation, and which frantically mimic each other's monthly obsession—Ice T! Ice Cube! Foxcore! Seattle!—and steadfastly insult their readers and listeners by implying that they are stupid if they disagree. And yet there used to be some beauty in that stance, a private exhilaration of discovery, an innocence no longer applicable to a world that now cares passionately about alternative music. Back in the early part of the decade, college radio didn't advocate obscurity and anarchy and noise because it was trendy or elitist; it did so from a purity of intention almost impossible to recapture now: because it loved it and understood the music and—in the unselfish, sacrificial nature of true love—expected exactly nothing in return.

Weiss smiles. "Stupid empty elitism is dumb and pointless," he agrees. "But back in 1981 it wasn't like that. I mean, people are starting to press up records all over the country all by themselves again; I get boxes of indies from all over every week now. But the reason a rare record is rare is because it's ahead of its time and great, not just because it's obscure. And in 1977 it was just more likely that the point of view you were coming from would make you good. Now, when almost everybody's in a band, their reasons aren't necessarily as warped or as talent-driven.

"I think it's important for people not to build icons," he adds, "because alternative music has become myth-driven instead of music-driven, and that's wrong. That's one reason I love to cut people down when they get big. I don't necessarily dislike bands because other people like them, I just dislike them because they've betrayed what they originally believed in."

Ten years ago, if you had told college radio disc jockeys around the country that come the nineties their playlists would be closely monitored by the music industry and that major financial decisions would then be based on their personal choice of songs, they would have stared at you in shocked disbelief. Moreover, once they stopped staring, they would have started laughing, because back then, the whole point of college radio was not to break bands or make money, but to provide an alternative to mainstream radio for the portions of society who had a burning desire to actually hear some of the more mannerless and obscure records, British, African, or American—independents, records they'd only heard of in English music weeklies and fine-print fanzines; records made in people's basements, records whose unfamiliar sound or speed had caught their makers in the grip of an industry that, for obscure reasons of its own, was willing to produce but not promote them. "Back then," says Weiss, "I wouldn't have taken a job in the record industry for any money. In fact, I was offered one and I laughed in their face."

These days college stations are seldom run by insane record fanatics combing their personal collections for their playlists; instead, it's a breeding ground for young record company executives. Weiss says kids walk into his office all the time with long résumés, pleading for an industry position. He should know; he's a young record company executive himself: product manager at Warner Brothers Records responsible for running the campaigns of bands like Babes in Toyland and Mudhoney, as well as those of Danzig and the Thompson Twins. Julie Farman Lovering is director of publicity at Epic Records in Los Angeles, where she works with Pearl Jam, the Screaming Trees, the Allman Brothers, and Motorhead, among others. Scott Becker runs *Option* magazine, which a friend from the old days once described as " 'MFO in print." Oedipus, the pink-haired deejay at MIT who ran the first punk rock show in America, is currently the music director of WBCN, Boston's largest commercial rock station, one of the most important radio taste-making positions in the country.

Weiss still listens obsessively to demos and rarities from all over the world of underground, but, he adds, somewhat wistfully, "I've stopped obsessing on whether a record came out this week or not."

In 1988 Weiss's parents' house in Vermont exploded, destroying much of his vinyl record collection. "And," he adds inconsequently, "I haven't listened to college radio since I left Boston in 1985."

FOUR

BUZZ OR HOWL

Adam Smith's invisible hands have got you by the throat. Don't buy things all across the land—let's rock the boat!

– Trotsky Icepick

Los Angeles: One night in the fall of 1980 I saw X play the basement of Barrington Hall in Berkeley. Kevin and Kenny and I stood in the kitchen, peering anxiously into the low-ceilinged gloom of the cafeteria, hoping for the occasional glimpse of a tiny woman in a miniskirt whose angry face popped up occasionally over the backs of everyone's heads. Her nylons were ripped. Her face was covered by a web of thick black hair. And she screamed over a guitar that sounded like gunfire: feedback raged along its furious top, while just beneath the lyrics' roar a faintly humorous suspicion of rockabilly kept us all unsuspectingly hot for the next chord and the next. Inside that room, we co-op residents stood in an awed circle around the band as it fumed through blasts of heat and rage directed at us. John Doe stared into our midst, contempt or irony or maybe just genuine amusement flitting occasionally across his pallid face. The unearthly grin of Billy Zoom kept leaping into focus. It was the first time I ever thought I might be looking right at a bunch of heroin addicts, and I must say, I got a big fat kick out of the feeling.

Barrington is closed now, shut down by the U.C. Co-op Association for various infractions, which included drug dealing, the harboring of runaways, house dinners featuring LSD punch and nude dining, and the occasional accidental death by misadventure, such as falling off the roof. By the time it closed I was sick of both its attitude and its antics, but back in 1980, when I first transferred to U.C. Berkeley and was placed there by the U.C. Co-op Association, its very existence was, to me, the quintessence of the difference between attending UCLA in the late seventies and attending Berkeley in the early eighties.

Because that's where I'd come from: UCLA, a university that certainly never made X (or me) feel particularly welcome. The L.A. I knew was totally pre-punk, even pre-hiphop. Can you even imagine the colorlessness of it all? The world was white on white: dueling neutrals, all blowdryers on high. Even the sunsets lacked color. In L.A. it always looked like morning: bleached baby blond people with shiny white teeth; it smelt clean like cocaine wherever you were; Ventura Highway, life in the fast lane, Malibu Grand Prix, "Stay."

When I remember UCLA at all, I think of the cracked old-gold carpeting in the dormitory lounge and the tiny purple flowers that bloomed along Sunset Boulevard, and the lardlike Jell-O in the cafeteria, and bad sex and bad music and bad movies and bad roommates, always telling me to turn it down. One night we went to Zuma Beach at midnight and made out with our boyfriends on blankets on the shore. When we came up the cliff side, we discovered that our car's windows had all been smashed into a zillion shards by marauding . . . marauding who? I don't think I understood till then just what an important element danger is to salience and empathy. It hints at other worlds where life is not like yours; it is the opposite of sterility, the birth of insight into all the places you are not.

It was the autumn after *Animal House*. Remember *Animal House*, the National Lampoon movie celebrating toga parties, hand jobs, and beer? That flick practically single-handedly brought back pre-sixties nostalgia, in the guise, of course, of Reagan world, and at UCLA it was not a comedy, it was a docudrama. Kel and I attended the official *Animal House* fraternity party along with stars John Belushi and Tom Hulce and with twenty thousand other UCLA freshmen. According to the next day's *Los Angeles Times*, it was the hottest September night ever—115 degrees—and we wore flower-patterned togas made of Wamsutta sheets pinned precariously over our bathing suits. We waded through beer and back to get there; stood dutifully in groups round a bunch of boys, barely able to suppress our boredom. It was supremely unfun. For years I denigrated the city of L.A. for not providing me with more fun as a freshman.

While I was at UCLA I lived in Hedrick Hall, a dorm so large that it ran its own general store in the lobby that was open all night. On Halloween of 1978, down the hill at Dykstra Hall, a band called the Urinals was making its debut, in Dykstra's fourth-floor lounge. Where was I? About fifty yards away, in the exact wrong place at the exact right time. So much for the phrase "you had to be there": I was there, all right, but all off-kilter, so near and yet so far.

John Talley-Jones, Kjehl Johanson, and Kevin Barrett were self-described UCLA art geeks with a penchant for punk. Their band began as a five-piece, but stripped down to three almost immediately, recording three singles while still lodged in Dykstra, the last one ("Sex") in the basement weight room, while some perturbed dumbbell kept dropping dumbbells, thus repeatedly fucking up certain key takes. For the next year and a half, the Urinals rehearsed in a UCLA parking structure on Sunday mornings at ten A.M. (Their accustomed location was lot 32. Lot 6 was taken up by the Leaving Trains, while Bridge, a band featuring Bruce Licher—later the founder of Savage Republic and the man responsible for helping launch both the Butthole Surfers and Camper Van Beethoven—played in the utility tunnels under the architecture building.)

The Urinals—later called 100 Flowers—aside, UCLA was hardly a hotbed of punk rock: the Hollywood punk scene was not particularly collegiate. In 1978 it was, however, at its zenith, having just negotiated the vague transition between the glitter rock scene and the true punk one, which included diverse types of bands, like the power-poppy Nerves, the girl-metal Runaways, the saccharine-fast Quick, and a strange arty band called the Screamers, which had a synthesizer and two keyboard players. Their drummer was placed off to the side, and everyone else stood around in a semicircle. Their songs were these weird melodramatic parodies of David Bowie and Western civilization, and the singer, Tomata Du Plenty, was, according to my sources, totally riveting.

L.A.'s first archetypal punk band, however, was the Weirdos. They were formed by John Denney and Cliff Roman, the latter a Cal Arts student whose taste lay in the direction of Captain Beefheart and John Coltrane. In 1977 Roman had read about the Sex Pistols and Generation X in art magazines like *Interview,* but he'd never actually heard their music. Still, he wanted to form a band that played "weird, loud, fast" original music, so he wrote seven songs in his living room and taught them to his friends.

One afternoon in March 1977, the Weirdos (a name their long-haired neighbors dubbed them) were practicing all seven songs at their practice space when a band called the Nerves knocked on the door. The Weirdos still didn't have a drummer, but the Nerves—Peter Case, Paul Collins, and Jack Lee—were so impressed with the music they'd overheard that they invited them to play at a show with them at a place called the Punk Palace in two weeks' time.

At that time, Roman remembers, the only possible gigs bands like this could get were self-booked and self-promoted in halls the bands themselves would rent out. After the Nerves had pretty much shown him how, he ended up producing one himself a few weeks later—this one at the Orpheum, featuring the Weirdos, the Zeros, and the debut performance of a band called the Germs, whose punked-out lead singer (soon to be called Darby Crash) he had met and invited along that afternoon at a Bomp record store meet-and-greet held for Blondie's Debbie Harry.

That show, in April 1977, was considered the first true punk event to occur in L.A. Greg Shaw, who ran Bomp Records, came to it with KROQ's influential Rodney Bingenheimer in tow. The Screamers showed up too, all excited, Roman remembers, about a new punk magazine called *Slash* that was going to come out soon. Belinda Carlisle was in the audience, as was everyone else who'd later form a punk band in L.A. ("later" being, like, two weeks later). The Bags were all walking around with paper bags on their heads. Even the Damned, in town for a larger showcase, showed up for the show, and Captain Sensible got up onstage and jammed with them.

A few weeks later, at a packed gig at the Whiskey, a photographer from *Time* magazine snapped the Weirdos' photo backstage, which appeared in a special *Time* article on punk. "All of a sudden we were L.A.'s answer to the Ramones and the Sex Pistols," recalls Roman, "and we'd only been playing shows for two months."

Led by the Weirdos, Los Angeles suddenly blossomed into an enormously active punk club scene, featuring bands like the Eyes (with D. J. Bonebrake) and the Go-Gos and the Germs and the Zippers. At that time the music was rather friendly, though, colorful, even flip: swift, loud, poppy punk songs, with a sort of wry cynicism, not too serious, not too dark. "It was the best pogo music," says Vitus Matare. "You'd always lose your tennis shoes on the floor of the Whiskey, and everyone would end up piled against one wall and then the other, like human ball bearings, bouncing back and forth."

"People would go crazy," agrees Roman from the stage perspective. "They'd be packed in the front of us with no stage at all, and everyone would have their hands up in the air with three fingers. That was the Weirdos' sign."

Unlike many of the more traditional black-leather-clad and safety-pin-pierced punks, the Weirdos were fluorescent. They used staples instead of safety pins, wore Peter Frampton shirts with big Xs drawn across his face, and attached iron-on transfers to their pants. In those days irony was like a brand-new discovery. They played really intensely, but anger was not in it. Their songs were called things like "Do the Dance" and "Teenage," and their clownish aura would later leave L.A. with a not entirely complimentary reputation for goofcore, shunned as a place where lazy rich surfers pretended to be punk. But for that whole year the Weirdos were beloved: top draw at places like Blackie's in Santa Monica, as well as clubs like the Hong Kong Café and the Masque.

By that time the Weirdos had a single out on Bomp. In the

next year, they'd put out two others, one on Dangerhouse and the third again on Bomp. Within the first three months of the band's public existence, Roman was approached by Seymour Stein, head of Sire Records, about signing a deal, but nothing ever came of the meeting.

The band didn't really tour either, other than taking frequent trips to San Francisco. On January 14, 1978, they were booked into the Mabuhay Gardens in San Francisco, but took time before the show to check out the Sex Pistols, whose drummer Paul Cook reciprocated the favor a little later in the evening.

That year the Urinals—now adept at Wire and Fall-laden buzz punk—broke into Hollywood with the help of a UCLA physics major named Vitus Matare, who was also the keyboard player in a band called the Last. He had come to Dykstra's Halloween party and immediately offered to put the Urinals down on tape. Their first recording budget was sixteen dollars, half of which went for one hour's worth of studio time to mix the damn thing. Then the Urinals borrowed a hundred bucks from various dorm mates in order to press up two hundred copies of the single. They sold those to Rhino Records, and such was the popularity of seven-inch singles at the time that all two hundred sold out almost immediately.

It was a fertile year and a half there, documented in part by Dangerhouse Records, a local label, kind of the Sub Pop of its day. Between 1977 and 1979 it released limited-edition seven-inches of bands like the Alley Cats and the Bags, X and the Weirdos and the Dils, the kind that had cool one-of-a-kind covers and multicolor screen picture discs and so forth. The label was run by two art-bound transplanted midwesterners, David Brown and Pat Garrett.

L.A. had everything going for it—great fanzines, great record stores, even a commercial radio station, KROQ, that was actually committed to playing local bands and punk quite early on, thanks to Rodney Bingenheimer, a.k.a. Rodney on the Roq. Meanwhile, numerous clubs sympathetic to punk rock abounded, even after the Masque closed down in 1978. "The Starwood," Vitus recalls, "was the best. It had a big dance floor and a balcony and a real high stage so everyone could see. There were these huge overkill monitors, initially used for seventies metal acts, and the result was the bands could hear themselves really well. Those original monitors got destroyed one by one, either they'd blow out or get trashed, but initially you always left the Starwood with your ears ringing. But you'd had a great time."

During that era my friend Lisa Fancher was growing up in the San Fernando Valley. Years and years after we became friends, when I mentioned I was about to interview Joan Jett, Lisa said, "Oh, I interviewed her once. I'll fax you the story." It was a piece in *Bomp* magazine that I'd read as an impressionable fourteen-year-old, and I recall perfectly the envy I felt, not for Joan, the sixteen-year-old guitar-playing rebel of the piece, but for Lisa, the sixteen-year-old writer, who lovingly described packing herself into the Cherry Pit, hanging out with Kim Fowley on the palm-ridden boulevards of Sherman Oaks and Sun Valley, and sitting in Joan Jett's bedroom listening to Sweet singles 'cause she was a bitchin' rock journalist.

Lisa was a lot more resourceful than me. She got into punk rock through Rodney on the Roq and hearing the Runaways, and hanging around with Kim Fowley on the fringes of the Valley scene. She ran the Quick fan club and wrote for *Bomp*. She was also a ridiculously obsessive vinyl collector: "I logged a lot of time on the freeways, whizzing between Bomp and Zed Records and JEM [then a new distributor that specialized in import singles]: running in to be the first to hear the Buzzcocks, or rushing over to get the gatefold Skids single, and buying vintage records at the Capitol Records swap meet, which was also the two A.M. to six A.M. social scene for anyone who had just gone to a punk rock show."

Lisa eventually got herself a job at Bomp Records, which led in turn to writing gigs with the *Los Angeles Times* (she reviewed the first Ramones and Blondie records) and then the

Herald Examiner. But by the middle of 1979 everything had changed. What happened, of course, was that as punk rock started getting popular, the attention of the media and of the moderate record industry started changing the audience—and the bands' aspirations. Dangerhouse was over, its cash flow murdered by distributors and by the oil embargo, which raised the price of vinyl and made even larger labels suffer.

Meanwhile the scene was turning distinctly darker, with the more dissonant presence of bands like Fear and the Circle Jerks and a complementarily more dissonant crowd as well, this one made up of runaways, junkies, misfits, and the like. And then there was the compelling and disturbing but ultimately unstoppable force, the excellence that was X. X was formed by John Doe, a Baltimore native who'd moved to L.A. to become a songwriter of the more traditional type, and Exene (née Christine) Cervenka. The two met at a poetry reading in Venice and within six months were collaborating on music. They drafted the drummer from the Eyes, but for guitarist they hired a pick from left field, one Billy Zoom, a former glitter rock dude and the current axe in a Gene Vincent cover band that played Hollywood lounges.

The resultant music was worlds beyond the abilities of the heretofore simple and fun punk scene: instead of funny little anthems about objects and fashion, X wrote about the dark side of Los Angeles itself. They were the Nathanael Wests of the seventies: "She had to leave Los Angeles." "The phone's off the hook but you're not." "Johnny Hit and Run Paulene." The band was riveting. And inevitably, they became enormously popular. But by upping the artistic content of punk X also unwittingly upped the ante for everybody involved in the punk scene in L.A.

Some people now claim that a definite shift in punk consciousness occurred in the scene after Darby Crash of the Germs killed himself, in early December 1980 (news of his demise was wiped off the front pages by that of John Lennon, which occurred a few days later). Before Darby died, the argument goes, the whole scene was so unself-conscious. No one thought they'd be signed or even had those aspirations. But right after that, X started getting more professional and cold on stage, and Golden Voice started running all the shows more professionally, and the Go-Gos and the Blasters started getting major-label interest, and people stopped writing songs about Idi Amin. X started saying they were part of a country folk tradition and got produced by Ray Manzarek.

And then the venues began to disappear, busted one by one by the LAPD. It got so hard for a band to get booked that the Last were reduced to doing these funky little bills at art galleries on Broadway. Vitus remembers a show of obscene mail art where the keg blew up, everyone in the audience was hurling art out the window, and the band was continually being rammed by the audience, till the drummer was reduced to keeping time on someone's head. It was hardly punk rock's finest moment.

And then it was 1980 and there was a sudden influx of bands from the Valley and the southern suburbs, Redondo Beach, Orange County. Black Flag and the Circle Jerks and TSOL and the Descendants took over the punk scene, along with the Adolescents, Middle Class, Social Distortion, and Red Cross (later renamed Redd Kross, when the real organization sued for trademark), along with a bunch of worse ones. Unlike the Hollywood punks such as the Screamers, whom Lisa describes as "really mellow culture collectors who'd invite you over to dinner to listen to Martin Denny LPs," these bands were real garage bands, made up of real live kids. Their art bespoke a sensibility they'd thought up all themselves, an electric race through rock 'n' roll, a naive little "bring me giants," a blunt kick to the very heart of the matter. "[The songs are] fast," said Ron Reyes, at the time, " 'cause that's the amount of energy we have, and they're short because that's how long our inspiration lasts." *"I sure hope things get a whole lot better/All I know is they fucking better/Depression got a hold of me/I've got to . . . break free!"*

Black Flag was really the band that linked Hollywood and the beach. Not only was its nucleus located geographically between the two (at a practice space/flophouse/recording studio called the Church in Hermosa Beach), but stylistically and organizationally the band walked both sides of the punk/new wave line. Black Flag's music was bluntly anthemic, the opposite of new wave: they were really the first band called hardcore. But its main importance to L.A.'s scene was organizational: more than any other early punk band, they were adept at finding places to play, getting permits for outdoor concerts and booking one-offs into town halls. And they were immensely popular. As Mike Watt, of the band firehose, put it, "The kids pick their kings."

Although Gregg Ginn, Black Flag's guitarist, was a fan of all types of music, he often put together bills with the Orange County bands. (Those kids had the money; the Hollywood scene was so tiny, and nobody in it had any bucks.) Unfortunately, those original Orange County bands were big trouble. They came from communities with little, tiny, persecuting police departments, and they were violent, and they were mean. "And young," adds Watt. "They were like, fourteen, fifteen, whereas we were all working guys, who'd moved out of our parents' houses. Also, what was weird was, the Hollywood punks and us were like misfits: the ugly people. The Orange County crowd were good-looking jocks. They weren't outcasts at all; they'd just chosen punk as a slice of their generation."

This was the scene that was eventually documented in Penelope Spheeris's *The Decline of Western Civilization*. Released in 1981, the movie was shot at various punk locations from December 1979 to May 1980. Instead of celebrating that movement's energy, the movie seemed to emphasize the violence and nihilism and a certain slightly humorous stupidity on the parts of the participating punks. The concert sequences—especially those by Fear and X—are exciting, but like the movie *Sid and Nancy* after it, what *Decline* never captured was the innocence and fun of that time, the positiveness, the joy. The movie makes it seem like anyone who dyed or cut their hair was a freak show with a problem, when in fact, most of the people who had the courage and the wit to do such things back then were exactly the opposite.

Spheeris wasn't the only one to glorify the negative aspects of the punk scene. Around the time that movie was released, *Rolling Stone* ran a large article featuring a huge picture of Derf Scratch with head wounds. The author, Woody Hochswender, archly describes the punk scene as being full of rich white skinhead poseurs with "no values" T-shirts and "fast hard-driving bands with whining textures cry[ing] out that the air is bad, America is materialistic, Rodeo Drive stinks, love sucks (and its corollary, masturbation is convenient). It's a scene," he added, "full of contradictions and more than a little blood."

L.A.'s punk scene at the time may well have been bloody and contradictory. But that image was exaggerated by the media, unwittingly making itself into a tool of the L.A. police department to help get punks off the street. "There was a lot of violence, but it really got blown out of proportion," says Lisa. "Not a day went by when they didn't have some dumb TV talk show or 'Quincy' episode about punk violence. That scene was really aggro and hormonal and crazy, but the bands were truly great and hilarious, and also really individualistic. You know, the Adolescents were superfast but melodic, and Black Flag was intense and political, and Red Cross was twelve years old and had thirty-second songs. They were totally indigenous, and they arrived in our midst fully sprung. They were too young to go to shows or anything, so they were just like mutating Damned and Pistols records in their garages, and for some reason it all came out at ninety miles an hour.

"The funniest place to see a show was always the Santa Monica Civic. Black Flag would headline there to a couple of thousand, and it'd be a madhouse and the kids would kick the windows out.

"And after that the hardcore scene completely died. Police just drove them out—busted all the really fun shows. They used to have them at these strange places, a Polish hall, the Fleetwood— and the cops would break it up so no band could get a booking anywhere."

But punk rock was never just about buying leather jackets and singing about Ronald Reagan; it was anti-record industry. That was especially true in Los Angeles, where the record industry lives and works. And in 1980 the six major labels, which control 95 percent of all record releases (Sony, then called CBS; Warner Brothers; MCA; BMG; Polygram; and Capitol), were all in the middle of a huge slump, brought on in part by the oil shortage (records are made of petroleum products) and partly by the well-documented failure of disco. The number of independent labels (labels whose product is not owned, manufactured, or distributed by majors) had been rising since the late seventies, mostly to deal with punk rock bands who were bound to be excluded from major outlets of production and distribution, from radio and media and the rest of the mainstream. But the indie label network's concentrated success rate dates from that time. Because of the economic slump, and because, blinded by the unprecedented success of a single record, *Saturday Night Fever*, they were still fixated on producing disco, majors were not interfering or competing with little indies.

Probably because of its proximity to the majors, L.A. has always been an area rich in independent labels: by 1980, L.A. housed larger indie labels like Slash, IRS, and Enigma, as well as the littler labels like Dangerhouse, Frontier, and SST. And probably the most positive aspect of punk rock—and the one that was most ignored by the mainstream press—has always been its economy. Self-made records, homespun bands, cheap shows, good art: mental liberation for three dollars a pop. You can't beat that kind of bargain at K Mart or K-Tel.

But perhaps it is this very aspect of it that has had—like all anticapitalist statements, from communism to Jesus Christ—to be crushed by the powers that be. Youth culture should always be subdued or co-opted, the argument goes, because if it isn't, money, and thus power, will be transferred into the wrong hands.

And those detractors are paradoxically correct, since the acquisition of money and power always ends up being detrimental to art. X being signed to Slash (and later Elektra) was seen by some as a victory and vindication for L.A.'s punk scene, but many other bands—the Weirdos, for example, and the Screamers, and the Urinals (now called 100 Flowers)—never even had a chance. The Dickies, who went to A & M in 1979, were essentially viewed as a novelty act (they did a punk version of "The Sounds of Silence") and the Go-Gos put out a sweet, poppy record that was nonetheless essentially bereft of the raw, speedy charm that had made them popular among their peers. Also in 1980, Black Flag underwent litigations with MCA-Unicorn, which threw them more than ever back on their own resources.

Black Flag was originally going to record for Bomp Records, but when the deal fell through, guitarist Gregg Ginn and drummer Chuck Dukowski decided to release the record on their own label. It was dubbed SST after Solid State Transformers, the name of Ginn's ham radio antenna company, which he quickly adapted to move records instead.

One of the first bands Ginn signed to his label was the Minutemen, a San Pedro trio of punk jazz aficionados whose specialty was, as their name implies, songs that clocked in at just under sixty seconds. "Dada with a groove," one critic called their genre. Like Black Flag before them, the Minutemen felt frozen out by the Hollywood scene. Mike Watt was the band's bassist. "We went to all those shows as fans, but we just couldn't get our bands booked there. There was this big prejudice against suburban dudes. We didn't get booked at the Whiskey until 1982, and by then we had some leverage because we had our own label and everything."

Before signing to SST in 1980, the Minutemen (then called the Reactionaries) had tried to get gigs going in their hometown, San Pedro, about forty-five minutes from downtown L.A. "We played a few times at a bar called Capone's," says Watt, "but in those days it was like, 'Fuck you, Devo!' every other song. And it was guys I went to high school with yelling that shit. . . . They acted like we were taking a stance on their whole life; drawing a line in the sand or something!"

"Punk," adds Watt, "is something you have to do to know it, and the only ones who understand it are the ones who did. Punk was about more than just starting a band, it was about starting a label, it was about touring, it was about taking control. It was like songwriting: you just do it. You want a record, just pay the pressing plant. That's what it was all about."

Because she'd worked at Bomp, Lisa Fancher knew that too. It had always been her ambition to save her money and start a little label, which she called Frontier Records. "There were hardly any indie labels at the time," she recalls, "and there were just so many great bands in L.A. that were really getting screwed. There were like *no* A & R people at shows. The bands would be selling twenty to fifty thousand copies of their records, mostly in L.A., and with virtually no advertising, and still no one wanted to touch them. I could see what was going wrong, so I knew what I could do right if I actually got into it."

Her first project was a band called the Flyboys. "It was the usual story," she says. "They were good guys but they'd had all these problems putting a record out, so I offered to do it. I'd worked at Bomp Records and knew people at Jem, so I knew all about pressing, jackets, and distribution. We paid for a couple of recording sessions, but the rest was done after hours at Leon Russell's studio because Jim Mankey [currently of Concrete Blonde] had a key. It was a kind of kamikaze thing. Of course the band broke up within days of seeing their LP in the store, and there went all my capital! Oh, I made back my investment of two thousand dollars, but only just. Still, that's a chance you take, and it was fun. I still had a job, and I still had the intention of doing another record sometime. It was a classic learning experience."

Her next experience was even more edifying. It was 1981 and the hardcore scene was at its height. "As it happened," says Fancher, "no one wanted to put out the Circle Jerks' LP *Group Sex*. It was total providence. I said, 'I'll do it!' I remember one of them hanging up on me: 'No girl's gonna put out our record!' But they checked me out, found out I was OK, and I did it. The weird thing is, I had no idea how popular they were, and I didn't really have enough money. I thought I'd press five thousand copies, but I had preorders for thirteen thousand and no credit at all. I ended up having to burst into tears at the pressing plant just to get the order filled."

Lisa had given the Jerks fifteen hundred dollars for the finished tape and, after expenses, split the profits fifty-fifty. "I thought that was fair at the time," she laughs. "But we all made a fortune! It's sold about a hundred and fifty thousand copies by now. It's a classic, classic punk record, and it's what made everything else fall into place for me. After them I did the Adolescents' *Amoeba* [sixty thousand copies sold] and TSOL's *True Sounds of Liberty* [eighty thousand]. I was on a roll. Word got out that I paid royalties, that I was a nice person, pretty easy to talk to, accessible.

"It was kind of terrifying though," she continues. "I mean, here I'd been getting checks from the distributors for more than I'd made in an entire year. I'd get checks for thirteen thousand dollars and write checks for ten thousand dollars all in the same transaction, never seeing any of it. I was terrified for the longest time to take any of the money home. I thought the company would crumble if I did. I wouldn't even hire an employee; I did everything myself."

Frontier's profits for its first year were about $30,000; by 1985, it was grossing $500,000, and by the nineties, after leaving indie distribution for more solid backing from BMG, Frontier grosses in the $1–2 million range, thanks to another growth spurt induced by the self-titled debut record of the band Suicidal Tendencies, which featured the novelty hit number

"Institutionalized," a noisy seesaw of a blues drone topped by an endless raplike monologue about teen–parent relationships by singer Mike Muir. In it, a character not unlike a male version of Darlene Connor on the sitcom "Roseanne" is quizzed by his parents regarding his delinquent activities, sullen demeanor, and general state of teenage mental health. The chorus consists of the singer screaming at his parents, "I'm not crazy—*Institutionalized!*—you're the ones that're crazy—*Institutionalized!*" At the end of the song, the parents commit the hapless lad to an institution, while he complains bitterly that "all [he] wanted was a Pepsi!"

That LP, released in 1983, has sold, according to Lisa, "absolute shitloads: five hundred thousand copies to date. Suicidal pays for everything," she adds, "a fact which Mike Muir harbors with great resentment to this day, which I can't understand. They got paid too!"

Lisa eventually bought a house based on the first surge of profits; after Suicidal, however, she was deep into the paisley underground, onward and upward and interested in other things. Suicidal Tendencies, she says, was a real last gasp for the punk scene. "The punk scene really had a sort of short shelf life," Lisa adds. "It was a lot like the hiphop scene is now, in that you had to have stuff out right when it was hot or forget it, it shifted. There's been a million hardcore punk records since, but after I did mine [the Adolescents and Circle Jerks] I felt like the scene had pretty much been mined. By 1983, all the best punk came out of Texas."

That may have been true as far as what was now called hardcore was concerned. But there were still great bands in Los Angeles. It was just that their musical preoccupations had radically altered, gone from dissonance and anger into hypnotic Velvet Undergroundisms and blues. The transformation was most apparent in the music of the Dream Syndicate. That band was known for playing twenty-minute-long guitar jams, about as far in spirit from the swift kick of punk as it could possibly be. And by the mid-eighties, Los Angeles was suffused with other post-punk movements as well, each with its own clique, label, and media-made following. There was, for example, a plentiful roots rock scene, exemplified in various different ways by the Blasters, the Long Ryders, Los Lobos, and even X (who'd long since abandoned the punk rock aegis for some real-world creed). There was the paisley underground—a loose conglomeration of neopsychedelic bands led by the aforementioned Dream Syndicate, the Bangles, the Three O'Clock, and Green on Red. Despite being closely tied up with the underground (the Dream Syndicate and Green on Red were initially on Slash, the Bangles on IRS, the Three O'Clock on Frontier), those bands seemed to be gunning for major-label deals from the start, and eventually got sanctioned in the mainstream by both Macy's and Prince. But as Vitus Matare points out, "All the same people went to see them who'd gone to see the punk shows, because by then everyone was addicted to going to clubs."

Lastly, there was the newly transfigured result of the hardcore scene, a strange, slow manifestation of blues rock and metal that revolved around the bands on SST. Although Gregg Ginn and Chuck Dukowski had begun SST in 1978 primarily to press and distribute the fruits of their own band, Black Flag, they were generous with their profits, and by 1983 SST was releasing vinyl by other artists, including the Minutemen; the Meat Puppets, from Tucson, Arizona; and Minneapolis's Hüsker Dü.

One of the things SST Records was particularly effective at was getting bands booked, early on in their careers, all the way across the country and even in Europe, with a reasonable guarantee. That was a crucial step in forming the whole independent network.

"Black Flag really blazed a trail for us," says Mike Watt. "That's what they should really be remembered for, making a circuit that even mellow little prim bands now have to follow. They found every anticlub in the country, and everyone chased after 'em down the road."

Tragically, the Minutemen's songwriter and singer, D.

Boon, died in a car accident in Arizona, at Christmas of 1985. But by that time the cult status of those four critically beloved bands—the Minutemen, Black Flag, the Meat Puppets, and Hüsker Dü—had made anything bearing the SST label hallowed by association. SST was like a *Good Housekeeping* seal of approval, guaranteeing that the music therein was, if not always entirely listenable, at least completely outside the mainstream, unacceptable to other labels. And at its best, in the years 1984–87, the label's roster was unique, uncorporate, and relatively eclectic. Many of its bands—including the Descendants and All, Vitus's new band Trotsky Icepick, the Divine Horsemen, and firehose (the band formed by the remaining two Minutemen and a Minutemen fan from Ohio named Ed Crawford)—were L.A.-based, but SST's roster wasn't confined to Southern California: they drew talent from all over the country. By the mid-eighties the label was on such a roll that it could cherry-pick the best independent bands from every locale—many of them, like Sonic Youth and Dinosaur Jr., already browned off at the original independent label they came from. Thus SST managed to reap what it had helped to sow, by releasing, for example, Sonic Youth's fifth and sixth LPs, *EVOL* and *Sister*, easily the band's most brilliant work. They put out Dinosaur Jr.'s second two LPs in 1987 and 1988, respectively. They even put out Soundgarden's *Ultramega* LP, thus helping to usher in the Sub Pop era.

SST also put out countless forgettable LPs by bands like Zoogz Rift, St. Vitus, and Tom Troccoli's Dog: in fact, one of SST's hallmarks was its sheer profligacy. In 1987, SST had eighty releases, most by new acts—way more than major labels like Warner Brothers or Capitol would dare introduce to the world. Of course, everybody knows that at a given time there aren't eighty great bands in existence on the planet, but for a short while people were buying bands on the SST label purely for their cachet. "At the time we were too inside it to see what our impact was," comments Watt, "but nowadays I've met bands who've told me it was always their goal to make a record for SST."

L.A.'s live scene has not really flourished since those halcyon days of old, however. The police still lean heavily on underground punk's case, and SST's roster is confined to Ginn's ever more peculiar taste and of course its still bright back catalog: Black Flag, the Minutemen, Hüsker Dü, Sonic Youth.

Meanwhile, Frontier is also still alive and well, busy releasing records by many vital indie bands like the Young Fresh Fellows, Flop, and Heatmiser. Although none of those bands are L.A.-based, Frontier still to some extent supports L.A.'s ever-etiolating local scene: in 1991 and 1992 it released two compilations of Dangerhouse Records' early singles, as well as a record by a regenerated Weirdos. Both are definitive overviews of the early L.A. punk scene.

The truth about L.A. was revealed to me quite early. Only a few years after I left it, I became aware that my time there had been unbelievably poorly spent. But going by my experiences alone, L.A. will always seem a dubious location for anything relating to art. It's much more comfortable to picture the place as home to Guns N' Roses and the Grammys, as the birthplace of all videos, and the graveyard of aesthetic credibility, integrity, and the like.

And yet, where better a place to subvert the mainstream than from its very bowels? Project: Mersh! Minuteflag! Don't Suck Corporate Cock! Friends Don't Let Friends Listen to Corporate Rock! These are the noble slogans of the Los Angeles underground in the years in between punk rock and now, when hardcore bands in their various incarnations buried themselves in the smoggy nights and forged the basis for a sound that would come to be called grunge.

And in my own time, from the safe distance of San Francisco, I ended up loving them all, the ones on these labels and all the others, L.A.'s finest: the Minutemen, 100 Flowers, Redd Kross, the Gun Club, Dream Syndicate, and Green on Red. I'd like to repair the rift in my memory of that time in Los Angeles, a faulty perspective of some sort, which blinded me to the beauty of the valley from the air. I'd like to relive those bad nights at Raji's and cruise down the freeway afterward singing softly along with Green on Red on KXLU: "*It takes money to make money, they say/Ain't it funny how love doesn't work that way?*" L.A. should have been my Paris in the twenties, but instead it was only my sad little Troy. We were the vandals, the infidels, the Huns . . . but even now I'm still not sure just who was sacking whom.

FIVE

MARGIN WALKING

Only the amplified truth of Ulysses shall be heard, as we reveal those who obscure their folly through a postured roll in the dungheap of yesteryear, puncturing aptly the validity its crust, dust, and odor supposedly impart (actually a veneer for the glamorization of those who and that which went before [read: abhorred parent culture] whose despised "Rock 'n' Roll" anthems and self-congratulatory Woodstock eulogy smatters us senseless, invading every orifice uninvited, reminding us at each turn what a golden age theirs was—yawn—and of their ineffectual epoch).

– Outline of the Nation of Ulysses Memorandum on New Programs for World Revolution: "13 Point Plan to Destroy America"

One cold November day in 1987, while attending an INXS video shoot on Balboa Pier in Newport Beach, I met an extra named Dave who'd been clad in a wetsuit for twelve hours straight. Dave, who was supposed to portray a skateboarding surfer type in the video for "Devil Inside," recognized me as some kind of a kindred spirit by my torn-off Black Flag T-shirt. He was, he said, from Huntington Beach, a member of the infamous HB gang who used to frequent punk clubs in packs, whaling on anyone who stepped on their turf. I told him I was from San Francisco. "Oh, God, the good old days at the Mab," he said fondly, with a quick, dispirited glance at the members of INXS.

I always think of Dave, who runs a sailboat business in

San Diego, when I think about that era: the danger and suggestiveness of inserting yourself into a mosh pit on Broadway; the glory days of punk. Certainly Californian beach punks invented hardcore (the term was meant to differentiate mere punk rock, like goofy clean Devo songs or arty Buzzcockian English stuff, from the more brutal, homespun sound of some of its successors). But there was another place where, in 1981, the genre was refined and exalted, where the music and its corollaries became intertwined with an ideology so outside the mainstream that even most punk rockers had trouble dealing with its strictures—and still do. The place was Washington, D.C., the band was called Minor Threat, and the label they played for was Dischord.

You know how every kid lives in hope of finding a way to blast through the falsest of their parents' values? I always have had a sneaking suspicion that D.C. kids' wholesale commitment to a creed of anticapitalism and meatless mayhem is due to having parents whose business it is to run the government. Living so close to the daily workings of systematic betrayal, the kids of D.C. found a way to truly madden their elders. No doubt the District of Columbia is not entirely made up of lushy red-nosed senators, but it is still somehow peculiarly fitting that, all throughout the Reagan years, the D.C. punk rock scene in particular was at the most extreme edge of leftist. D.C.'s punk rock scene has been political since day one, but the rest of the planet hasn't exactly leapt on its bandwagon: more than once in the last decade, the city's scene has closed ranks rather than touch pitch.

Ezra Pound once wrote, "Civilization depends on local control of purchasing power needed for local purposes." He also wrote, "Damn you, sing: Goddamn. Goddamn. Goddamn, 'tis why I am. Goddamn." Either statement could be the guiding precept for Dischord Records, the label of Minor Threat and the business end of the powerful personality traits of Ian MacKaye, guitarist for Minor Threat and co-owner of Dischord. Ian grew up in D.C. and attended Woodrow Wilson High School, where he hung out with a bunch of skateboarders. At the time, WGBT, the Georgetown University radio station, had one punk rock show, called "Mystic Eyes," which all the hipsters at Wilson listened to, but he himself listened to it only twice: "I listened to the doo-wop show instead."

In 1978, Ian recalls, he thought Ted Nugent was hot shit. "Some of my friends were into the Ramones and we'd go, 'You're all just new wave faggots!' in a playful kind of arguing way. Then at Christmas of 1978 my sister lent me the Tuff Darts album. And then I heard the Clash and the Sex Pistols and the Jam and the Damned."

That fall Ian got hooked. Meanwhile, over at Georgetown, WGBT had just gotten in trouble for running a Planned Parenthood ad. The station was being sold for a dollar, and a protest punk rock show was being held in honor of its death. Ian, then seventeen, went to the show, which featured the Cramps.

"It was such a life-altering experience for me," he recalls now. "It was the greatest show I'd ever seen. It had everything: overcrowded hall, people climbing in through the windows, chairs breaking, total chaos. Lux Interior threw up onstage. . . . It was just so different from anything I'd ever seen. I clearly remember seeing Nick Knox taking a piss and it scared the shit out of me, because he was in *the band!* It was like, I shouldn't be having any contact with him!"

Next day, Ian cut off all his hair. A week later he saw the Clash, with Bo Diddley opening. There was no turning back. At that point, Ian formed a band called Slinkees with his high school friends Jeff Nelson, Geordie Grindle, and Mark Sullivan. Ian played bass. They did really goofy songs, he remembers, meant to piss off their hippie friends. "There was one called 'Conservative Rock' and one called 'I Like Milk,' and all this mean stuff about Trans Ams and the Grateful Dead, because that's what we hated. It was kind of my first straight protest stuff."

Presently, Mark went to college, so that band mutated into the Teen Idles. "There was the commune here called Madam's

Organ, a bunch of yippies living in a row house, and they'd do shows every weekend for two dollars, and we finally got on a bill with the Bad Brains. They were considered, like, this real inner-city band and we were the first real suburban band—although actually they were from the suburbs and we were from the city. At that time there were a lot of arty bands, playing scientist rock, discordant no-wave stuff. But we just played really, really fast."

The Idles were still in high school, but, Ian recalls, "whenever we got paid, we never split the money, we put it in a cigar box. We were totally frugal and did really cheap shows from day one. I remember the first interview I ever did with the Wilson High newspaper. The girl asked, 'Are you playing music for the girls or the money?' and I was, like, totally befuddled. It just never crossed my mind to do it for either."

Slowly, the Idles, the Bad Brains, and several other bands—including Ian's little brother's band, the Untouchables—started to make a local scene, helped on by knowledge acquired through the clerks at Yesterday and Today Records in Rockville, Maryland (the same Rockville as in R.E.M.'s song "Don't Go Back to Rockville"). Ian and his skateboarding pal Henry Garfield (later surnamed Rollins) were insane record collectors, especially fixated on seven-inch singles from California. "I remember we'd all pile in a car and drive out there and we'd be bracing ourselves on the balls of our feet as we pulled into the parking lot in order to jump out of the car before it even stopped moving and be the first person to get to the bin of new singles. The Dils' single was just so incredible . . . and everything on Dangerhouse, which I thought was the coolest label ever. I started getting *Damage* and *Slash* and English magazines and learning all about other scenes."

Because they were obsessed by California, Ian and his friends decided that the Teen Idles would tour California the summer after they graduated—1980. "We thought California was where it was at. We had heard Black Flag's single, it was our favorite, and *Slash* and *Flipside* were like our Bible. Besides, we hated New York City because it was full of English punk clones and junkies.

"So we booked two gigs, one at the Hong Kong Café in L.A. and one at the Mab in San Francisco, and we took the Greyhound bus out. Henry and Mark were our roadies, and we only had our guitars and drumsticks, and we borrowed people's equipment out there."

Of course the tour, though now a fond memory, was a disaster. When the Idles arrived at the bus station in L.A., they discovered their one L.A. contact's phone had been disconnected. Drummer Jeff Nelson got arrested at the bus station for jokingly grabbing his ass as a gesture toward an undercover cop who'd called the (pink-haired) band members "faggot" and "clown." Ian had to call a distant great-uncle and invite himself and his five friends over. The gig at the Hong Kong Café was a bust as well: thirty people showed up; the band made fifteen dollars.

Then the Idles split to San Francisco, where they discovered that the Mab's owner, Dirk Dirkson, had bumped them off their intended bill—which also featured the Dead Kennedys, Flipper, and the Circle Jerks—because he thought their photo was cheesy. ("And it wasn't cheesy, it was cool!") The Idles stayed at Target Video in the Mission and attended the show as spectators, which may have been the scene of the first ever instance of stage diving. "We met the HB—Huntington Beach—crowd there, the Alva Brothers and Gregg Gutierrez [later of the Three O'Clock and Mary's Danish], and they were totally insane! They came to our gig the next night—we played with the Wrong Brothers and Lost Angeles—and got in all these fights. Gregg got hit on the head with a bottle and it sent him to the hospital.

"But we were totally intoxicated by it. The whole thing was just mind-boggling. We loved them and they loved us. They were blown away because our style was so different from theirs. It was like this huge meeting of regions."

The Idles returned to D.C. with renewed ambition. Other bands began springing up from their crowd—Government Issue, Youth Brigade. "We thought, 'This is so cool, we'll do a little label, and everyone will get their own seven-inch,' " recalls Ian. "We thought we'd document the D.C. scene."

Thus it was that he and Nelson formed Dischord Records in the fall of 1980. The Idles had just broken up—but the band still had eight hundred dollars in their cigar box, so Dischord's first release was the Teen Idles single. "We had already recorded a tape and we just knew no one would put it out, so we just went, 'Fuck it, we'll do it ourselves.' And Skip Groff [of Yesterday and Today] showed us how, since he knew the guys in England at Stiff Records and he had his own label called Limp. We put eight songs on it because our songs were so short, and that was that."

Distribution? "The first concept was just selling it at shows and local stores. We'd take 'em up to Bleecker Bob's [in New York City] and Newbury Comix [in Boston] when we went up on weekends to visit our friends who were in college there. It was supposed to be on consignment, but they only cost a dollar each. So the store would ask for five singles and tell us we had to wait for the money, and we'd be like, 'Jeez, can't you just give us the five bucks?' "

Slowly, Ian recalls, a network started to form. "We saw a copy of *Touch and Go* magazine at the Tape and Record Exchange and we sent them a record. It arrived broken in four pieces, but they taped it together and played it anyway and raved about it in their review section and ordered a bunch more. That was how it went."

Pretty soon—damn soon—the Teen Idles sold out all one thousand copies of their single. Then they sold another thousand. And another. The second single was Henry Rollins's band SOA (State of Alert), which Henry paid for himself. It had ten songs on it. Each single, Ian recalls, cost about eight hundred dollars to make. 'But we didn't give a fuck about money. We just made back the investment. I had all these day jobs—I worked at an ice cream place, a movie theater, and driving a newspaper truck. I drank tons of Coca-Cola and never slept."

When the money came back, Dischord did the third one: Minor Threat's *In My Eyes*. And one way or another—word of mouth, mail order, whatever—Minor Threat caught on big-time. And, Geoff Weiss's championship up in Boston aside, they did so with an incredibly minimal amount of college radio airplay. "We could always have given a fuck about college radio," Ian laughs. "We're from D.C., we don't know about radio. Besides, we thought college sucked. It's funny now, because nowadays colleges are nothing *but* punk rockers, but back then I always thought punk rock and college didn't mix. I remember going up to visit Mark at Colgate, in upstate New York, and walking around in midwinter in our chains and spurs and people just regarding us like shits. There were no punk rockers there.

"We did hook up with some stations early on: KPFA, KUSF, WERS. For the most part, we didn't get any airplay. Besides, on *Minor Threat* I say *fuck* on all but one song. I never thought punk rock was about radio anyway. It's about playing, and being contrary and rebellious and not accepting the status quo."

With that theory in mind, that summer (1981) Minor Threat did a two-week tour of the Midwest with Youth Brigade. "It was fifteen teenagers, two of them only fourteen, in a van, a Volvo, and my Plymouth Duster," Ian recalls. "We booked Chicago, Madison, Detroit, Reno, San Francisco, and San Diego, but we never got beyond Madison. The whole tour got aborted when somebody's parents ordered their minivan back."

Throughout 1982, Minor Threat drove up and down the eastern seaboard, gaining speed, distributors, and fans—cutting itself a new swath of audience made up of some outcast breed of minors, an unheralded and unnoticed constituency whose presence wouldn't be felt or included in the college radio or metal world or anywhere else, for that matter, for years to come. Meanwhile, at home in D.C., the live scene was so happening, so inbred, and so very loyal to its own that, according to Ian, for years even big touring national punk acts had to open for local bands, like Minor Threat and the Bad Brains.

In 1983, the band released "Out of Step." It sold thirty-five hundred copies in one week. "And all our money was tied up with the distributors for six months," Ian recalls, "so we couldn't afford to reorder it. We had slated the record by Faith—my brother's band—up next, and it was kind of this big moral dilemma, whether to use the money we had for reorders of "Out of Step" or to release the new record by Alec's band. We borrowed money from friends and then this guy John Loder showed up at a Minor Threat show in New York from London. He had this business, Southern Studios, and he could get credit at the pressing plant and stuff . . . so he helped us reorder five thousand copies, and that was it." Ian pauses. "Bombshell."

In the world of punk and hardcore, Minor Threat still stands alone in its ability to convey its beliefs, in its blind emotional momentum. Its music is not exactly melodic—you don't hum *Out of Step* to yourself when you're feeling nostalgic for 1983. But there's something forever undated about its sheer force of delivery. Its tempos charge along at ninety miles per hour; Ian's vocals are a scratchy shout, and the lyrics, which state that most people are fucked and intolerance is intolerable, are starkly stated manifestos, bluntly uttered discoveries spit out by boys whose outrage is so innocent it is positive, pure. Minor Threat's power is tribute to the credo that an electric guitar in the hands of a dedicated fifteen-year-old can be as expressive and as true to, say, Brian Baker as a pen was to Alexis de Tocqueville or a sword to Attila the Hun. "Out of Step" has a kind of clarity that shreds through rock 'n' roll cliché; its immediacy is so precisely rendered, its feelings are so real. *"Sit in the same room . . . we look the other way . . . fuck conversation, we've got nothing to say . . . I'm sure we both hate to be ignored—haven't we met someplace before? Haven't we met before?"*

Minor Threat's sound has never been improved on; it is still the Beatles of hardcore, the be-all and end-all of that era. There was a downside to D.C.'s development, however, and that, unfortunately, was its fierceness. The local loyalty factor somehow created a scene that, like L.A.'s scene before it, was riddled with serious punk rock violence. Nowadays a lot of people remember only that aspect of the movement. "The violence and anger of it wasn't the only thing going on here at that time, but it was part of it," recalls Ian. "It really crackled. People were so defensive about the scene and stuff . . . and so jacked up. It was so exciting, the music and the interplay between people; it was just so obviously heavy. But there was this massive amount of ferociousness waiting to come out."

And Ian was usually at the center of the storm. "It was like, the Slinkees were my fun band, and then the Teen Idles were more angry, and then by the time Minor Threat came along, I was just so pissed off," he recalls. "I guess I'd just gotten so marginalized. Maybe I marginalized myself, but I was always considered such a kook because I was straight, and that was always such a goddamn big deal to other people. I got ridden like a motherfucker for it, always, and there I was—I was so angry over the choices I'd been given, and then I was being ridiculed for the choices that I made. I got beat up and treated like shit, and I guess it made me angry.

"I mean, here we were, we were nice and straight and honest, doing harmless stuff like skateboarding and listening to music, and yet the revulsion level about us was pretty high. We were chased in the street! I guess that's how the anger factor crept in. I used to have to fight a lot. From '81 to '84 I got in hundreds of fights, almost always at shows. We weren't jumping people, there was this strong family concept among our friends, but there'd always be some asshole or drunk guy, and we'd just get into it.

"I think," says Ian now, "I always had this deep desire to be taken seriously. I'd been laughed at all the time by people who were trying to decide how I was going to act. I'm really not a cruel or hateful person, but now I see it was so empowering to fight. I mean, you can't imagine the satisfaction of having some high school guys cruise by calling you 'faggot' out the window, and you and all your friends start chasing their car down the street and them getting so terrified that they run a red light to get away from you, and us all standing at the intersection laughing at them.

"I guess I thought of threatening people as a way to make them take responsibility for their actions. I can see how effective violence as a form of communication is. But it becomes uncontrollable. And by 1984 it was just so ugly. And I'd confront people who were fighting at gigs and they'd say, 'But we're just trying to protect the scene like you did, Ian,' and I was like, 'Oh my God, what have I done?' "

Minor Threat broke up in 1983. After that, Ian concentrated on working at Dischord, producing and releasing records by other bands (though he did play in a purely local band called Embrace). Ian is currently revered in the underground for his long-standing integrity, for running Dischord and belonging to Minor Threat, for his successful translation of his ideals into a profitable business, and lastly for Fugazi, a band he formed that year with Joe Lally and two former members of the Rites of Spring in 1987. That came later, though, after 1985, when, Ian recalls, there was a resurgence when "all the punk rockers woke up and went, 'What have we got?' We decided that everyone would form a new band and fucking start over. That was when Embrace, Gray Matter, and Rites of Spring began. And we came out and said, 'OK, we're big pussies now; we're wimps, that's cool.' "

But it wasn't just a style change, it was one that went deeper. It was more like an adjustment, a sort of correction, within the bands themselves. They began flying in the face of the macho virus that had become hardcore punk rock. They still do.

These days, the D.C. scene, as documented by Dischord Records, is the Galápagos Islands of the independent music world. It is the control group by which we can trace the seeds of corruption that afflicted everywhere else. By isolating itself for those crucial four years when the rest of the alternative world was busting its ass to get bigger, it ultimately retained its ideals. Of course, D.C. might have developed a blistering punk rock scene without Ian MacKaye—after all, the Bad Brains existed there before he was even out of high school—but it's doubtful if it would ultimately have had the same level of integrity. I can't for the life of me think how Ian has managed to maintain his shiny-eyed idealism throughout a decade in which every single aspect of postpunk rock and the Amerindie movement has been incorporated, corrupted, or disabled by the machinations of the record industry—or how he maintains it in a world full of children whose brain cells have been colorized ugly by MTV. But since he has managed to do it, it is only fair that we take note. Respect, as he and his label mates often say about other bands, is due. Respect is fucking due.

Southern Studios still works as a pressing agent and distributor for Dischord, and Dischord has sold over a million copies of combined titles. Fugazi alone has done 160,000 sales per title (there're six) and hit the top of both Rockpool and CMJ charts—although Dischord is cautious about advertising and sends out very few promos. Twelve years down the line, like Minor Threat before them, Fugazi's gloves are still up regarding crucial issues such as local control of money. They stick to a strict all-ages policy. They are selective about which magazines they'll do interviews with, because they believe that not everyone on the planet needs to know about their mere existence: a sadly novel concept in this world of media overload. They still—in 1993—try to never charge more than six dollars per show. (I once paid six dollars, for a pro-choice benefit. I also once paid $3.75.)

"But it's never been a matter of being didactic," says Ian. "It's never been telling people what to do or think. It's always been what was happening here at the time. Dischord just documented it. We've never had an agenda, at all. You know, certain scenes come and go, they're like explosions that fade away. This community has been around for quite a while. I suppose someday it'll go away, and when it does, so will the label. I would never force the issue, or put out crap. . . . I want Dischord to be like a book, with a beginning and a middle and an end."

"When I was a child, I spake as a child . . . but when I became a man, I put away childish things." That has always struck me as being the biggest home truth in the Bible. I do not agree with its sentiment or import, but I keep seeing it enacted, even within the boundaries of the punk rock scene, over and over again. So many punks, like hippies before them, have seemingly divided their life into two distinct modes. The first mode is childhood, all aggro and out of control, crying out against injustice, liberty, and individuality. The other? Staid and stopped and even stooped—all of it somehow in direct contradiction to the wildness of youth. Suddenly they think it's time to put away childhood things, and the first thing to go is always the electric guitar.

So the slam dance grinds to a halt. The punk rock scene, kept nominally alive through the fringes of hardcore, is now mere embers, burning and bumping against one another, driven into hiding, where it starts to mutate strangely, alone in the dark. Now we are alone in our love affair, huddled together in a still inviolate group, circling our wagons. There are always ways and means, of course—places to go and people to see—and always there are garages. All over the country, kids are locked inside the house, fomenting contents that will spill forth soon enough.

Out there, where the music industry watches cannily over what's going on in our world, they know nothing of all that. Out there, they're busy playing games with their tainted cash, purchasing the services of former college radio program directors, stocking major label staffs with underground experts who've decided to go corporate, ruining real rock bands by promising them the moon, and, of course, concocting MTV formats by which to sell our once-lovely youth movement back to unsuspecting squares. They think that punk is dead, and that we've given up our childish things, but actually we're just resting. We're reflecting on all that has passed. We are waiting, and watching out of the corners of our eyes, whiling away the time thinking about, oh, I don't know, sex, death, and God's great silence. We are thinking about our glorious past and hoping that somewhere, somehow, the embers are still smoldering.

TWO

IN BLOOM

SIX

SHAKING THROUGH

Something's missing from my head, where a mouth should be, I'm all ears instead. I've swallowed everything you said, I've been well-fed . . .

– Big Dipper, "Impossible Things Before Breakfast"

Francesca is staring fixedly at the stage. Slowly, she bends her knees so her mouth is right by my ear. "Dance," she hisses into it. "It intimidates people."

We begin to flail wildly away in time to "Wolves Lower," our arms swinging in slo-mo, fancying ourselves a lot like Morrissey in the "How Soon Is Now" video. Soon we've cut ourselves a hole a full arm's length in circumference in the crowd around the stage. It's June 1984, and she and I are standing nose to nose with R.E.M. at the Catalyst in Santa Cruz, an hour's drive south of the Bay Area. We'd heard the gig announced on the radio that afternoon and, convinced it'd be sold out, each left her respective workplace on a trumped-up excuse ("That was my mom. I have to quick take the cat to the vet!") and bought a pair of tickets, one for the other.

For Francesca and me at that time, R.E.M. was already bigger than the Beatles, smarter than Einstein, more spiritual than the Pope: we kept forgetting that the world at large had never heard of them. But when we got to the Catalyst, as early as was humanly possible, it was clear the gig was going to be a bust. So we ate our extra tickets along with our dinner at the café next door to the club. We were, I remember, sitting directly across from Michael Stipe, no doubt unnerving him with our worshipful stares. Later on we had a long, though essentially boring, conversation about tamales with Bill Berry at the bar.

Those were the days when you could do that kind of thing, though: worship a band's music, but still exchange pleasantries with its members in social situations. Invite them over to dinner. Ask them to scrawl the chords of "Don't Go Back to Rockville" on the back of a cocktail napkin. Let them sleep on your floor. It wasn't like with the bands who were a little older, a little more jaded, the Gun Club, or the Cramps. Those bands betrayed their late-seventies origins by clinging to the concept of the backstage pass. In 1984 I used to run into members of bands I absolutely loved and be able to talk to them as if they were normal human beings. For God's sake! Would I ever have acted so familiarly to Chrissie Hynde? Ray Davies? Keith Richards? Rod Stewart?

The members of R.E.M. were like regular guys—a little on the rude side, kind of drunk, not too good-looking. But they put on shows that left us standing there, in the middle of the dance floor, gaping, the kind of show that went by in an instant in some other time warp, stumbling, as Stipe put it, through our ABCs. After they were over, we couldn't speak, couldn't clap, or anything. We just stood there with our peers, nobody leaving, nobody talking. Awestruck.

That's why everything else that followed was entirely their fault. The success of college radio, the Amerindie scene, the formation of alternative music departments at record companies, the International Pop Underground, Nirvana. Ultimately, you can lay it all at R.E.M.'s feet, as if the whole damn subject were a dead mouse or a bird or something equally unsavory. Pretend you're a faithful doggie, and they're your kind masters. Sit still, now . . . walk.

Because even though college radio had created a way for bands to be heard by those who cared coast to coast, even though there were splinter scenes well before R.E.M. came along; even though punk rock denizens had started independent labels everywhere already; even though they took off from already established groups like the Velvet Underground, Big Star, the Byrds, and the Feelies, and even though there was already a core network of underground people stretching back to a time well before the invention of a group called R.E.M. (stretching backward past New York's no-wave scene, CBGB's, Television, Patti Smith, the Talking Heads, the Ramones, and the New York Dolls, and by now we're in, like, 1974), even so, it was R.E.M. and only R.E.M. who galvanized the entire subculture and made it into a community.

Before that, there were a bunch of different local scenes, made up, for the most part, of highly knowledgeable record geeks who worked in college radio. After R.E.M. came along, there was really only one.

The thing about them was that their music was all-inclusive. There was something about the murky lilting chime of Peter Buck's guitar; the piercingly private one-note howl of Michael Stipe's voice and lyrics and the subsequent jointure of the two that tolled of liberty right from the start. When you heard them, you looked up, and all you heard were sky-blue bells ringing.

This is the effect R.E.M. has had on everybody who has loved them, from the beginning of their time to the present, through the course of eight long-playing albums. In 1983 my sister, then a construction manager at Bechtel Corporation in downtown San Francisco, bought their EP *Chronic Town* at the record store based entirely on the cover: a grainy black-and-white close-up of a snarling gargoyle, with the white parts washed out in a vivid sky-blue. It reminded her, she said, of Flannery O'Connor. One day she played it for me as if it were the aural equivalent of *Wise Blood* only better, because this was a story that was only about us. I drank in that music like it was water in a desert, and I hadn't even known I was thirsty.

From then on its four songs rang out of our separate apartments over and over again, for years and years to come. That R.E.M. were from Georgia, were on an independent label, were unlikely to appear on MTV (which barely existed then anyway)—the significance of all these things escaped us entirely. All we knew was how much we loved that record, its strum-and-drangle pop, with its Byrdsian country overtones, its lyrics about sound, its furious halloo. There was nothing violent or passionate or frightening in their seduction, we weren't enslaved by the seedy romance of drugs or rhythm or bowled over by ideals or proselytized to or anything vulgar like that. R.E.M. were so ordinary. They made it seem like ordinary people could love them without wearing weird clothes or being embarrassing in public. They said, "Hi, how are you?"

Later on I was surprised how simple the band's easy chord strumming and open tunings were to effect. But the sound of "Wolves Lower" is so much more than its mere parts: its electrically charged howl in the midst of sonic simplicity is a classic example of that strange third element, neither music nor lyrics, that rock 'n' roll sometimes evokes, some inhuman emotional presence rising up of its own accord off the vinyl, something invoked from wood and wire and four different minds in concert, something singing off the instant synapses of silences, sudden snaps between fingers and electricity, actual feelings murmured into your mind, unintelligible, yet heard by all of us as clearly as if they were being screamed in the chambers of our hearts.

Now I know so many people for whom R.E.M. was the catalyst for complete personal redemption: people who, after hearing the band, formed their own groups, or started record companies, or moved to other cities, or joined college radio stations, or quit grad school, or wrote books. Their music spoke so truly. It still does. Over the years, I've probably reaped more pleasure from their songs than from any other band's. Nothing they've said has been as painful or as true as even a minor number by Paul Westerberg, and yet in some other way they've colored everything: graced the pages of my memory with hues that I cannot possibly describe but love so very deeply: private colors and sounds, which I know each of their lovers and listeners shared dumbly along with me.

R.E.M. have always been generous, though: blind to smallness, completely and unwittingly righteous. Back in the days when R.E.M. were a little band, their niceness stood in bright relief against the scary world of angst and pain that the rest of rock 'n' roll celebrated. I mean, there were still skinny girl groupies and guys with blow hogging up all the mirror space in the bathrooms of every club, and there were still all the people who said sniffy things like "Oh, they were OK on their first record," or "I saw them before you," or "Oh, they've ripped everything off from the Feelies." Those people have always existed, even before fans of *Spin* magazine and Sonic Youth managed to give that point of view some kind of fascist credence in the underground. But in R.E.M.'s glory days—back when people used to be able to debate for hours as to whether Peter Holsapple or Chris Stamey was the better songwriter in the dBs—you could be a neophyte, you could have not heard Big Star, you could have missed their first performance here, and no one ever made fun of you. You didn't have to belong to belong.

R.E.M. changed our whole perspective. From the moment we first heard *Chronic Town* we were galvanized. They were our mirror, put on earth to reflect what we were, in case we didn't know, and what we were, it turned out, was sick of anger and ugliness and anti-everything cant. R.E.M.'s music was reflective rather than nihilistic, spiritual rather than self-righteous, elegiac rather than mad.

R.E.M. formed in Athens, Georgia, in 1980, after Peter Buck met Michael Stipe at a record store where Peter worked and where Michael was shopping with his sister Lynda (later a member of OHOK and Hetch Hetchy). Bill Berry and Mike Mills were friends from high school in Macon who ran into Buck and Stipe at a party. Thanks to the proximity of the art-ridden University of Georgia, Athens already had something of a post-punk live scene: the B-52s, Pylon, and the Method Actors had already fashioned for the town a sort of twisted, campy, gothic music renaissance. Athens had everything a person needed to be cheerful: cheap rent, good weather, and an art school, and for a while there in the late seventies and early eighties, I picture life for the underground like an Annette Funicello movie set packed with stray extras from "Star Trek." Bouffant hairdos and Jetson clothing, lipstick traces and loud garage rock. About as far from the grime of punk as you can get.

Athens was always all about atmosphere and artiness, and the genuine romance of the great lost South. Soon after they met, some of R.E.M.'s members lived in a church that had apartments built in it, plus pews, a stage, forty-foot ceilings, and preachers buried under the floor. Legend has long since liked to elaborate on this haunting aspect of the band's origins, and it is true that here is where they rehearsed and played parties, where, as Buck once told *Creem*, "people liked us, probably because there was free beer and we played for free."

Originally, the band members discussed naming themselves Cans of Piss or Twisted Kites, but decided they'd rather be called something they could tell their parents. "R.E.M. was nice—it didn't lock us into anything." Two months later, R.E.M was headlining gigs in Athens, plus roadtripping weekend gigs to North Carolina, South Carolina, Nashville, Memphis, and Atlanta. As Peter Buck told *Rolling Stone* in 1990, "It wasn't so much there was an audience [for us] but there was a lot of dissatisfaction. We weren't sure where our place in the business was, or even if we had one, but we did realize something was going on when there seemed to be so many people, the smart people in town who would come up and say things [like] 'Have you heard this band or that record?' Sometimes the towns we went through didn't have any bands of their own, and the local New Wave band would only do Cars covers. But people would go see that because, 'well at least it isn't Eagles covers.' And in every town, no matter how small or how we did, there would always be from twenty to a hundred people who would say the same thing: 'The radio around here sucks.' "

In late 1981 Hib-Tone approached them about making a record: the single "Radio Free Europe," which, allegedly as a joke, they sent out to college radio with no liner notes or i.d., just to intrigue people. It worked.

*

By the time I started working at a college radio station in late 1983, R.E.M. had two and a half records out, the EP *Chronic Town* and two LPs, *Murmur* and *Reckoning*, on the independent label IRS. Me, I'd just crawled back from college, having just spent every penny I ever managed to scrape together on bumming around Europe, and now I had to live in my old bedroom and be persecuted by the specter of adulthood and feel incredibly embarrassed and inadequate because I did not have a life. (This is my mom: "Honey, have you ever considered technical writing? My friend's daughter has a degree in English from Stanford and she's making thirty grand at Apple!") Instead of something proper like that, I had a stupid job stage-managing *Peter Pan* at the local children's theater, putting on the Indians' makeup and making all the Lost Boys hush.

So just for fun, I volunteered at the college radio station, putting together their little program guide, and deejaying four-hour fill-in shifts beginning at midnight. But I was never a very good deejay. I was almost entirely ignorant of everything between the Buzzcocks and Howard Jones. I could play the Ruts, but Wire had passed me by. It was only my newfound love of R.E.M. that made it all right that I didn't know any songs by Freur, that I didn't understand why people thought the Birthday Party were a good band, that I had never heard of the Minutemen. The only thing I knew about was circa 1978 punk rock—the Clash, the Jam, the Ramones, and the Undertones—plus a little Elvis Costello, the Pretenders, Television, and T Heads, stuff like that. I wasn't adventurous enough with the new stuff, plus I hated the sound of my own voice. I'd be OK for an hour or two, playing my favorites by Gang of Four and XTC, but the last ninety minutes would be sheer hell, searching among the C library, pulling out "Burning for You" by Blue Oyster Cult or something by Stiff Little Fingers. Then I'd get pretty darn slipshod, hurling the headphones down on old album covers, or throwing the longest song I knew,"Marquee Moon" by Television, on the turntable in order to finish up some novel or the new *Rolling Stone*.

That's what I was doing the day I had my great Amerindie

revelation; hunching up on the deejay stool, monitor on loud, headphones off, seven or so minutes into the great masterpiece by Television. I was reading *Record* when I came across a quote from Peter Buck in an article about R.E.M. that completely turned around my way of thinking about rock. He said: "I guarantee that I have more records from 1983 in my collection than any other year. I mostly buy independent records by American bands, and there's a lot of good ones. All over the country we go, and every town has at least one really top-notch group. Maybe they're too uncompromising or maybe they're all not pretty boys, or maybe they're just weird. From Los Angeles, which has a million good bands now—Dream Syndicate, Rain Parade, Black Flag, Channel 3, Minutemen—to the Replacements and Hüsker Dü from Minneapolis, Charlie Burton and the Cutouts from Nebraska, Charlie Pickett and the Eggs from Ft. Lauderdale, Jason and the Scorchers from Nashville, there are good bands all over America doing exciting things, and no one really hears them."

Well, there I was, surrounded by all the records he mentioned. What would you have done? I leapt off my stool and shoved aside my boring old punk rock picks—a song by X Ray Spex, the new one by the Smiths ("Jean"). I scrabbled frantically among the vinyl. Headphones on, I carefully re-cued. And the next minute I was on the air, reading the above-mentioned paragraph aloud, before bopping the button, before turning up the news. *"Don't know what to do when pink turns to blue . . ."*

That winter Hüsker Dü played a benefit for the station in the cafeteria, and before I knew what had happened, I'd suddenly become an Amerindie devotee, shunning all things British, dreaming of a world full of kudzu and mimosa and people who shopped at the Piggly Wiggly. Then suddenly it was spring, and me and my friend Francesca, renamed Jane From Occupied Europe and Divine Discontent, began hosting an early-morning show once a week that was entirely devoted to the American underground. Midwest and South, the Northeast and Texas, portions of the country we'd never thought about in our California cloud, took on all this significance in our poor little geographically deprived brains. No longer did we long to go to Paris or Tahiti; instead we pined for Athens and Minneapolis and Boston, creating in our minds' eyes a new America where every small town contained exactly four cool people and one large garage. Elvis Costello went by the wayside in our fury to follow Buck's advice. We played everything he'd told us to and then some, ranging across the map of the United States with exactly the results he'd foretold. From Boston, Mission of Burma and the Lyres and the Neats. From the New York/New Jersey area, the Feelies and the Bongos and the Individuals and the dBs. From Ohio, Pere Ubu and Human Switchboard. The Violent Femmes, from Milwaukee, Wisconsin. The Windbreakers, from Mississippi. Defenestration and the Embarrassment, both from Lawrence, Kansas. We played the Woods and Let's Active and the dBs and the Young Fresh Fellows, the Wipers and the Fastbacks and the Pontiac Brothers and more. We played Savage Republic and Redd Kross and the Meat Puppets, Camper Van Beethoven and 10,000 Maniacs, TSOL, Minor Threat, Black Flag, Soul Asylum. We played everything that came our way as long as it was American, and Buck was right: it was all really, really good.

And so, girls and boys alike, from coast to coast, we were spoken to not by the band's members, but by its music, heard live, heard not in our brains but deep down in our souls. Listening to R.E.M. was like watching the landscape flicker by on a train from the inside, not the sexual rock 'n' roll churning of Aerosmith, Jeff Beck, and Muddy Waters's "Train Keep A Rolling," but the prismatic impressionism of "Driver 8" and everything that came before it: Television, the Velvet Underground, Tom Petty, the Byrds. "Come on aboard, I promise you, we won't hurt the horse," sang Stipe on a B side called "Bandwagon," and that welcoming gesture, that basic ethic of hospitality was what really distinguished R.E.M. from both its predecessors and its peers. Throughout the early eighties, other alternatively oriented artists talked incessantly about avoiding the bandwagon: busting trends, keeping clean, not selling out and just generally being hipper than the masses. R.E.M. just invited everyone to come along for the ride.

To make up for the misfortune of having been born on the cutting edge of California, I took to traveling a lot. One weekend I drove to Southern California to see a bunch of people I knew from college. There was this boy I had a crush on who was actually in a paisley underground band, and one night he invited me to a paisley underground party. He didn't take me there or anything. He had to go rehearse or record or do some band-related thing, saying he'd meet me at this party.

The funny thing is, I didn't even resent it: I thought, in my twenty-two-year-old idiocy, that this was how adults behaved. And so I worked up the nerve to go to this party alone. I really don't know how I managed it—probably I just felt like I had to have something interesting to report back to Fran. It was horribly scary, first trying to find the place—driving alone around Los Angeles, a city I knew almost nothing about—and then going in alone to a party full of what I considered famous people. The first person I saw when I walked in was Chris D. of the Flesh Eaters, and I was so awestruck with delight that the whole evening took on this rosy glow. I was way too shy to take any food, but I sat there quite contentedly, all alone in a corner, and looked at everyone chatting away about subjects I cared about: Raymond Chandler, R.E.M., the new Green on Red album. Hovering around the kitchen area, I saw actual members of the Bangles and Dream Syndicate and the Leaving Trains interacting with one another! Presently, someone began banging on a pot and then the whole party joined in, playing rhythm section on table tops and utensils, while other people took turns singing nonsense verses for half an hour. I felt like I'd stumbled into my personal version of paradise.

The boy who'd invited me there never showed up. After a time I slipped out of the house, found my way to a freeway entrance, and drove back to Newport Beach, where Fran and her friends were getting ready to go to some local seaside fern bar. I remember walking across the little bridge to Balboa Island with them silently, contentedly, that night. Here was the world I came from: pretty girls with perfect figures, pink gin fizzes and keggers, boys in O.P. shorts, beaches and booze; a world I could not belong to and never had. Over there—thirty miles north, in that house in the flat part of Hollywood—there was the world I wanted to be in. I had finally found my milieu.

I've stolen only two things in my life: a paperback edition of a Nancy Mitford novel from a country house in Ireland, and an original copy of Big Star's *Radio City* from—well, I still can't tell you where. It was a place, however, rest assured, where its value was quite unknown, and when I found it, I remember, I slipped the disc out of its pristine jacket and ran my finger shockedly across the dust. I couldn't ask the people for permission to own it, because what if they'd said no? And I knew that I couldn't just leave it there unplayed, unloved, uncherished in the dark.

I don't think I'd even heard the record yet, I just knew it was something I had to own. Some boy I liked had told me that, and of course I had believed him. Big Star's leader, Alex Chilton, was, I knew, a huge influence on R.E.M., though all I'd heard of him was the bizarrely rendered punky blues incantations of *Like Flies on Sherbet*, which we had at the station, and a production credit on the Cramps LP, and, of course, the Box Tops' "The Letter," on which he sang lead. But I already had some sense that this was the record that was crucial to the zeitgeist of much of 1983.

Before CDs began a mania for reissues, Big Star's three obscure records (there's another excellent record called *#1 Record*) were extremely difficult to find. But when I put the one I'd stolen on, I knew for sure that I had done the right thing. *Radio City* and *Big Star Third* (recorded in 1973 and 1974 respectively, though the latter was not released until 1978) were monumentally influential to the music I loved at that time—to R.E.M., to the dBs, and most of all to the Replacements (who'd later write a song called "Alex Chilton" in obeisance to Big Star's leader). *City* is a jangle pop-lover's dream, all harmonies and Rickenbackers and culturewise poetry about white American nights. *Third* is a slower, sadder, late-night meditation on the death of love. They are the records that define that era. And if I had to leave one behind on my way to exile, I couldn't choose between them if I tried.

A few months after I nicked the first one, I broke up with the boy who'd tipped me off to it all in the first place. He was a person whose acquaintance I could have done without, but whenever I listen to *Radio City* or *Big Star Third*, I know that I got the better part of the bargain. "Regret nothing" doesn't even begin to describe the thankfulness I feel to him for adding Big Star to the soundtrack of my life.

Years passed, as they are wont to do. In 1987 *Document*, R.E.M.'s fifth LP (and, incidentally, its last on an independent label, IRS), shipped gold and generated a top-ten hit called "One I Love." Just before that record's release date—on a day that happened to be my birthday—I was instructed by the powers that be in my life to go to a secret hotel room and interview the band.

Sitting amid a welter of empties, downed during the previous five interviews, Peter Buck and Mike Mills were holding court. As we spoke, a bevy of hangers-on were gathering in the lobby for an evening on the town with the band, and the phone kept on ringing with messages from people with no last names who had met them two years ago ("You remember me?") inviting them to come to gigs or bars or parties later on. "Come to hear the party line on *Document*?" cracks Pete Buck, as I'm ushered into his presence. "Oh, pleeez . . ."

By that time, of course, the party line on R.E.M. was getting infinitely intricate. In his *Village Voice* review of the LP before this one, Tom Carson had called R.E.M. reactionary, their music "lulling and delusive," and concluded by saying the band represented "the emotional syntax of Reaganism." The *Voice* conveniently chose to ignore the fact that R.E.M. had never taken corporate sponsorship, never lipsynched on television, insisted on live vocal tracks even for "Solid Gold," and had hand-picked opening acts such as the Replacements, X, Camper Van Beethoven, and the Minutemen, even at points in their career when it would clearly have been easier not to. But Carson's assessment of the band's work was part of the überhip's inevitable anti-R.E.M. reaction, a reaction that's both predictable and traditional in alternative rock circles. It happens every time a band's fan base grows beyond the confines of those you could personally meet.

Carson would no doubt defend himself by saying that over the course of four albums, the band had gotten worse—different—in order to appeal to the masses. I don't think that is true, but things had definitely changed in other ways. I guess it was only natural that five years of leading a following of fanatics would take its toll on a band's ego: that day, I remember, Mills told me a matter-of-fact story about a time he and Peter showed up at a college radio station for a surprise interview, and the deejay in charge "was so freaked out she had to go outside and throw up." Buck talked without irony of "this rock star lifestyle." Mills, also without irony, bluntly interrupted my flip comment that the Chills (from New Zealand) were the best band in the world with a serious reprimand: "You mean the *second* greatest, don't you?"

That night, between a dissertation on high school ten-year reunions (Buck attended his with "this really gorgeous girl in tow and everyone was jealous," Mills said wild horses wouldn't drag him to his), unfair pot busts, a brief but definitive overview of the life and works of Flannery O'Connor (Buck) and the pros of owning an Acura (Mills), as well as the inevitable reordering of ever more drinks, I reminded Peter that the last time I interviewed him we had talked about the ghetto of college radio, and he'd said, "I can't help it that I'm not Schooly D—I'm white; I went to college—I'd sound totally dumb if I did a street rap." It seemed, I added, that what the band was saying on *Document* about the state of the world contradicted

R.E.M.'s prior intentions just to express a kind of collegiate zeitgeist.

"Well, just because these things [social ills] don't touch us personally doesn't mean we aren't affected by them," Buck amended. "Some transcendental thinker in the 1880s once said, 'What degrades any man degrades me,' and it's true. You've got to believe that what's happening to the lower man is an indignity to all men. I mean, I have money, I can eat, I have all the clothes and records I need and stuff. But that other world is going to become a part of my world anyway."

As Buck spoke, I nodded, but I had long since turned my head away. I was looking out the window at the dusky night sky. Outside our room, the harbor lights were scattered like temporary starlight on the ridges of the bay; they reminded me of something, perhaps the unknowable notes in an R.E.M. song. "Music," said Paul Verlaine, "before all else, and for that choose the irregular, which is vaguer and melts better into air." "When I see the glory," said Tom Verlaine, "I don't got to worry." I knew, right then, that the other world was encroaching—not the one Buck meant, of poverty and sadness (though that one was out there too), but the mainstream world of regular people, the ones whose values and pettinesses I had escaped through the love of this very music. Soon they would be back, Buck said, a part of our world, whether we wanted them to be or not. Soon I was going to have to share. My undistinguished colleagues, my thoughtless co-workers, my peers, the girlfriends of my youth who used to plug their ears and hum when I tried to play them records by Blondie and Bruce Springsteen; they were waiting in the wings, pressing their faces on the glass. The light was beginning to dawn.

Oh, life! Rushing forward, always too fast, always upon us like an oncoming train. *Document* marked the end of R.E.M.'s five-record deal with IRS, and because it was a hit, R.E.M. had the leverage to sign a lucrative deal with Warner Brothers. That's one of the things that made their sixth LP, the chartbusting *Green*, a hit, and themselves as beloved worldwide as they should be. The other was their sheer greatness.

The next time I saw the band, at the Universal Amphitheater in Los Angeles about two months later, the whole world was different. We'd all gone public, like a corporation; our stock had split: I was an official rock critic for the *Los Angeles Times*, arguing with my editor about leads and column inches; they were legitimate superstars rather than cult ones, pissing off the powers that be by refusing to play the hit. R.E.M. played furiously that night at the Universal: I remember, near the end, them hurling themselves into "Wolves Lower," inevitably catapulting me into their arms. That night they washed me clean of any grimy bitterness or sticky nostalgia about who heard them first; reconciling me to anything the future might bring. It seemed to me it would be more graceful—more courteous in fact, more R.E.M.-like—to relinquish my hold on them right then and there. Ladies and gentlemen, I give you R.E.M.

SEVEN

UNSATISFIED

How I wish that I didn't know now what I didn't know then.

– the Young Fresh Fellows, "Hank, Karen and Elvis"

My friend Michael once claimed I live in Mayberry, a remark elicited solely by the fact that my mailman's name is Andy. In fact, far from living in Mayberry, ever since moving out of the 'burbs, I have lived in the Haight, or as near as makes no difference. Two blocks from my abode is the beginnings of it: a couple of head shops, a comic book warehouse, café upon café, a triad of used record and clothing establishments, Bound Together, the Anarchist Book Collective, and, across the street from the latter, a shop with my mom's favorite oxymoronic name, the Obfuscation Awareness Clinic.

To the unobservant eye, the six-block stretch of Haight Street from Central to Shrader hasn't changed much since 1967, despite the advent of a Gap, a McDonald's, and, inevitably, a Ben & Jerry's ice cream shop at—where else?—the corner of Haight and Ashbury. It's still run over with hippies and street people and black-clad youth, skinheads and faux jesters and grunge boys in backward baseball caps and others even more modern whose pickup line is inevitably "Hey, wanna see my piercing?" It's a street where it's a lot easier to buy a Perestroika T-shirt and Cat in the Hat-striped tights than it is to find a quart of milk. But I knew almost nothing about Haight Street when I first moved into the Hotel Hell, a four-story Victorian on the corner of Lyon and Fulton, in 1984, not even its proximity to my new locale. Nor did I then associate my lifestyle with the lifestyle of the hippies in the sixties who'd made the district famous, even though, like them, I bought all my clothes at junk stores, rejected the goals of my suburbanized peers, and lived for the nights when we'd go see rock 'n' roll shows at any of a row of nearby nightclubs.

The house I lived in at 560 Lyon is a historic building: a picture of it in far better repair than I've ever seen it adorns the cover of a famous coffee-table book on Victorians called *Painted Ladies*. It had—has—six bedrooms, two bathrooms, and no heating apparatus whatsoever (a shortcoming we naively failed to notice on the July day we moved in). In a lot of ways living there was like living in northern England. In 1912. The plumbing broke regularly (and spookily, we thought: only on Friday and Saturday nights), and the wiring was so bad that a blowdryer or microwave used to pop the whole system. But I loved living there more than anything I've done before or since: lazy afternoon parties in the skylit attic we called the greenroom, Sunday brunches with bands on the roof looking over the city, strange run-ins with junkies and the police when our block's crack houses got out of hand, weird urban incidents involving naked ladies and TNT, nighttime burrito feasts, twelve and fifteen strong, before our weekly Monday night tromps up the Panhandle to the I Beam, where for years we'd check in just to see what was going on. One week it'd be the Meat Puppets from Tucson, the next, the Replacements from Minneapolis, then, in quick succession, the dBs, Flaming Lips, Soul Asylum, Zeitgeist or Green on Red, Hüsker Dü, the Minutemen, 54–40, Redd Kross, Savage Republic, Sonic Youth, Glass Eye, Robyn Hitchcock, Love Tractor, the Young Fresh Fellows, and on and on and on.

Soon after I'd become established at the Hotel Hell, I began commenting naively on how felicitous it was that every rock nightclub in the city moved to within walking distance of my home, but not for years did I see a correlation between my punk rock life there in the mid-eighties and the recent hippie-ridden historical past of the sixties. In retrospect, though, one thing living in the Haight taught me was that time goes slower than one thinks. God, when we moved into the Hotel Hell, R.E.M.

had only been together for three years, but we thought it had already been forever; we thought we were over them. How could we know 1984 would be our 1965? Rock 'n' roll time isn't fixed like real time; it goes by in fits and starts that don't always match up with one's memory. Led Zeppelin lasted for only ten years beginning to end; the Cure is now going on fifteen. The Beatles' entire career span was longer than the time lapse between their demise and the formation of the Sex Pistols—a mere six years. The Clash covered Bobby Fuller's "I Fought the Law" in 1978, only twelve years after it was first a hit; the Buzzcocks' "Ever Fallen in Love" was twelve years old when it came out again done by the Fine Young Cannibals. Anyway, that year was the height of the Amerindie scene's glory—Amerindie, a word coined by *Village Voice* critic Robert Christgau to describe American bands on low-budget independent labels, labels that we trusted so implicitly to bring us the news that we didn't even have to hear the band's records to know we'd like them live.

That's how things stood when we first heard the Replacements; *Let It Be*, and from that moment on, "Unsatisfied" was my favorite song. I remember that moment I first heard it exactly: four in the afternoon, a Saturday in late September; lying flat on my back in the greenroom under the skylight and waiting for the needle to drop. It was Chuck's record, and he was almost in tears of reverence before he even played it: that keyed-up state you get in when you've rushed all the way home from the record store and you just can't get it on the turntable fast enough. "*Look me in the eye and tell me that I'm satisfied. Are you satisfied?*" I remember lying quite, quite still during the opening notes to that song, and as they ascended the scale into the crash landing of the chorus—"*I'm so I'm so . . . unsatisfied*"—I was riven with a rush of adrenaline that welled on up and over, pouring the seeds of a heedless obsession into my soul.

In October the Replacements came to town to play the Berkeley Square and the I Beam. Francesca and I went to both shows with the girls around the corner, Laura and Mary (like in "Little House on the Prairie"), who also had this thing about the band. One night the Replacements were playing at the Berkeley Square, and I had a bad cold, so bad I didn't want to go. But Laura called and begged so hard that I went anyway: refusing her would have been like watching an animal in a trap gnaw its leg off to get free.

I think that was the show where I first met Paul Westerberg—afterward, I mean, at a party at Rory's house. We were hanging around in groups, waiting for the band to arrive, when he walked in the room, all hunched up, too big for his clothing, black eyes peering out of a mess of moussed-up hair. I was looking at an eighth-grade science textbook. "Look," I said to him, "did you have this book in Minneapolis?"

"I don't know, I cannot read," he said, moving on. A moment later, I saw Laura holding her unlit cigarette out appealingly to Paul, eyes as big as a Bil Keane character, begging for a light. Laura didn't smoke at the time.

But of course, like most hero worship, this love of ours had nothing to do with Paul himself. In fact, as regards to his poor person, it diminished in proportion to the amount of respect we felt for his songwriting ability. When he sang, "*I hate my dad/someday I won't,*" we could easily think of him as a skinny sex object. A year later, when we heard him say, " 'Ha' is the first word in happiness, and the last word in lonesome is 'me,' " we started to become strangely silent in his vicinity. After I heard "Unsatisfied," I was a tongue-tied wreck in his presence. Years later, at a postparty show in the upstairs room of the Fillmore sometime after *Pleased to Meet Me* came out, Paul pushed his way through a throng of eager well-wishers and plopped down at a table right beside us. My friends and I looked down at our shoes for three straight minutes as Paul gazed out the window smoking, then we politely excused ourselves and left. "What," said my friend Elizabeth bitterly, "were we going to say? 'Oh, Paul, when you sing "ooh" after "Alex Chilton" I just want to die?' " As Wayne and Garth so eloquently put it, we weren't worthy. We weren't worthy.

Poor Paul! I see now the isolationism of our response. But

what could we do? All those years of great Replacements shows had wrecked us for plain conversation. Looking back, it's difficult to describe what was so great about those shows. It was never the sheerly visceral pleasure of noise and abandonment—they were hardly ever tight enough to pull that kind of thing off. Usually their sets wound up flat on the floor, playing "Help Me Rhonda" three times in a row, each time worse than the last, or they switched instruments after the first half and then threw every guitar into the drum set, knocking Chris Mars almost unconscious, and then sitting on the floor to finish the set. Nor was it the cathartic pleasure of their mayhem: they weren't ever really angry, and their mayhem usually ended up in ugly befuddlement and confusion. When you went to see the Replacements, you'd almost always go home disappointed, thinking, "Maybe next time will be perfect." It was like being captured midair in a swan dive off a cliff. The landing might be a disaster—in fact, it was sure to be. But those moments while you were flying, suspended in that beauty with the sea still such a long way down, it was pure, pure bliss.

So where was the pleasure? It wasn't in the sight of their incompetence and disgrace. It came instead, somehow, from someplace so deep, so much more purely physical. You know the feeling you get when you see a person get embarrassed, and you reach out a hand to that person to help them through their humiliation? That is the feeling that the Replacements could always effortlessly evoke, both in themselves and in their audience. Friendship, goodness, warmth; some nascent, struggling niceness, bubbling up from a pile of dirt. United in their loneliness, generous, ebullient, careless, but fun. Looking back over that catalog of virtues now, it is clear, they were the archetypal eighties Amerindie band—slipshod and sincere, dogged by disaster, completely off the cuff. Brilliant.

So it was that "Unsatisfied" came to be our personal anthem, our mental cleansing agent—played, top volume during our breakups with boys and our get-togethers with others, played after horrible evenings spent reviewing Huey Lewis, played to initiate some new household member or other, played to say farewell. I still can't hear "I Will Dare" ("*meet me anyplace or anytime or anywhere, if you will dare meet me tonight, if you will dare, I will dare . . .*") without being reminded of that time, so secret, so funny, so hopeless, so sad. Life in the Hotel Hell, with its perpetually revolving door of roommates: John the bike messenger with his backward-spinning record player and endless jars of psilocybin mushrooms in the fridge, Tom the heroin addict from West Virginia, and an endless bunch of others. The radio always blasting out songs by Big Black and Love Tractor; bands always sleeping on the floor. There was always something to do in that house, after all our dumb day jobs were over, something to look forward to, like the next time the Meat Puppets or the Replacements were coming to town. Look me in the eye, and tell me that I'm satisfied. For a minute there, I almost was.

When I first saw the Replacements—at the Keystone, Palo Alto, in November 1983—I thought they'd been around forever because they already had three LPs out. Hüsker Dü's first appearance at that time—opening for Angst, Slovenly, and the Dead Kennedys (the latter of which, incidentally, I considered positively hoary) at the Foothill Junior College Cafeteria—was equally mind-altering for me: both bands blew doors open I didn't even know were shut. And both bands served to turn my eyes toward Minneapolis, a place that until then I had associated only with "The Mary Tyler Moore Show."

Since then, even now, in my mind's eye, Minneapolis still lies peacefully like a Christmas card all covered in snow, and under that white blanket, the cosy clubs all warm and rocking blast out music every night: Hüsker Dü and the Replacements, the Magnolias and Soul Asylum, and later, Run Westy Run and the Jayhawks. Just once in my life, I'd like to be one of the Minneapolis faithful, the kind who makes it out to the club in the middle of a blizzard. Only one band's even made it to the venue through the dark and stormy night, so they have to play three sets, filling up the last two with hundreds of rash covers, from "Kumbaya" to "Roundabout," from "Tear the Roof off the Sucker" to "The Cross." By the end of the last song, all four paying customers are onstage singing too. And of course it's way too gnarly out to risk going home, so everyone has to sit up all night in the back room of the bar drinking peppermint schnapps and bonding while waiting for the thaw.

That, I believe, was nighttime in Minneapolis in the middle of the eighties. Imagine Seattle, only colder and less scenic. Who would ever have thought that the spirit of punk rock was being sheltered and bred there, appreciated so thoroughly by a bunch of placid descendants of Nordic dairy farmers? And yet such, apparently, was the case. "The day the Sex Pistols' single arrived in Minneapolis," Minneapolis native Peter Jesperson recalls, "we had people lined up at the store for hours waiting for the UPS truck to unload. We sold forty copies of 'Anarchy of the U.K.' right out of the box."

New York and L.A. were scene-driven and radio-driven. Minneapolis was store-driven: its punk rock scene revolved around a tiny mom-and-pop record store called Oar Folkjukeopus. Peter Jesperson managed that store for eleven years. From 1978 on, he also co-owned a label called Twin/Tone with Paul Stark and Charlie Hallman, as well as deejaying at a club called the Longhorn. And he unofficially managed and produced most of the bands he signed to the label. For years, Jesperson was an integral figure in the Minneapolis scene, but gives the credit for its beginnings to a single, ahead-of-its-time rock band. "In Minneapolis, when we heard the Ramones' first record," he says, "we all kind of laughed and went, 'Wow, there's a band in New York that's doing exactly the same thing as the Suicide Commandos!' "

The Suicide Commandos, with their goofy, Stooges-driven garage rock sound, weren't exactly popular, but leader Chris Osgood used to get them gigs at high school dances and the like, where they were invariably kicked out. After being touted early on in their career in the *Minnesota Daily* by a University of Minnesota student named Andy Schwartz (who'd go on to found *New York Rocker*), the band put out two singles on Paul

Stark's P.S. label, and then got signed, along with Ohio's Pere Ubu, to Polygram, a label that was cashing in on the new wave movement by beginning a new wave label subsidiary called Blank. The two bands did a U.S. tour together, the "Coed Jail Tour," and then were immediately dropped from the label, which became insta-defunkt.

The Suicide Commandos broke up a few months later, dropped by Polygram little more than a year after signing their contract. Meanwhile, the club that the Commandos had commandeered as their live home, the Blitz Bar, had moved its clientele to a more accommodating place across the street, the Longhorn. By that time, Jesperson recalls, there was a plethora of good bar bands in Minneapolis, though they were more on the bad-boy rock trip than a punk one. Jesperson began auditioning bands for Twin/Tone, most of which appeared on a compilation double LP called *Big Hits in America Volume 3.* (The best known was called the Suburbs.) Soon after that, he turned down the demo tape of a struggling hardcore Saint Paul band known for breaking television sets onstage at the Longhorn. "And then I was, like, 'Oh, by the way . . . I think you're going to have a problem with your Scandinavian in-joke Minnesota name,' " Jesperson recalls.

The band was called Hüsker Dü, and its candycore style—rage-meets-ability-meets-the-Beatles—predated grunge rock by a good ten years. Hüsker Dü angrily formed their own record label, which they called Reflex (because it was a reflex action against Twin/Tone), and released two genius records on it, *Everything Falls Apart* and *Metal Circus.* Hüsker Dü was such a powerful band, but they looked like farmers or something: two solid-looking fat guys and a total square, and the contrast was incredibly startling. They'd stand up there, the picture of seriousness, pouring wicked hot clangor out of their instruments, creating this gigantic wall of sound that occasionally seemed to knock singer-guitarist Bob Mould off his feet. He'd lunge this way and that, caught up in the act of building big noise. It was like he was trying to liberate every particle of sound on the planet, hurling meaning and music together in a positive orgy of anger. Atomizing, detonating, exonerating, screaming . . . I think in retrospect what I loved about Hüsker Dü was their lack of sentiment. I never thought something so angry could sound so sweet without simultaneously sounding corny or boring.

Meanwhile Jesperson continued running what was in effect the only game in town. "I didn't book the Longhorn, but I had a lot of input into opening acts and stuff, so people used to give me tapes all the time, as well as giving me tapes in the hopes of getting on Twin/Tone. So I was getting tons and tons of tapes, all the time."

One day in May 1980, a kid named Paul Westerberg dropped off a tape at Oar Folk Records (where Jesperson still worked) in the hopes of getting an audition to play the Longhorn. "I know it sounds like a fairy tale," recalls Jesperson, "but I knew how special it was the minute I heard it. I was really backed up on tapes, and I remember he had to call me a couple of times to ask if I'd listened to it yet and I'd go, 'Nah, haven't got around to it yet.' And then, one day a few weeks later, I was sitting in the back room of Oar, slapping tapes into my boombox, one after the other, and about seven or eight tapes had gone by and they all sounded like the Stooges. And then I put it on. Literally one minute into the tape, I called, like, three or four friends of mine, going, 'Either I'm crazy, or this is the greatest band I've ever heard.' "

The song he was listening to was called "Raised in the City," and it was by a band called the Replacements. (The rest of the demo included "Shut Up!," "Shape Up," and "Don't Turn Me Down.") "It was obvious they were influenced by punk," Jesperson says about the demo, "but the words to their songs, they were like updated Chuck Berry, or something. And the music! The joke was, Bob Stinson's favorite guitarist was Steve Howe."

Jesperson dialed Westerberg's number. "I said, 'So, do you want to do a single or an LP?' and he's silent for a second and then goes, 'You mean you think this is worth recording?' " He was incredulous. " 'I just wanted a *gig!*' "

Jesperson got him one. Until then, the 'mats had played only a couple of dates, kind of horning in on their friends' shows at weird places in East Minneapolis, getting things thrown at them, getting thrown out. But the Replacements played the Longhorn under Jesperson's auspices on July 2, 1980, to fifty people. ("Of course four hundred people now say they were there.") From that time on, the 'mats were the vortex of a whirlwind around which not just Minneapolis but the entire country revolved.

"It was so explosive," says Jesperson. "It was so amazing. They'd been playing in the Stinsons' basement every single night, so they were really tight. They were ragged and drunk, but it was so exciting. . . . I mean, their bass player was twelve years old! And Paul is so charismatic, even then . . . he was twenty years old and there was no question, he was just such a powerful presence.

"They were real young upstarts with no way in. They weren't part of the clique at all . . . they didn't hang out with other musicians. And I remember Bob Mould at that gig going, real bitterly, 'Oh, and I suppose the red carpet's gonna roll out for these guys now *you're* involved.' "

Jesperson felt a little sheepish, but that didn't stop him from rolling the red carpet—such as it was—with all his might. Disgusted, Hüsker Dü took themselves off to SST Records in Long Beach, California. In the next few years they released four brilliant records—*Metal Circus, Zen Arcade, New Day Rising,* and *Flip Your Wig*—which had more vision and impact than almost any band before or since. Hüsker Dü's brilliance cannot be equaled, but the Replacements were so stupid and contagious. The Replacements were true love.

In 1981 the Longhorn folded, and the scene, such as it was, moved over to a club called the 7th Street Entry, the converted kitchen quarters of an old Greyhound bus depot. Twin/Tone released the Replacements' *Sorry Ma, Forgot to Take Out the Trash* in September of 1981, and the band started touring: "We originally got out of town by opening for the Suburbs in Duluth or Madison or Milwaukee," Jesperson, who managed the 'mats, recalls. "We played Fargo, North Dakota, and Sioux Falls, South Dakota. We used to go down to a place called O'Banion's on Clark Street in Chicago and drive home right after the gig, seven hours straight."

One night in February 1981, the Replacements played the song "Kids Don't Follow" at O'Banion's. Jesperson was so excited he told his partners at Twin/Tone he had to do another record with them immediately. "And they were, like, 'Nah, we just did one'—they had other projects and stuff—and I said, 'I'll do anything to get this out now. I'll cut every cost there is to cut.' "

The Replacements recorded eight songs in the studio on a Saturday and mixed them on a Sunday. Next day Jesperson went out and bought five thousand white jackets and a rubber stamp, hand-stamping each cover with its title, *Replacements Stink*. Meanwhile Paul was still writing, as the liner notes for one record put it, "songs more often than most people go to the bathroom." Brilliant songs. Jesperson recalls driving to Duluth with him and Chris in a borrowed car. "And Paul had this real furrowed brow, and he goes, 'I just thought of a line for a song I got to tell you: "I can live without your touch/but I could die within your reach." ' " Once again, Jesperson was floored.

The band toured almost nonstop for the next year and a half—as well as recording *Hootenanny* and *Let It Be*. Of course neither the band nor the record company ever had any money: the gigs were all low-paying, sleep-on-floors kind of things. "We [Minneapolans] always knew they were extraordinary in our own minds," recalls Jesperson, "but we didn't see their influence as it was happening. I remember the first time we heard something like that was in Oklahoma City. It was the last gig in a six-week trip, we were just, like, straggling home from the West Coast and it was a Sunday night, and I was thinking, 'Oh, God! What a drag this one will be!' We drove up to the club—it was called the Bowery, and it was in this old church—at around six o'clock, and the owner met us at the door and he was raving. He was going, 'It's the Replacements! My favorite band ever! *Let It Be* is my favorite record of all time! Everything's on the house!' We were just looking at each other going, '*Wow!*' "

Up till then, Jesperson recalls, "I thought I was so crazy for thinking they were the best rock band on the planet. I thought I was unhinged." But that night's gig was so extraordinary that Jesperson called his girlfriend up during their set twice and held the phone up to the stage so she could hear. After it was over, the band's roadie confiscated a bootleg tape from some hapless fan in the balcony, which the band listened to in the van on their way back to the Twin Cities, cracking up the whole way home. "And Paul's like, 'We'll put this sucker out, and we'll call it *When the Shit Hits the Fans*.' " Which Twin/Tone subsequently did. Cassette only.

Jesperson first got the 'mats to New York in March 1983. "We'd had a real hard time booking them there," he recalls. "It was thirteen hundred miles away and we didn't have any idea where to go. We were, like, 'Do people still play CBGBs?' We didn't know."

Luckily for him, a young booking agent at Singer Management in New York City named Frank Riley decided to take the band on. "It was an insane thing to do at that time, and they subsequently caused him a lot of trouble," recalls Jesperson, "but he did because he'd had some luck getting his bands into Minneapolis clubs and he had an affinity for our music, and it really made all the difference to their career."

The Replacements played New York's Folk City on April 13, 1983, booked in by *New York Rocker*'s Ira Kaplan and Michael Hill. "They had a tiny p.a. and the idea was for rock bands to come in and turn down their instruments. Of course the 'mats turned them *up!*"

Glenn Morrow was at that show. "No one could have cared

less. They did a cover of Alice Cooper's 'I'm 18,' and that was kinda the only thing anyone remembered. There was something really off about it: they were terrible but compelling. I remember thinking they were bad, but feeling just *compelled* to go see them again a few weeks later with Hüsker Dü. After that I was sucked into their sick vortex."

Thanks to *Let It Be*, the Replacements legend was growing. One day, Jesperson recalls stopping at a pay phone on the highway near Chattanooga to call the Twin/Tone office. It seemed, they told him, that *Rolling Stone* had agreed to review *Let It Be*, but they needed to know one thing. "So I looked across the highway, and I see Paul just standing by the van, and I yell, 'Hey, Paul!'

"And he goes, 'Yeah?'

"And I yell, 'You know the line in "Unsatisfied" where you say, "Everything you dream of is right there in front of you?" '

"And he goes, 'Yeah?'

" '*Rolling Stone* wants to know, what's the next line?'

"And Paul yells: ' "Liberty is a lie." ' Right across the highway. *Liberty is a lie*."

The Replacements returned to New York several times in the next six months. One night they played at CB's unannounced, as Gary and the Boners (Alex Chilton, who was opening, insisted on having a pseudonym as well: he picked the name the Deteriorating Situations). Though the show was unannounced, the entire room was filled with, Jesperson says, "guys in polo-necked shirts with great big question marks hovering over their heads": A & R men, wondering what the big deal was.

In December 1984 Seymour Stein saw the band at Irving Plaza on Long Island: Jesperson remembers his lawyer leaning over to him and saying, "He says he'll have you signed to Sire before you even get home." Hüsker Dü was also placed on Warner Brothers in 1985. But neither band fared particularly well with the mainstream population. It had been six years since the Suicide Commandos had been dropped by Polygram, but no lessons had been learned on either side of the equation since: record company, radio, and band alike still didn't have a clue of how to make the world listen. The Replacements were in *Rolling Stone* and on "Saturday Night Live," but their music was underproduced—which meant it sounded like the sound that is now celebrated as "grunge"—and the lyrics were far too buried for a popular taste more inured to the crystallinity of synth pop and the overdubbery of Motley Crue.

Moreover, neither band was really willing to do the video thing: indeed, the Replacements, in protest, made a video for "Left of the Dial" that depicted nothing but the broad side of a stereo speaker for two and a half straight minutes. Fans laughed their heads off at the sight of it, but Sire was not amused.

Hüsker Dü's *Candy Apple Gray* and *Warehouse Songs and Stories*, released on Warners in the same year (1985–86), died an even more ignoble death. Replacements fans may not have liked the shininess of *Pleased to Meet Me* and *Don't Tell a Soul*, but they always thought the whole world should hear their heroes. Hüsker Dü's hardcore audience, however, deserted them for the treachery of dealing with the corporate ogre, and needless to say, no new audience was forthcoming. By 1986, both bands were in debt, as well as dealing with varying degrees of substance abuse problems (a perennial theme in the cold Upper Midwest). Just after the release of the ugly-covered *Tim*, the Replacements kicked Bob Stinson out of the band for overindulgence, replacing him with Slim Dunlap, but even this emergency measure didn't stop the remaining members from leaning on alcohol and cocaine. "They were a scary bunch of guys to deal with," Jesperson says now. "They alienated people right and left. Like, they only ever did two in-store appearances. The first was at the Georgia Mall in Athens, and two of the band members would not even go into the store. Or they'd show up at radio interviews and be really drunk and rude."

Hüsker Dü, though slightly less crabby, had similar problems. Drummer Grant Hart struggled with a heroin problem, singer/guitarist Bob Mould with an alcohol one. In 1988 their longtime manager, David Savoy, committed suicide. Soon after that, the band broke up.

Meanwhile, Jesperson (who continued to manage the band for a couple of years) was compensating Twin/Tone for the loss of the Replacements to a major by developing other bands from the Twin Cities. Fueled by the Replacements, Minneapolis's scene was still raging: young people were even moving there to take part in it. Jesperson was swamped with tapes, but his favorite was one by a band called Loud Fast Rules, which was fronted by a local kid named Dave Pirner, whom Jesperson had known since he was a little bitty tenth-grader, cutting school to hang out at the record store. "I remember when he was so thrilled because he'd been added to the Twin/Tone mailing list," Jesperson recalls.

Pirner's band quickly became the Replacements' band of choice to take on out-of-town dates. "One night," Jesperson recalls, "at a club called Merlyn's in downtown Madison, Tommy [Stinson] and I walked into the club real late and Loud Fast Rules were onstage just ripping it up. I was just getting chills it was so insane, and I went backstage afterwards and said to the singer, 'We've *got* to make a record.' "

Loud Fast Rules became Soul Asylum, Twin/Tone's next big-selling act. They were a sort of sunnier version of the Replacements, and their live shows were everything that band's were not: tightly wound, furious, one long blue blurry haze of noise and fervor and excitement. Thus, by 1986, Minneapolis had three bands, any one of which on any given night could literally have been dubbed the best band on the planet. It was total punk rock mecca, everything that Seattle would later be lauded as without any of the brouhaha. As Michael Hill, the man who originally booked the 'mats into New York City, and the guy who now runs A & R at Warner Brothers Records, says, "There wouldn't be a Nirvana without there first having been Bob Mould and Paul Westerberg."

*

Grunge's dominance in the mainstream came a tad too late for Soul Asylum, who in many ways—what with their wit and niceness and Pirner's good looks—would have been a far better Nirvana than Nirvana themselves. "You can't be bitter, though," says Pirner now. "You have to be happy for their success. They've just fought the same battle we did, and they did it right. When we were breaking all that ground, it was just because we wanted to have fun. So I don't take it personally—I think it's nice to see somebody making it work. After all, everybody who ever loved this type of music always knew it was worth something, and it's good to have the public finally realizing that at last."

Minneapolis's scene, sound, and spirit still rage on, but sometime in the late eighties its cachet wafted mysteriously over to Seattle. Twin/Tone eventually signed a distribution deal with A & M, but it went awry. Then they suffered losses in the late eighties when their distributor, Rough Trade, abruptly folded. The label currently houses bands like the 27th Various, the Dashboard Saviours, and Ticks, but it's no longer the only game in town: in 1987 ex-Marine Tom Hazelmyer, guitarist for a Twin/Tone band called Halo of Flies and for a short while a citizen of Seattle (he once played bass for the U-Men), moved back to town to start his own independent, which he dubbed Amphetamine Reptile. Am/Rep—the label has the word "Noise" emblazoned across its logo—was meant to accommodate several midwestern hardcore bands that were seriously outside of Twin/Tone's sphere of interest, and began by doing seven-inches. Its roster—exhibited on the seminal grunge compilation of LP *Dope, Guns, and Fucking in the Streets*—included the Cows, Hammerhead, the God Bullies, Surgery, Lubricated Goat, and Helmet (along with the future grunge rock staples such as Jesus Lizard and Seattle's own Gas Huffer).

In 1991, after Nirvana's success piqued major-label bidding wars among soi-disant grunge bands worldwide, Helmet was detached from Am/Rep in a deal with Columbia that brought the band over a million dollars. The label didn't do badly either. "They used to rent space here in our office," sighs Jesperson, "but they just bought the entire building across the street."

In September 1990 the Replacements released their seventh and last album, *All Shook Down*. Instead of taking off on an immediate tour, however, the band sat back in Minneapolis while Westerberg, two months (or, as he put it to me the day I interviewed him, "nine weeks, four days, and twenty hours") into his second-ever attempt to halt his consumption of alcohol, went from major metropolitan market to major metropolitan market, there to speak personally to radio stations and retail outlets and the occasional members of the press both about the record and about the current, confusing, and extremely misunderstood state of his band's fortunes.

I met up with him in San Francisco one morning in October 1991 at Miss Pearl's Jam House on Eddy Street, the café of the Phoenix Hotel. He looked up from his coffee, black head still mousse-tousled, eyes all sad. He looked strangely sophisticated, I thought, compared to the days of parties at Rory's house: kind of like a rock star, at last: his jeans finally fit and stuff. But he was no less guarded for all that, and no less embarrassing to be around. I remember we were waiting for something or somebody—I forget now what—and he was flipping through the pages of a special issue of *Rolling Stone* called "The Eighties," for which he'd been interviewed. He looked and he looked, flipping backward and forward, skimming the article on the underground, searching skeptically for his quotes. "Oh, there we are," he said bitterly, finally, pointing to a single sentence uttered by Peter Buck: " 'We worked with the Replacements a couple of times—before they started getting really drunk all the time.' " (I found out later Buck's quote actually continued. "They were just wonderful," but Paul didn't read that part to me.)

It was a depressing day. Paul and I went to Haight Street, where Paul drank Clausthaler after Clausthaler and I ate french fries and he told me about the downside of being a Place Mat.

"I suddenly got caught up in being a performer," he explained, "and what do you turn to? Drugs and alcohol, and every fuckin' escape you can possibly imagine . . . surrounding yourself with people who in your mind make you a star. And I haven't come totally around yet. It's not like I'm totally in control and in command of my talent and stuff . . . it's still scary as hell."

I said, "Doesn't that make the idea of making records and touring seem awfully hard?"

"Mmmm," he agreed. "It poses the question of, 'Am I in the right business? Or am I doing a totally perverted thing that goes against my very nature?'

"I hate people who disown someone for doing something bad," he added wistfully. "The Rolling Stones' last record had some stinkers on it, but I don't hate the Rolling Stones for it. Everybody makes mistakes, but if you make a mistake at the office it's forgotten the next day, but when we do it, someone buys it and writes about it and holds it against us. We've had to make all our mistakes in public where they can be listened to forever.

"You know, when [a band] starts out," he continued, "that one hour onstage is the best hour of the day. But it had gotten so that the only part I enjoyed was the other twenty-three: you know, hanging out, listening to music, taking drugs, and drinking. 'Yeah! This is my job! I'm people's hero for this!' And that's totally fucked up.

"When some people go to rock shows," he added sadly, "they want to be taken by the hand and told, 'Sit back, don't worry, we'll take over.' And our attitude has always been, 'Help!' "

Paul was still quick with the one-liners at the radio stations where he was interviewed that afternoon—at KUSF, he told the deejay that "Merry Go Round" was about child abuse—but in private he said, all shyly, it was "about me as a little girl." Then—"Oh God, I can see it now: 'Paul Westerberg thinks he's a woman!' You won't have that be your headline, will you?"

I shook my head furiously, while he toyed with the label of his Clausthaler bottle. "It really is about me, you know," he added anxiously. "It's not me walking around with a ribbon in my hair at the carnival, but the line 'They ignored me as a child,' that's definitely about me."

Later on, we went over to a commercial station, colloquially known as Live 105, where a deejay called Steve Masters was waiting to interview him. "Could I go to the bathroom first?" asked Paul, full to the brim with nonalcoholic beer.

"Hey, man, can you wait till we're done?" snapped Masters nastily.

"Do I have a choice?" Paul asked wonderingly. It turned out there was a key to the KITS bathroom, which Masters refused to hand over. I thought piteously of olden times, of the warmth and worship all my friends and I feel toward Paul Westerberg. I used to say I'd throw myself in front of a bus for him, but what I should have done, right then and there, was throw Steve Masters under a bus.

"So," said Steve, "what's 'Merry Go Round' about?"

Paul: "Uh . . . a girl."

Masters: "A girl called Mary?"

Paul: "That's right!"

Presently, Paul and I went over to the Paradise Lounge to wait out a couple more hours till Sister Double Happiness went onstage at Slim's. World Entertainment War was soundchecking, and we confided in each other our hatred of bands with keyboards. Then, because we had nothing to say to one another, we started a game of rock 'n' roll hangman.

Paul protested. "I don't like this game, it's too easy." But I still drew a little scaffold with an eleven-letter clue beneath it.

"*U*," guessed Paul.

"Fuck you!" I gasped.

Paul shrugged. "I told you. I'm kinda psychic." As he bent his head over my notebook, drawing his own scaffold, I supposed it wasn't really that weird that he'd got my choice. It is, after all, most people's favorite Replacements song. Then I smiled, thinking back. "Unsatisfied" was the name I wanted to give my column in the *East Bay Express*. My editors had made me pick another, and I chose the title of an obscure Ricky Nelson song: "Fools Rush In."

All this seemed too complicated to explain to Paul, however, who would certainly never have seen or read my column, so I concentrated on guessing his choice.

"*E*," I guessed. Nope. "A?" "B?" "M?" "T?" Nope, nope, nope. Somehow, in a very few guesses, I was hung. "Oh, well, you probably don't know this song," Paul apologized, filling in the blanks.

The song he'd chosen was "Fools Rush In." Shuddering, I made us stop playing. I suddenly realized that when Paul Westerberg sings, "You be me for a while and I'll be you," he's not making a suggestion: he's asking us to share his lifelong burden.

The last time I saw Paul Westerberg, he was in the corridor behind Freeborn Hall at U.C. San Diego. He was walking by at a brisk pace, over to the tour bus, while a boy named Dave, whom I'd met at a Replacements show the night before, and I swept past in an opposite direction toward my car. Paul said, "Bye, Gina, see you soon," and this boy Dave's eyes bugged right out of his head. He stopped short in the street, took quick shallow breaths, clutched my arm in glee. For a moment everything was quiet, and then he looked at me, his eyes all shiny. "Paul Westerberg knows your name!"

And I thought, this is as good as it gets. To stop and talk to Paul would have only been embarrassing, filled with huge pools of silence. To be with him any longer would only have been sad. But just saying hi—that's bliss. Like in high school, remember? "OK, so don't say hi." It meant so much, and yet so little. Just for a moment there, a single pristine instant, that punk rock illusion came true: artist and fan were equal. "Hi, Paul." "Hi, Gina." There was no barrier of fame or genius. Just for a moment. And I wanted to say to Dave, "You don't have to know him to get him at his best. The best you can get from him is to be in the audience while he's playing; and that's something anyone can have for the price of a ticket."

That was the apex of my love affair with Paul Westerberg. January 17, 1991. It was soon after that, I think, that I bought

Margin Walker, at which point it all faded into a childish dream, and I felt a twinge of that horrible foreknowledge of betrayal, the knowledge that one day even your most sacred heroes, your Bob Dylans, your Bruce Springsteens, your Paul Westerbergs, will not matter as much as they once did, because someone else will matter more.

Last year, the Replacements turned ten—seventy in dog years, and even older in the fast-aging mentality of punk rock. In the spring and summer of 1991 they toured the United States for five months, then quietly they broke up. Chris Mars released a solo album in 1992. Tommy Stinson's band Bash & Pop released a record in 1992. Paul Westerberg wrote two brilliant singles for the soundtrack to the movie *Singles* and, as far as I know, is still on the wagon. Lisa said she saw him skulking around with Tad Hutchison at a Pop Llama picnic in Seattle last July. A few months later, he started recording a solo record at Matt Wallace's studio in San Francisco, and wound up staying in the room right next to Kurt and Courtney. A friend of mine watched interestedly as Paul and Kurt passed each other one morning wordlessly in the lobby. "I don't think Kurt had any idea who it was, but Paul certainly did, and he just wasn't interested in making contact."

With Nirvana and Pearl Jam at the top of the charts, I can't help but wonder why the selfsame triumphs never happened for the Replacements. It makes me feel really bad that they didn't, because nobody ever deserved better, nobody better ever deserved more. I comfort myself with the words Westerberg himself once uttered about that topic, that one last psychic night at the Paradise Lounge. "My gut feeling is, we wouldn't even be around if we'd gotten big early, we would have gone over the edge and not come back. Massive success would have been a dream come true, but a person's dreams are so different at thirty than they are at twenty. Maybe my dreams did come true and I didn't notice . . . or maybe they weren't such great dreams to begin with.

"Anyway," he added wistfully, "I try not to dream so much anymore."

EIGHT

WHAT GOES ON

People think I'm a rich musician. Let me describe my position. Way down.
– Alex Chilton

New York City in the middle of July. You know those steamy afternoons when the air is, like, mud brown and every building drips dirty water from its ceiling, and even the pigeons are suffering from inertia? People sit on the stoops of dingy brownstones hoping that the shade made by the jagged rooftops will block out the patches of thick dull sun. By nighttime it's gotten so that even the sky has started to sweat, and the music from the nightclubs leaves you all burnt and deafened. A cabby grabs you up in Times Square, stopping briefly halfway down Ninth Avenue in the middle of Hell's Kitchen just to get into it with a bum who's ill-advisedly begging him from the pavement. "In my home country of Liberia, we don't have bums like that," he sniffs, dusting off his bloodstained hands.

"Neither do we in the rest of America," I say, untruthfully, but with some spirit. The guy nods into the rearview mirror, wisely but unconvinced. "But bums are like bad apples at the bottom of a basket," he opines. "You leave them there, they'll rot the rest."

I take his point: the America that I know, the regular America, full of mini-malls and parking lots, had best be on its guard. There are no garages in New York City, but that doesn't stop the people there from gathering in lofts and warehouses and basement bars and practice spaces, plying drumsticks between the strings of their twelve-string guitars, strumming them with violin bows or hammers, deconstruction, reconstruction, the sound of the city splattering across the room. *Fau naïf*—or is it *naïf vérité*? All arrogance and shit: never once acknowledging their mere allegiance to that basic human impulse: "Hey kids, let's put on a show!"

So if I die from a terminal disease twenty years hence, I guarantee you I caught it in the ladies' room at CB's, on just such a night like this. Because New York is where it started: at least, New Yorkers want you to believe that they began the whole shebang: the Ramones and the Dolls and the Heartbreakers and the whole damn sensibility, torn T-shirts and leather jackets, just caught up and magnified and reflected westward from a mirror held up across the Atlantic Ocean. Television, Patti Smith, the Voidoids, the Velvets. As usual, New York had it all: great bands, smart people to like them, progressive radio (WMFU), and an early punk rock magazine, *New York Rocker*, which made it its business to spread the gospel far and wide.

In the late seventies, bands like the Dead Boys, Talking Heads, Blondie, and Richard Hell were signed and then mistreated, cruelly dubbed new wave and then summarily dismissed. Their place in the underground was briefly taken by a movement called no wave, all art jazz and irony, sort of the emotional opposite of hiphop. And then there came the Feelies, a couple of twisted white kids from Haledon, New Jersey, whose truly bizarre take on the Velvet Underground would subsequently shake up the next decade's underground. The Feelies sounded like rain smacking a corrugated-tin roof, a storm warning of melody, a muttering lilt. The Feelies were one of those bands, like the Velvets and Big Star before them: hardly anybody bought their record (*Crazy Rhythms*, import only), but everyone who did went out and formed a band.

Unfortunately, the Feelies—at least the two main guitar men, Billy Million and Glenn Mercer—were truly peculiar people. Shifty is the word. Not in the usual New York street sense—they didn't do heroin and steal people's amplifiers. No, their personal bizarreness took the form of never going to Manhattan ("We get real bad headaches going through that tunnel"), insisting on five-hour sound checks, not laying down vinyl, and, uncharacteristically, knowing how to jog. They were science nerds making their mark on an unprecedented milieu: recreating rock 'n' roll in their own nervous image. They used, I'm told on good authority, to take chlorophyll and coffee before concerts, the better to jitter and speed through their ritualistic sets. They used to want to play shows only on holidays. They lost drummers like some people lose socks, even pissing off the famous Anton Fier (who'd left Ohio's Pere Ubu especially to join them) because they played too seldom, and that was particularly a pity because their appetite for percussion demanded that they have two.

And yet the Feelies were, according to a *Village Voice* cover story in late 1978, "the best band in New York." *Voice* writer John Piccarella had caught them opening for a then-unresuscitated Alex Chilton at Max's Kansas City, a gig attended by six people, and that was that. With their seditious melodies and mantralike lyrics, their insistence on the unpunk ethics of sharp sound, the Feelies proved false the rest of the world's sense that New York was no longer a fruitful rock scene (unless of course you were black and down and owned a turntable and a bunch of twelve-inches). After the Feelies, the world was forced to cast its glance on the other side of the river. We looked at Hoboken, and Hoboken started to hum.

"The Liverpool of the Eighties"—that's what *New York Rocker* called Hoboken, early on. The big accomplishment of the no-wave movement—those bands like the DNA, the Contortions, and the Bush Tetras—had been that they made a clean break with sixties rock. Hoboken's scene, on the other hand, was completely steeped in the sixties, producing band after band with a strict iconography: psychedelia, pop, and Velvet Underground, Velvet Underground, Velvet Underground.

So, with the dBs' Holsapple and Stamey playing the parts of Lennon and McCartney, Hoboken's scene grew ever more Beatlesesque. Unlike Boston or Athens or L.A. or D.C., Hoboken's scene was based entirely around a nightclub—Maxwell's, a two-hundred-capacity two-room bar right around the corner from the Maxwell's Coffee Plant. The club was bought in 1977 by Steve Fallon and his three siblings; the first show—July 9, 1978—featured a band called "a," whose four members eventually split into two bands, the Bongos and the Individuals. Those two bands would, over the next four years, typify the Hoboken scene's aesthetic: jangly guitars, jagged rhythms, vague lyrics, and a dance-y groove.

The latter band was the vehicle of songwriter and guitarist Glenn Morrow, an NYU student who worked by day as the managing editor of *New York Rocker* and by night as the booking agent for Maxwell's itself. Morrow lived in Hoboken even before it was cool to live in Hoboken, because it was cheap and his girlfriend lived there. "The whole city was a ghost town. My first apartment there cost eighty-five dollars a month for six rooms."

From the first, Maxwell's worked out well, because touring bands could stop there and do a set near New York without pissing off New York club owners. So here was this unpretentious little club that could get a full house of hip, interesting people from New York City. Morrow used the opportunity to book lots of local acts—the Bongos, the Fleshtones, the Nervous Rex, Come On—who created a social scene somewhat anti-no wave.

Morrow: "I read a Sonic Youth interview recently in which Steve Shelley said, 'We were really down on all that Hoboken pop squirm,' and I think that describes it exactly. 'No wave' was real rooted in the New York 'everything is ugly, the world is such a bad-ass place, let's crawl in a hole together and die' thing. I learned a lot from those bands, but we just weren't that nihilistic. In fact, we had this delusion that we could be these real commercial, popular bands, only on our own terms."

Meanwhile, Hoboken's music scene, along with aesthetically similar scenes all over America, was being financially aided across the Hudson, where the downtown dance club scene was blooming. "It was like all of a sudden there were a million kids going out at night. We could make really good money playing places like Danceteria, the Peppermint Lounge, and the Ritz—up to a grand a night, which is amazing given we were playing all original material," Morrow recalls. "Those places were packed all the time, but that doesn't exist now, there simply aren't the bodies."

That was the apex. One night after a particularly scintillating set a girl called Madonna came up and kissed him after a concert. Another night, Morrow recalls housesitting Lester Bangs's apartment, and the MC5's late Rob Tyner called up, all depressed, and the two commiserated as to the probability that Reagan's era would usher in the actual end of the world. Meanwhile, Stiff put out a no-wave compilation called *Start Swimming*, which was a recording of a British concert by the Bush Tetras, the Ray Beats, the dBs, and the Bongos. "We thought it was like the Crusades," Morrow says now. "We were all like, 'Farewell! God speed!' And then the English simply slammed it, and from then on we hated England. Some early Rough Trade stuff was OK, the Raincoats, the Slits, the Swell Maps, Gang of Four. But then they became like a fucking factory, regurgitating these perfect images of rock 'n' roll. Spandau Ballet and shit."

In 1982 the Individuals recorded their first LP at Mitch Easter's Drive-In Studio in North Carolina during the same block of time that a band called R.E.M. was booked in to do an EP called *Chronic Town*. (The connection came from Hoboken's adopted house band the dBs, whose members came from nearby Winston-Salem.) The bands didn't have to cross-pollinate their ideas, since they somehow already had. "We did share some aesthetics," Morrow recalls. "I know we didn't want to write love songs, but about other subjects entirely, with the result that our lyrics were real surreal, so people could read into them what they wanted. Certainly R.E.M. shared that with us."

The Individuals' record, *Fields*, released in 1982 on a tiny independent label, was critically well received: the *New York Times* named it one of the year's ten best (alongside X's *Under the Big Black Sun*, Lou Reed's *Blue Mask*, and *The Message* by

Grandmaster Flash). But despite the rave reviews and sold-out local shows, the Individuals' career faltered. Their record label went bankrupt, and no major-label offers were forthcoming. One night in 1983 Glenn went to see the Replacements at Max's Kansas City with co-band member Janet Wygal. "I immediately wanted to break up the band," he remembers. "Janet said, 'Gee, I wish we could do this,' and I remember thinking, 'Yeah, but we *can't*.' "

And then Manhattan suddenly languished. Its club scene was reduced to a series of arty performance spaces, the Knitting Factory, and the Bitter End. New bands had been priced out of living in the city; and besides, hiphop was the only sound that really mattered: however artsy the outfit was, forever after that time, from now to the present, there would always be the sense that Stetsasonic—heck, even the Beastie Boys—would speak more eloquently to and about the citizenry of New York than Controlled Bleeding or Rat at Rat R.

Stamey left the dBs. The once-beloved Bongos, then on a major, made two bad records that nobody liked. Maxwell's, however, has thrived, eventually becoming one of the premiere rock venues in the New York area. The club's owner, Steve Fallon, began Coyote Records, releasing albums by Jon Klages, a newly resuscitated Feelies (*The Good Earth*, produced by Peter Buck), and later the Mekons, the Neats, and Yo La Tengo. But the seminal days were over. Glenn Morrow: "The social scene ended. It was like people went there and met and fell in love and that was that. It had all just been a mating ritual and they stopped going out and got a life." "*All my friends thrown into the fire/Lost in a sea of their own desire/I'm a big fish in a little pond/Oh my God, all the water's gone*,' sang Glenn on an Individuals song called "Rain," which he later recorded for the *Rage to Live* album.

"I think," he continues, "we were the last generation to think we could be the next Beatles. But then we finally looked around and noticed that the industry was just totally ignoring all these incredible bands like Pylon and Mission of Burma, and we were just outraged. After that, the next generation of bands like Hüsker Dü and the Minutemen, who did *really* uncompromising music, they came to terms with that. They were like, 'Fuck it! If they don't get signed, we sure won't.' No wonder SST could sign anyone to a one-off deal: it'd be, like, 'Do a record with us; no one else wants you.' And the bands were, like, 'OK.' They weren't going anywhere."

Parents might say otherwise, but I think there's really only one thing every American should graduate from college with, and that's at least one close friend who's moved to Manhattan. In this day and age, it's simply imperative to know at least one person who braves the insurmountable costs, the housing shortage, and the fear factor, and just goes for it: someone who doesn't mind squishing into a one-bedroom walkup with a bathtub in the kitchen or whatever for a year or two. A person with a couch.

I was lucky. I got that out of college, if little else; a friend's floor on East 97th Street, always available, and a spare set of keys. My dad used to give me frequent-flyer coupons for services rendered, and for years I used to crash at Annie's, tiptoeing in at three or four A.M., leaving her long notes on her kitchen table detailing my evening's fun: how I'd spent the night at CB's canteen seeing Nikki Sudden while the Meat Puppets pounded flesh in the room next door; had been up all night waiting for the Lunachicks, Das Damen, and Band of Susans to perform at a disgustingly large dive called the World; watched the Wipers, Thelonious Monster, and the Dead Milkmen at an upstairs club in Times Square ironically called Nirvana, or taken the PATH back from Maxwell's after a Chills gig in 1987.

Ann had to go to work at seven in the morning, so I used to go stay with her for days on end and never actually see her. I remember long, long cab rides bombing up Lex listening to Billie Holiday or "To Sir with Love"; I used to keep a list of my cabbies' names because I thought they were so funny. Oh, those cab rides! A person like me never had a red cent in New

York City, because of having to save up for them: I used to treat my friends to dinner at the Burger King across from the Marriott in Times Square but only if they treated me back. Beer was simply out of the question.

Given the difficulty of just being a rock fan, I always wondered how a person could ever form a band if they lived in New York City. Most that I knew about were either rent-controlled natives with parents in the West Seventies or suspected cases of trust-funditis, neither of which are necessarily crippling to brilliance, but both of which are rare enough to lessen the pool of possible talent in a place.

In the late seventies you could live in Hoboken or the East Village really cheaply, and during that time there were great bands there. After that, not so many—those that did come up were noisy, arty outfits, dense, humorless, snobby: Live Skull, Pussy Galore, and the Swans. Those bands all played music that was, like the city they lived in, grimy and noisy, passionless, hard to hear. To me, they also reflected a certain New York attitude problem, a line of predictable elitist cant dispensed through the *Village Voice* and, slightly more secretively but also more powerfully, through *Conflict*, a fanzine begun back in Boston by one Gerard Cosloy and transplanted to New York when Gerard took over the helm of a Long Island-based indie called Homestead Records.

Gerard is really one of the great personalities of the Amer-indie underground. He radiates a kind of curmudgeonly combination of entrepreneur and knight in shining armor that's unique to American life. He's always reminded me of that quote from Yeats, "The best lack all conviction, while the worst are full of passionate intensity." In direct opposition to the grand music industry tradition whereby record companies provide all writers with product and no questions asked, Gerard used, so it's been said, to scratch the name of each intended critic into Homestead's vinyl promos before mailing them, and then go through used record store bins to see which one had sold them back. Then he'd call them up and berate them for it. (CDs put a stop to that game. More's the pity.)

Gerard's a real First Amendment kind of guy: getting into year-long feuds with the *Village Voice* over the artistic merit and political correctitude (or lack thereof) of the Frogs or G. G. Allin (an artist known for assaulting women in the audience and shoving microphones up his own ass) is life's own delight to him. And during the time period we're talking about, Gerard was at the helm of Homestead, or Homostead, as my friends and I liked to call it.

Ah, Homestead! Pigfucker central. Unlike the other labels, which were begun and run by self-invested entrepreneurs, Gerard was merely the tool of Dutch East India distributorship. But even using other people's money, he managed to put out records by the likes of Nick Cave, Scraping Foetus, Sonic Youth, Big Dipper, the Volcano Suns, Squirrel Bait. He licensed the original Flying Nun New Zealand stuff, like the wonderful record *Juvinalia* by the Verlaines and eventually a reissue of the Chills' monumental *Kaleidoscope World* (the first really important import release by the now trendy label Creation). And then of course—Gerard has always been so cutting edge it kills me—the first record by a Seattle band called Green River, which later became Mudhoney and spawned a whole 'nother thing of its own.

Gerard is no capitalist, however: he's lightheartedly rejected demo tapes from bands that have gone on to sell millions of records—the Smithereens, for example—without losing a moment's sleep over it, while bands he has signed—like the Shams, and Teenage Fanclub—have never sold, well, great. But almost every one of the bands he's helped has gone on to charm and/or influence legions of alternative/indie rock faves.

Still, what Gerard has released has never been as important as his attitude, which he managed to disseminate pretty thoroughly throughout the entire United States by means of *Conflict* and which, I might add, absolutely haunts the zeitgeist of college radio today (albeit in the much-watered-down guise of cheap cynicism and pointless dumb mouthiness). *Conflict*'s constituency, Gerard recalls, was "pretty broad. People who bought records, people who hung out. My friends. Shut-ins, basically." This is Gerard's stance on reggae music, as gleaned from an old ish of *Conflict*: "Only thing in this world that's worse than listening to some spliffed out moron who ain't washed his hair in 3 years singing 'I love jah' is watching white college students throw frisbees around to the strains of the above rasta fool, although jazz-influenced fusion hardcore comes pretty close . . . why doesn't everyone just admit that the Bad Brains peaked with the ROIR cassette and that they've sucked ever since?" "In some corners of the universe, pop this listless might impress someone as original—like if you had never heard anything before." " 'The Thing That Just Goes' cooks hotter than Ed Asner's relatives at Dachau."

Offensive as these words are (and were), *Conflict* exists now as a document of a time when such prose was considered standard fare. All of Gerard's words, childish, offensive, witty, or whatever, jumped off the page at you, so strong, so committed to his belief in the music he wrote about. Bands often sank or swam—or rather, filled clubs or didn't—on the strength of a fuzzy, photocopied paragraph by Gerard. What made Gerard powerful, after all, wasn't his hateful wisecracks, but the fact that his musical opinions were usually right on the money. What was great about *Conflict*, and fellow fanzines like *Forced Exposure* and *Matter*, wasn't the dialogue they created between underground people all across the country, but the music they were speaking about and the passion its adherents felt for it.

Nowadays *Conflict*'s attitude can be seen in a watered-down form in the pages of modern, irony-laden magazines like *Spin*, but it's an attitude that has little merit when wasted on bad records and aimed at people with no opinions of their own. Gerard himself thinks it's questionable whether it had any validity even then. "I cringe when I see what I wrote back then," he says. "I must have been on such a mind-control trip! It was all so reactionary and sloppy. It cut so many people out of the picture. I grew up in an era when Democrats and Republicans weren't that different, and the distance between the left and the right was nonexistent. I guess I thought that preaching to the converted didn't matter, and that throwing slurs around was funny. At the time I thought it was a reaction to the hypocrisy of the times. I thought, 'Yeah! this is for the Volvo drivers! This is for the kids at Hampshire College!' I thought, 'Everything is wrong here and it's up to me to fix it.'

"But the world changed around me and I didn't catch up. I think it took me a long time to understand that this country if full of fucking mean-spirited people and that my slurs were just reinforcing really shitty, shitty things people did and thought. There were so many people who didn't get the joke. And, I see now, all the in-jokes prevented so many people from picking up on it all along. . . . I guess I just wish I'd left the door open a little wider."

Cosloy may well have been alienating people who might otherwise have joined the bandwagon earlier. But his label opened the door for numerous bands who might not have been allowed in quite so soon either. "I signed stuff from New York but also from Chicago and Boston," Gerard recalls. "I guess I was trying to document the entire national scene as it was at a certain time, and how I thought the sounds were all interlinked. To my mind, there was this overlap between all the bands who just created themselves and weren't influenced by what was currently on radio and television. They were bands who had a traditional rock lineage but that was a little hard to trace . . . that fit in some thin gap, as it were, between Ray Davies and Thurston Moore.

"But in the end, it was a very unfocused kind of policy. Looking back, I think we bit off a bit more than we could chew. The real indie labels, the ones started out of people's houses, have done a much, much better job of documenting their scenes. Like, Neutral, Glenn Branca's label, really put New York noise bands on the map more than Homestead did."

It was Neutral, not Homestead, that released the first two Sonic Youth EPs, *Sonic Youth* and *Confusion Is Sex*, thus quietly launching the career of the band that would become possibly New York City's greatest contribution to the independent underground. Sonic Youth was started around 1980 by the longtime punk rock fan Thurston Moore and his girlfriend (later wife) Kim Gordon, a transplanted L.A. art student who'd formerly been associated with Oingo Boingo. The band was originally conceived as a deliberately mistuned noise band, which included a keyboard player and the actor Richard Edson (*Stranger Than Paradise, Do the Right Thing*) on drums: in those days, the outfit was called first Male Bonding, then Red Milk. According to Moore, it sounded more typical of the downtown New York art scene than of hardcore: the band's offerings were cold, lengthy musings on the generation of pure noise, rather than one-minute songs about assassinating Reagan. But, says Moore, "we always wanted to write pop rock songs, not for experimental reasons but because we like them. We're not trained—I always just plug into the stereo and play my guitar with a hammer, and Kim only took up her bass the day she joined the band."

Thus, in the course of three years, Sonic Youth evolved into a more straightforward rock act, albeit one that combined the principles of feedback, distortion, dissonance, and wretched excess with more melodic songs about the dark side of pop culture. Slowcore, some people called it: a genre that encompassed songs about violence, celebrity, and Charles Manson: "Death Valley 69." "Kill Your Idols." "Madonna, Sean, and Me."

Sonic Youth then followed the example of more isolated Amerindie bands by getting out on the road early. That made them different from many another arty New York band, who were content (as Morrow mentioned earlier) with supporting themselves by the goodwill of the disco scene, when a band could play the Peppermint Lounge or Danceteria and make three thousand dollars a night.

Three thousand dollars a night sounds like a good deal for any band. But Cosloy thinks it wasn't actually that conducive to band development. "No one was there to see them," he explains. "They'd all just be in the other room dancing. The band was the sideshow, communicating with no one. It was like a grant system, only instead of the NEA they were funded by the Ritz. What bands should have been doing was getting out of town, or making records or something."

Sonic Youth did just that: Cosloy recalls seeing them at Storyville in Boston in 1983. "There were only four people in the audience, and the band had been promised a hundred and fifty dollars and the promoter just didn't have it. But they refused to leave till the guy had gone to a bank machine and gotten it."

And so from small things big things one day come. Presently, being from New York and all, Sonic Youth were lauded far and wide in the hinterland as kings and queen of the underground, masters of guitar torture, the holiest purveyors of jagged-edgiest dirty art rock row. Their topics of interest grew to envelop sonic life, sonic death, and sonic silence, all in one. The band's subsequent records, *Bad Moon Rising* and *Death Valley 69*, reached wider distribution by appearing first on Homestead; they became larger still with the release of *E.V.O.L.* and *Sister* on SST. By the time the band wound up on Geffen in 1990, Sonic Youth had seemingly learned from their peers' and forebears' mistakes. Though their records *Goo* and *Dirty* have not been major sellers, the band was later credited with having somehow ushered in the Nirvana mania. As one New York scenester put it to me the other day, "It's like, what's more important, the fact that Sartre discovered existentialism, or that he became a weird fascist at the end of his life?"

The members of Sonic Youth still live and work in New York City. Rents are still too high there, hiphop is still king, and there still aren't any garages. But word on the street is that things are picking up: "There's a new level of consciousness here, and a bunch of bands with their own followings and cliques and flyers and stuff, that seem to have nothing to do with radio or media or what label they're on," says Cosloy. "And that's great. There's a sense that people are paying to get into clubs again, that it's not all totally media-supported."

In 1986 Glenn Morrow joined up with Tom Prendergast's fledgling new indie label, Bar None, in order to release his own records under the moniker Rage to Live. The next project Bar

None took on was a quirky Brooklyn-based performance art duo called They Might Be Giants, whom Glenn saw as an updated version of the Bonzo Dog Band: in 1987 their self-titled record spawned a surprise video hit on MTV called "Don't Let's Start," which has funded the company ever since.

Meantime, Cosloy has gone from doing Homestead and *Conflict* to running his own label, Matador. He still has great taste and lots of influence, but—as befits a label exec—his opinionated manner has become significantly more subdued. After years and years of proud personal poverty and a determined habitation of the demesne of the fringes, Matador Records is about to sign a multimillion-dollar, seven-year joint venture agreement with Atlantic Records, thus, Gerard says wryly, "preventing me from backing out of this business until essentially the end of time."

Does the idea bother him? He pauses. "Well, this isn't a hobby or an experiment anymore," he says. "It's a job that lots of people depend on and stuff. In the old days people went to a lot of effort to convince themselves it wasn't a business. And denying it just made people rotten business people. Now there's no denying it.

"I mean, I believe in our stuff and I like it, but it's not, like, the most important thing in the world to me. With Homestead, I probably did believe that. It was really stupid of me, but yeah, I guess I did. I went from living at home and going to shitty punk rock shows to living in the most exciting city on earth and working with my most favorite famous people in the world—Sonic Youth, Big Black, Live Skull, Nick Cave. So it was a really big deal to me, it was probably too much of a big deal. Now that I have some historical perspective on life, I can see that a record is a record, and to tie your self-worth to the accomplishments of others is so stupid.

"But I think people have to find that out for themselves."

NINE

AS BEAUTIFUL AS THE DAY

Is the compulsion to great refusals a virtue, a neurosis, a mark of oppression, or some combination of all three?
– Robert Christgau

Austin, Texas, 1988: Beneath me lies an enormous high plain of crop-brown rock cut across its very middle by a great flat river and hills that hide a host of creeks and dragonflies and cicadas, all resting peacefully beneath a hot afternoon sun. Austin's Main Street is made up of a lot of long, low wooden buildings, and outside all the bars and taquerias, dogs with red bandanas round their little necks wait patiently for the patrons to take them home at two A.M. Time passes. Presently, music blasts out of every storefront; the human contents of the sidewalks spill over into the street, where they weave between huge RVs and Bronco 4 × 4s, which are lumbering along majestically at a motorized snail's pace. There's a large contingency of fluff-brained Texas cheerleaders in Lady Longhorns sweatshirts, which they periodically lift, to cheers from the rows of frat boy jarheads who loiter boisterously up and down the strip. Luckily, the vast quantities of Shiner Bock they've all swallowed since sundown have long since made them tolerant. Here, the foibles of the black-clad go unnoticed by the jeans-clad; here, the two groups nearly get along.

So there I am, jostling my way between the Ritz and the Cannibal, when the body of my friend Glenn shoots out in front of me, spit like a gumball from the doorway of some club or other. "There's a band in there you'd love," he remarks genially, as he picks himself up. "Four guys doing Thin Lizzy covers. Their underpants show through their jeans." My eyes light up and I bolt inward, turning once to wave to Glenn as he attempts to thread his way back out into the fleshpots.

In Austin, every house has a porch, and every porch is drenched in shade, and every shadow is made from an oak tree, and every oak tree has a hammock hanging on it, and every hammock conceals a boy, and every boy is strumming a guitar. The city of Austin boasts a population of 468,000, and according to the Chamber of Commerce, which has long taken an interest in the subject, that figure includes nine hundred rock bands. Nine hundred bands equals thirty-six hundred potential rock stars, pumping your gas, serving you dinner, selling you records, bumming a beer off you at Antoine's or the Cave Club or the Continental on a Friday night. Nine hundred bands, all lined up along Sixth Street and South Congress and Guadalupe and beyond. Chances are everyone you meet could show you the chords to "Stepping Stone." As Pat Blashill, an Austin music fan and rock photographer, once described it, "One day, you're listening to your favorite band. The next day, someone says, 'Here, hold my guitar for a while, I'm goin' for a beer.' And the day after that, you're driving the van for the band's national tour."

This is Texas, then: legendary home of country-and-western outcasts, burnouts, and Texan eccentrics like Waylon and Willie, Butch and Jimmie Dale, Janis, Roky, and more recently, Daniel Johnston. Austin has always been tolerant of deviants, just as it's always been a center for popular music, dating way back to the 1880s, when William Sydney Porter—better known as O. Henry—made an uncertain living there as a sales clerk, bank teller, draftsperson, and musician. In his free time he published a magazine called, ironically enough, *Rolling Stone*.

In the 1950s blues great T-Bone Walker resided in the capital of Texas; by the sixties, the Sir Douglas Quintet had come to the fore, as did Janis Joplin and a crazy acid-rock scene led by Roky Erikson and the Aliens (two of whose members had to be forcibly sequestered in mental institutions) and Red Crayola (known for jamming to the amplified sound of an ice block melting). Willie Nelson, Waylon Jennings, Jerry Jeff Walker, and a whole slew of country artists created Austin's "outlaw" scene in the seventies—a network of crossover country artists divorced from the syrupy sweetness of Nashville.

Austin had its share of miscreant one-hit wonders, like the Crazy World of Arthur Brown ("I am the God of Hellfire and I Give You Fire!") and the equally hell-spawned Christopher Cross. And it's had its share of punk rock bands too—the Skunks, the Violaters, the Huns, and the Big Boys come to mind, as do Austin punk expats littering either coast: Kathy Valentine (later the Go-Gos), Carla Olsen (later of the Textones), and M.D.C. (Millions of Dead Corporations—or Cops).

And then there's those hick-ridden indie bands with little or no contact with the industry, mainstream or otherwise. Legions of bands with no idea of how to get a record contract, but a sizeable built-in audience and the indolent, weathered, low-rent life of ease that most rock bands only dream of: bands like Glass Eye, Zeitgeist, the True Believers, the Wild Seeds, the Hickoids, the Big Boys, and Scratch Acid (later called the Jesus Lizard).

But despite the propitious circumstances, Austin's place in the independent scene has never been as solid as that of, say, Minneapolis, Boston, or Seattle, mainly because there are no thriving local independent labels based there, and no real eloquent voice on college radio. Austin's musical richness is based entirely on its unusually thriving live scene. Whereas in most other American towns, combatting the natural couch potatohood of the citizenry is a major battle for club owners, in Austin things are way different. There is instead a local population that loves to go out and see live music late at night.

Perhaps that is because the town's made up of slackers. Or maybe it's the weather: in the summertime the locals can get fever-high from rock 'n' roll, thus saving themselves the cost of actual drugs. Austin has no parking problems—you ride your bike everywhere—and even the lowlife looks different, since nobody, but nobody, wears black. You check out the Liberty Lunch, a ceilingless warehouse on Second Street by Town Lake some July night, and you'd be amazed at the cavalcade of social types who've broad-mindedly gone to see some punk rock bands: kickers, hippies, bearded country-and-western freaks, and of course the thousands of other band members who reside within the Austin city limits.

But the greatest progenitors of the myth of Austin have got to be the Butthole Surfers, an acid punk band that originated in San Antonio and wound up a decade later frightening the horses in the up-for-anything Austin area. They were out of their heads, all right: it'd be the hottest day of the year, and they'd set their drum set on fire and hurl it into the audience. Or Gibby Haynes, the singer, would bash all the other band members on the head with whiskey bottles. Once, word has it, a person died at one of their gigs, thus ensconcing them forever in the hearts of a thrill-seeking (but essentially namby-pamby) underground. I myself once keeled over in a dead faint at the mere sight of a bloody car accident they had projected on a screen behind their stage. A typical fanzine description: "Dance to it? I don't know. You could kill to it."

I first saw the Buttholes opening for the Circle Jerks at a gig in Sacramento. A few days earlier in San Francisco, the band had sold out the Mabuhay Gardens and caused some kind of mini-riot during the gig, but here in the heartland, a host of fifteen-year-olds watched nervously as the Buttholes destroyed all music as they knew it. Blinded by their relentless strobe, confused by cacophonous lyrics shouted out through a bullhorn, daunted by the tape loops and satanic echoes, many of these children backed out of the room well before the set was over. So they didn't see, as I saw, Gibby fling the drummer, Teresa, over his shoulder and carry her off still beating on a flaming kettledrum he held before him. It's a moment I still treasure, lonely, defiant, brave, and beautiful. The Buttholes were warriors, all right, some kind of twisted advance guard, put here to warn the natives. Punk rock originally dreamed of a world where the most outrageous act could put on the status quo, a world where people who spat in the face of authority were king. Punk rock postulated that the only way one could ever live out that dream was never to give in to the powers that be; to do it yourself and be damned—or rewarded—for it. But even punk rock couldn't have dreamed of anything as rash and wild as the true story of the Butthole Surfers.

Thirty miles south of Austin, in the midst of fields full of wildflowers and a big sky so blue you could lose your mind looking at it, lies the town of Driftwood, Texas. Situated a ways off the interstate on county road 666 (not), it sleeps year round under a green-brown blanket of rolling hills and birch trees, a million miles from anything urban, from parking spaces and shopping malls and Burger Kings and crack houses.

The civic center of Driftwood consists of one weathered wooden store with an old gas pump in front of it, and with the volunteer fire department building across the way, an equally weathered structure set within a grove of trees. The storefront sports a hand-lettered notice that tells of a town meeting that'll take place sometime in the far distant future, but for the moment there is no future. There is only the dead calm of afternoon and a long wait in the shade. I buy myself a pop at the general store and sit down on the rickety porch. The air is so still I can hear the sound of woodpeckers pecking at the nearby tree trunks. Nothing happens for a long, long time. And then, far off down the road, I see a guy on a bicycle coming toward me. The road he's riding is giving up dust, and as he draws closer I can see he's the same guy I last saw a few weekends ago swathed in hot colored smoke while torturing an electric guitar in front of a screen displaying a bloody film, his lips drawn back in a terrorizing grimace, his body bathed in a sinister haze of noise.

Presently he gets off his bike and we stand face to face in the middle of the road. He looks around at the fields and sky without speaking. "God's country," says Paul Leary, finally, nodding approvingly at some horses cavorting in a nearby field, and I agree: it's as far as one could possibly imagine from the world where Surfers vocalist Gibby Haynes shrieks the lyric "Satan! Satan! Satan!" over and over again.

I say as much to Paul as we drive slowly over a road that wends along field and creek on our way to the Butthole Surfers' ranch. He nods. "Yeah, but that's the whole point. It's really great out here: we just love it. Hays County is dry—you got to drive thirty miles just to buy a six-pack. See those horses?" he adds inconsequently, pointing toward a herd of ponies gamboling along a yellow ridge. "I been watching them ever since they were foals. They used to never get more than a foot apart from each other, and now just look at them!"

Soon we've turned up the road to the house. "All this land," remarks Paul, pointing out toward the brush-covered horizon, "we own. Going to buy another ten acres soon. Oops! Watch that little bitty bridge—don't worry, if we can get over it in our van, you can do it in a Toyota . . . the Meat Puppets once wrecked that fence over there though, with their big ol' RV."

Inside the house we're met by Gibby and Jeff, who are whiling away time watching an Oprah episode on "Men Who Love Fat Women." "And people think we're tasteless," Gibby comments, shaking his head ruefully. The television is static-ridden, and Gibby and Jeff aren't really paying much attention: "We don't get too good reception," Gibby shrugs, unconcerned. Mark Farner, the Buttholes' brown doggie, and Papillon, the cat, are curled up on the carpet in front of the set. "We have two blue jays and some hummingbirds and some mockingbirds that come round too," Paul says proudly. "You should see the bluebirds. The females are really cool. And last week there were three days when there were about a hundred robins on the lawn. There's doves too, and when they all take off at once, it sounds like fucking Vietnam!"

First stop on my tour of the Buttholes' house is the studio, one room crammed full of about $100,000 worth of equipment.

There's a DAT machine, a thirty-two-track mixing board, a Dolby II sound equalizer, all kinds of speakers and reel-to-reel tape axles, sound-muffling foam on the walls, the usual home studio stuff. "We're always allowed to bring equipment home from the music store," Gibby explains. "They just love us 'cause we spend *tons* of money there. If we like it and use it, we pay for it. Otherwise, we just bring it back."

Gibby obligingly winds up a reel-to-reel of the band's most recently recorded track, one that Paul just wrote on a sequencer. "I write the drum parts," he explains, "then add guitar parts over there"—he points toward the bedroom, where he plays under headphones to eliminate distortion—"and Gibby adds the vocals."

Paul switches on the tape, and the room fills up with the relentless thud of sequenced drums. At this volume they sound like a giant hand using the Empire State Building and the isle of Manhattan as pestle and mortar. Paul's vicious guitar comes in, then Gibby's insane chant. It sounds great. Paul shrugs. "That's just some of the stuff we've been working on out here."

When not on the road, this is where the Butthole Surfers now live and work. Or at least, where some of them do, sometimes: the band's last record, *Hairway to Steven*, was recorded in a studio. The band owns the land and the ramshackle ranch-style wooden house that was already on the land and all this equipment, on which they write music, experiment on tape, record demos, and just plain have fun. "I'd much rather make money making records than putting myself through the touring meat grinder," Paul states flatly.

"Studios are expensive," he continues, "and we've recorded in a lot of them. But the best stuff comes out of our own house." The Buttholes have been doing nothing but recording on their own out here for about six months, one of their more extensive periods of time off the road in the last eight years. They have many, many songs on tape now, some of which are just fragments, some of which are in an almost finished state. Within the next few months they'll release a limited-edition double live set (as a bootleg), a new Butthole

Surfers record, and a record by their alter ego band, the Jack Officers, which Gibby says is "like synthesizer music, neat dance music, space music. It's just got a few singing parts . . . it's like acid house. No, it's hick house!"

"You have to admit," Paul adds proudly, "it's pretty neat that Driftwood, Texas, became hip to Eazy E and NWA before New York. Forget all about punk rock music; rap music is what punk rock always wanted to be. It's accessible, but they want to piss people off, and they don't hold anything back."

Working on tracks for those three releases, the guys in the band have been busy enough, due perhaps in part to the lack of good television and radio reception to distract them. But there's a little bit of tension in the Butthole camp at the moment: though the band claims to prefer recording at home to the "stiffer" sound of the studio-recorded *Hairway to Steven*, there's intermittent talk of flying to New York to record with Bill Laswell. Additionally, their label situation is up in the air. Although Gibby says they're happy with Touch and Go (the label that has released most of their albums to date), he admits that the band is attracted to the idea of a major and is in fact now talking to one in particular.

"The big thing would just be distribution," he says. "We went into a mall in Tulsa recently, and we saw these bootleg Butthole T-shirts for sale, but the store didn't carry any of our records! That means that bootleg T-shirts get better distribution than our albums. With better distribution, we'd sell more records. But then again, to a major, maybe selling under a hundred thousand records is a failure."

The Buttholes are exceedingly cagey about any information regarding record sales; direct questions about financial figures tend to be met with gaping silences. When asked how many copies a Butthole record sells, Jeff says, "More than the Fabulous Thunderbirds, and less than Suicidal Tendencies." Gibby adds that they'll be pressing twenty thousand copies of the live LP, all of which are already presold, and adds, "We could easily do double that." On the other hand, Paul says, "There's only a limited dollar for Butthole Surfers records."

The limited dollar of devoted Butthole-ees is one reason the band is so virulently opposed to all bootlegging activities—so opposed, Paul tells me, that whenever the band discovers another bootleg on the market, they immediately press a better recording of the same show, copy the cover art, and flood the market. This is the impetus behind the upcoming live album. Still, there are bands in the world who probably wish they had such problems. For the Buttholes to get to a point where the Springsteen-like quandary of how to counter bootlegging is a major concern is a pretty great accomplishment, given that for years all they wondered about was where their next meal was coming from.

The Butthole Surfers got together in the spring of 1981, when, Gibby says, he and his longtime high school and college pal Paul Leary began playing music together in a San Antonio living room. Gibby had known Paul forever ("First his family thought I was a bad influence on him, then my family thought he was a bad influence on me, and then they just went and figured we were bad influences on each other"). Their affinity for calculated outrage predates the formation of the band—before that, the two of them, then graduate students at Trinity College in San Antonio, had a T-shirt company that sold silk-screened shirts of David Berkowitz (Son of Sam).

It was while selling those shirts on Venice Beach that they met Bruce Licher, the head of Independent Project Records and a member of Savage Republic. Licher, Gibby recalls, "turned us on to a bunch of music—Black Flag, Fear, the Circle Jerks, X—hell, even Oingo Boingo seemed cool in those days."

Subsequently, Gibby and Paul returned to Texas. "And one time the Big Boys were playing at the Lake [Travis] and they asked us to play a couple of songs right before they went on. That used to be the punk rock thing to do if you were a new band, remember?"

"And then they offered us money to come back and play a gig and we thought we was going to get rich!" Paul interrupts, cracking up.

Before that experience, Paul's last band had been when he

was in the fifth grade: he played covers of Monkee songs in front of his elementary school. But after playing at Lake Travis, Paul and Gibby and the rest of the then-Butthole lineup decided to move back to L.A. to make it in rock 'n' roll. "I remember trying to impress my mom," Paul says, " 'cause she was so disgusted that I was gonna quit my job selling lumber at the lumber mill and go play in a punk rock band. I go, 'But Mom, there's these guys in California called the Minutemen, and D. Boon, he writes ten songs a day!' And my Mom goes, 'Yeah? That's because he can't stand any of 'em after he's written 'em!' "

True fact: to this day, Mrs. Leary has yet to pronounce the name of her son's band out loud.

The Butthole Surfers played their first real gig as such at L.A.'s Whiskey on July 4, 1982, with the Dead Kennedys and TSOL. "It was fucking great," Paul recalls. "Most fun I ever had. We sounded like hell, and they loved it. In fact, to this day, the better we sound, the worse people like it."

"And the worse you sound," Gibby adds, "the better it gets."

After that, things went downhill for a while. At one point, the band broke up when their bass player at the time (they had fourteen prior to Jeff, who's lasted longer than all the others put together) forgot he owned an amp. Another one went into the desert and tried to light himself on fire; a third ditched the band to try and get on "Jeopardy" when he had a dream indicating that the first stop on the road to becoming the Messiah was to win at "Jeopardy" five days in a row. ("We used to know the formula for how you could win, like, five million bucks on 'Jeopardy' if you got, like, a double jeopardy at the end of all the hardest categories," Jeff recalls.)

Eventually, the Buttholes ended up back in San Antonio, where Gibby went so far as to get a haircut, a suit, and a job at an accounting firm. "But at every job I'd get there'd be someone I used to work with, I was just so notorious. Like one time there was this guy I was working with and he was going down the steps and this eighty-year-old lady whom we were auditing was going up them, and I saw him coming, so I stooped down under the steps and pretended to be looking up her dress. And he didn't get the joke at all, he just thought I was the most disgusting human being alive."

"Another time," Paul recalls gleefully, "we put out this magazine called *Strange V.D. Magazine* that had all these pictures of really wicked venereal diseases with humorous descriptions of what it actually was. And we made copies of it in the copier and left one of the original pages in the machine by accident and it got returned to him personally by one of the partners."

Soon the only career option open to Mr. Haynes was to re-form the Butthole Surfers. This time the band (augmented by present members Jeff, King and Teresa) began recording (*Cream Corn* and *Rembrandt Pussyhorse*) by breaking into a recording studio whose tool shed they were sleeping in at night. They began, slowly, to gain a certain amount of notoriety, especially by means of their live shows, which were—well, colorful. The band's name, originally intended as a little kid's joke ("Really, if we wanted to be nasty we would have called ourselves the Shit Up Your Mother's Pussy Surfers," comments Gibby), got them immediately banned from the mainstream press, but in some ways that ban has ultimately worked in their favor. "Other famous bands would be interviewed, you know?" Paul notes. "And they'd make these really disturbing remarks about the Butthole Surfers."

So the legend grew. Giant Texans carrying flamethrowers. Dueling drummers playing in strobe-lit unison. Rock 'n' roll with lots of aggressive guitar chops, over-amped chords and meandering, psychedelic leads, tempered by an unsettlingly abrasive aesthetic: things at wrong speeds, layers of noise, and lyrics grappling with horrid subjects like Julio Iglesias and bodily functions. Naked women, ugly movies, the last word in scary, mind-bending, morally disturbing music. It was irresistible to the artiness in all of us in the underground. And what about art? "*Art*," explains Gibby patiently, "is just the last three letters of *fart*."

By 1985, the Butthole Surfers were entirely committed,

heart and soul, to the road rock lifestyle. What followed was a three-year period of complete homelessness.

"Living on porches and floors," Gibby recalls.

"Once or twice a week, we'd sneak into one motel room at a Motel Six and sleep for twenty-four hours straight," Paul reminisces.

"It was this big breakthrough when we bought sleeping bags. It was like a revelation: 'Wow! Why didn't we have these the whole time?' "

"Yeah, we'd had flu for six months of the year without realizing if we'd just had a sleeping bag in winter we'd stay warm all night."

Grueling though it seems in retrospect, Paul and Gibby claim to have enjoyed the experience. "Sure, it had its moments," Gibby says. "I don't regret it at all. We met a lot of wild-ass, cool-as-shit people doing it."

Additionally, it was through touring that the band earned enough money to buy the equipment and living space they now occupy. "You know, all the people who've come after us, all the other bands have been ripped off by the exact same people as us," Gibby notes. "We all made the same mistakes. It's weird. A lot of people really freak out that we write our own songs, record our own music, do our own artwork, and just about distribute our own records, and are doing as well as we are. But that's just what you've got to do. It's not that it's any harder today than it was before."

But isn't it true that the Buttholes have done it better than anyone else?

"No, I wouldn't say that. It's just that we've more or less invested what we made back into the band. We've done a bunch of records, and we haven't gone into outside studios and recorded a whole lot. I mean, a cheap-ass fucking record costs fifteen thousand dollars to do—and that's a cheap-ass one. Twenty thousand dollars is the budget we've had for the last few, and a hundred thousand wouldn't even buy coke spoons for a Guns N' Roses recording project. And so it's been, like, five records for twenty thousand each: a hundred thousand total. So we just bought it all, did it all ourselves.

That's what we spent our money on. Instead of spending money on rent, we just bought equipment, just gritted our teeth and stayed out there on the road.

"It's been a lot of work," Gibby continues, "and most bands don't have the stamina to last through the really tough years. Most bands break up after they're on the road 'cause they can't stand each other for extended periods of time. But we get along amazingly well compared to most bands."

"Or," Paul speculates, "maybe they just have other priorities. But when you do this for a living, these kinds of things naturally develop. You've got to sell records to go on the road, and you've got to go on the road to sell records. So that's what you do."

"First we got one projector," Gibby explains, "then we got two projectors. First we got one little light, and then one little smoke machine, and then this ex-con sold us twelve hundred dollars' worth of strobe lights for, like, fifty cents."

All of which eventually developed into the full-blown Butthole Surfers shows of today, the ones with the smoke and the fire and the naked dancing girls ("We don't even hire 'em anymore, they just show up," grimaces Gibby). The ones with the gross-out films in the background ("We just check 'em out of the University Film Library here," Paul tells me). The ones that KLM's in-flight magazine plugged in a recent issue as follows: "Obscenities, perverse humor, chaos, and bad taste are the ingredients for a live performance by this Texas band. Be sure and see them while in Amsterdam!"

The shows come equipped with audiences that have what Jeff politely terms "such a heavy grunge factor in them. . . . It's amazing, you light one guy on fire and he'll follow you all around the country wearing his scorched jacket—try and get backstage and everything."

"It's weird how for such normal people we know so many freaks," comments Paul.

That evening, as the sun set on Driftwood, I offered to drive Gibby into Austin to meet his dad for dinner. Gibby grinned impishly. "Can I have control of the tape deck?" I shrugged, steeling myself for forty-five minutes of Butthole noises and sonic discontent. Instead, Gibby came out of the house clutching his favorite tape, an advance copy, he told me, of a band he'd first heard in Europe. "I know you'll love this," he gushed. "It's so incredibly cute." The tape was of De La Soul's *Three Feet High and Rising,* and as my red Toyota rushed homeward across the hills of the Edwards Plateau, Gibby and I chanted and giggled, giggled and chanted: "Me Myself and I." Now I can't hear "Plug Tunin' " without practically smelling Texas.

Soon after I said good-bye to the Buttholes that afternoon, they signed to Rough Trade Records (reputedly asking a $100,000 advance, thus helping to hasten Rough Trade, which went bankrupt in 1990, to its end). For a while after that, the Buttholes went labelless, before signing to Capitol in 1991. They'd long since sold the ranch by then, but are still able to command a reputed fifteen thousand dollars per gig. Their shows are still automatic sellouts, coast to coast, putting them in a position to book one-offs on either coast without having to drive those hellish distances between dates, without having to kill themselves every night.

But that was still all in the far distant future. Back at the ranch that night, Paul pointed out across the long grass. "We want to buy that other ten acres over there so nobody can build on it and wreck our view. And we want to build more, so we can have a studio out there and each have a nicer bedroom in here."

"And we want a swimming pool that we can do laps in."

"A circular swimming pool, and an ice-skating rink and a basketball court," Gibby continues dreamily. Mark Farner yawns. Papillon stretches. The mockingbirds make mocking noises, and the sun sets on Driftwood. The band is just joking of course, and yet, the reality isn't such a laughing matter: somehow or other, in the teeth of all odds, the Butthole Surfers have succeeded on almost everybody's terms.

Everybody, that is, except Paul's mother, who still threatens her grandchildren with certain death if they ever reveal to any of their schoolteachers the name of Uncle Paul's rock band.

"Actually, my mom admits we're doing well," Paul concedes. "But then she'll add in the same breath: 'Yep. And so's crack!' "

TEN

LET'S SAY WE DID

Sure it's pop. But I still wouldn't bake a soufflé next to it.
– unattributed K quote

Thirty miles south of the Canadian border, nestled between the San Juan Islands and beautiful Mount Baker, Bellingham, Washington, is a notably scenic locale even in a state chock full of vista points. Its tiny downtown features numerous old-timer bars and cafés, and there's not one single tract development or condo complex anywhere in sight. There are three good record stores within a two-block radius, however; and on my one visit there in 1992, I had the great pleasure of thrifting at a junk store whose dealer insisted, before I left, on dressing himself in a huge Mr. Peanut costume. The outfit came complete with a cane, onto which he'd tied a dollar bill with a string. This he dragged along the pavement in front of him in the hopes that I'd stoop to pick it up. "Make it ten, and maybe I will," I jested. He said he'd never heard of Nirvana. "But people keep saying that whenever they see me like this," he admitted.

Around the corner, the teeny-tiny 3 B Bar on State Street was busy gearing up for their annual Garage Shock rock festival by offering dollar pitchers of Lone Star and showing cheesy horror movies all day to an abundance of large-tummied and bearded mountain-male rock fans. Many wore Harley-Davidson Bellingham T-shirts, the back of which read, "Acid Wash makes my butt hurt."

Sponsored by Estrus Records, Garage Shock ran for four nights with, according to the festival organizer, Estrus Records label head, and guitarist for Bellingham's own Mono Men,

Dave Crider, "no headliners, no openers, no guarantees. Just eighteen bands from the Pacific Northwest," including Crider's own Mono Men, Clackamas's Dead Moon, Anacortes's Gravel, and a ton of other bands from Idaho, British Columbia, Oregon, and environs, whose unifying philosophy seemed to be only a thoroughgoing belief in reverb. "There will be no political statements made at Garage Shock," adds Crider. "And no major artistic statements, that's guaranteed. Whatever this is, it is not art. A lot of people think garage rock means guys in paisley shirts and Vox guitars. But it's not that at all. What it is is American roots rock 'n' roll, whatever that means, to whoever plays it. I mean, I think Motorhead is garage rock."

Garage Shock's ethos, as stated by Crider, could double as the motto for Pacific Northwestern rock in general. The festival wasn't meant as either a civic event or generous communal offering, but the length and breadth of the resulting entertainment unwittingly displayed the unnerving depth of interest in rock 'n' roll that exists in and around Washington State and the rest of the Pacific Northwest ("Cascadia" to many who live there). Seventy miles south of Seattle—180 big ones from Bellingham—a whole other aesthetic is underway, and it's just as rich a vein of garage rock as ever you may find. But in Olympia, the hippy chicks and bicycle boys still believe passionately in punk rock. Young as they are, they know full well that the coming American revolution will be grrrl style, that major labels are the corporate ogre, and that all rock stars must die. Unlike in Bellingham, in Olympia, politics, art, and rock 'n' roll are not mutually exclusive activities. But their relation to one another is knit into the very fabric of Washingtonian society: it's a pattern that was cast in the community irrevocably. It's as sticky as a Beatles song, sung to its mothers such a long, long time ago.

Olympia is the capital of the state of Washington, at the

southern end of Puget Sound. There, the enormous blue body of fjords and waterways that scoops a huge chunk out of the Pacific Northwest winds up in a river called the Deschutes, right next to an unbearably cute public statue of a giant wooden salmon.

Olympia is also home to The Evergreen State College. (The "The," which is included on signs on the freeway and everywhere, has always bugged me, because for the longest time I didn't realize it denoted that Evergreen was a state college; I thought it meant it was the College of the Evergreen State. I'm like Christopher Robin every time I see it: "Don't they know what 'ther' means?") Everywhere east of Denver, however, Evergreen is known as hippie central: it's the Antioch, or the Reed, or the Hampshire College of the Northwest.

The difference is that it's a state school, and thus cheaper than the aforementioned ivory towers. Ever since the seventies it has attracted the cream of America's smart but not snobby, adventurous, alternative youth. It'll never win any prizes in *Playboy* for being a party haven for naked wild women, but for a brief time in the late seventies it was certainly the secret center of media deconstruction and infiltration, a place where underground theories were put nobly into practice. And its impact since that time has been strangely pervasive, wending its way through the id of American pop culture—from Matt Groening's "Simpsons" to the genesis of Sub Pop itself.

Evergreen graduate Bruce Pavitt now calls Olympia at that time a "cultural think tank," but it was also something much less stuffy: a little while later, in 1984, it was the pristine green set of a practically private teenage punk rock explosion. Between the two times, the city has nurtured so much that is integral to the alternative rock scene today.

In the early seventies Evergreen State had a ten-watt college radio station, KAOS, which, like many FM stations at that time, had a free-form policy. Thus much of its musical airtime was devoted to the works of Joni Mitchell, Keith Jarrett, Dan Fogelberg, Phoebe Snow, and the Grateful Dead. But in 1975 the station was commandeered, so to speak, by one John Foster, a nineteen-year-old who'd drifted into Olympia a few months earlier.

Foster grew up in Kent, Connecticut, a longtime radio head who made himself familiar from an early age with countless nearby stations: WNEW-FM, in New York, and WABC, the original Top 40 station, and numerous smaller ones as well: WGRG in Pittsfield, Massachusetts, and WKBW-AM in Buffalo, New York. "I was the kind of kid who'd be up on the roof swiveling around my antenna in midwinter and using icicles for better reception. And because I came from a real small town, I had a real appreciation of what local radio could mean to people in small towns."

In 1974, when he was eighteen, Foster began doing the Jack Kerouac act, winding up at last in the far western corner of the country, in Olympia. There he wangled, through a community youth organization, a full-time job that was paid for by the state. His title was music librarian, and one of his main duties was to put the station's library into shape. "I had to listen to every record to decide which category it went in. That was the way I became really aware of how much wasn't being represented on the radio, even at a really uncommercial radio station like KAOS. It seemed like the continuum of what was hip to play was just really narrow, that not a lot of records were even allowed into that category."

Foster decided to rectify that situation. He wrote to the New Music Distribution Service, a distributorship that catered to a lot of free jazz outfits and what he now calls "postindustrial weird music" labels. The organization sent him a list of over one hundred names and addresses of tiny labels, which he then started contacting for promos.

"Then," Foster recalls, "I started getting little publications, like *Cadence*, and *Coda*, and *Blues Unlimited*, and expanded into finding out about other kinds of labels, like cajun and bluegrass, and I just became fascinated with this grass-roots movement. It seemed like there were so many subcultures, and so many regional scenes, and none of them had *any* airplay."

Foster wrote to all of them for promo copies of their

records. Many of the labels, excited to hear there was a station that might play their product, wrote back. Pretty soon, the station was being deluged with new records. And Foster, for one, played them all. "At that time," he recalls, "I had a lot of airtime. Sometimes the station would go off at three A.M. and I'd get up and go in and crank it up again and play things. You know, the kind of thing you do when you're young and so in love with what you're doing."

Foster's musical eclecticism was aided and abetted at that time by an incoming Evergreener, Toni Holm, who'd worked as a teenager at WOSY, the community radio station in Antioch, Ohio. Holm believed—much as did the Christian Slater character in a cheesy movie called *Pump Up the Volume*—that the airwaves ought to be for everyone. "Her thing," explains Foster, "wasn't so much music as the idea of having different people in the community other than college kids on the radio. She was more like, 'Let's get gay people on the radio,' or refugees, or Mexican Americans, or old people. And that was seen as a really threatening idea, even in what was considered an enclave of hip college kids. But it wasn't as threatening as the idea of playing stuff that wasn't readily available."

Foster's and Holm's ideas quickly became politicized. "I took a real nuts-and-bolts economic view of the whole thing. I mean, there were six major record companies controlling everything heard on the radio, and that included the Grateful Dead. So I thought if we were really serious about being alternative, then we had to play all the more disenfranchised stuff out there instead. It was a political rather than a musical approach. So I created the green line system, whereby records that had independent distribution got a green line on their spine, and everything else had a red one. In 1977 the new regime at KAOS passed a policy whereby we would play eighty percent green-line music. I think I tried to get it to ninety-five percent, but they balked at that."

This was a particularly radical policy when you consider that, in 1977, the nascent state of independent labelhood was such that even records by the Ramones, Patti Smith, and Talking Heads all had to be red-lined. What was left to play? "Plenty," shrugs Foster. "Because I had really good contacts at that time. The material was available all right, it just wasn't comfortable to listen to all the time."

In 1978 Foster started to put together a written central source to enable other college stations to hook up with independent labels. Originally begun as a school project, the Lost Music Network started out as a nonprofit clearinghouse—for credit, of course, at Evergreen, where Foster was by now enrolled. The project began as an insert in the KAOS program guide, which got mailed out to station subscribers and other stations. But Foster kept expanding the mailing list to clubs and record stores around the country. After the fifth issue, he and his friend Dana Squires changed to a 24-page tabloid format much like that of early *Rolling Stone*: this became *Op* magazine. *Op* was the perfect vehicle for Foster in that it made use of every aspect of his interests, his networking and radio theories, and his huge library of independent label releases. *Op*'s policy was that it would review every single piece of music on independent labels it received. "I used to lock people in my bedroom and make them listen to singles for hours, and it drove everybody but me crazy."

By 1981, Squires and Foster were working full-time on *Op*, and Foster was in a band called the Pop Philosophers. Olympia was already well on its way to establishing itself as a focal point for regional punk—a circumstance that was certainly due to the presence of *Op* and KAOS. But Foster himself likes to downplay his own role in the formation of the scene. "Olympia could have happened anywhere—it could have been at Thomas Jefferson College in Michigan, but it wasn't. Scenes are based on individuals, not on places. Olympia goes through its highs and lows, but a lot of the reason it's so vital is because of Calvin Johnson [and now Candice Pedersen]. Calvin is the real constant here."

*

Calvin is the Calvin of K Records and Beat Happening, the organizer of the IPU (International Pop Underground), and the human Hello Kitty of rock. He grew up in Olympia, and in 1978, when he was fifteen years old, a high school friend of his found out about the Evergreen State College leisure education program, enabling Olympia citizens to learn aerobics, basket-weaving, and the like. Calvin wanted to take a class in the history of black music, but his friend convinced him to enroll in a class (instigated by Holm's theories on the importance of community radio) called Radio for Everyone, which trained volunteers for shows on KAOS.

The year before that, Calvin had been to London with his family, where he'd purchased the Sex Pistols single, and records by the Jam and the Damned. "So I thought I'd get a show on KAOS and play cool punk rock music. Little did I know the station had been playing more punk rock than I'd ever dreamed of for the last two years. Up till then, I had no idea there even was a station in Olympia."

Unbeknownst to Calvin, KAOS was of course already over-ridden with punk rockers, many of whom had their own bands. Within two months, Calvin was at one with them. In May 1978 a group of KAOS deejays, including Calvin, drove up to Seattle together to see Patti Smith perform there. One of the deejays, Steven Rabow (who later worked at KZOK), had arranged to interview her, so the KAOS crowd welcomed her at the airport. Then they caravaned over to her in-store appearance at Tower Records. There, all the KAOS deejays asked Patti Smith for her autograph. Not Calvin. "I thought that would be really lame and not punk rock, so I said, 'Can I autograph *your* jacket?' " Smith declined the honor. After the show, they all went to a party at a loft, which Calvin later found out belonged to a recent Evergreen graduate named Lynda Barry.

The next month, Calvin got his own show—ten to twelve on Friday nights—which he's had ever since, barring one year (1979) when he moved with his family to Maryland. He returned to Olympia, this time as an Evergreen student, in 1980, to find that his time slot on KAOS had been kept warm

Courtesy of Pat Blashill

Monday MAY 12
Tuesday MAY 13
Wednesday MAY 14
Thursday MAY 15
Friday MAY 16
Saturday MAY 17
Sunday MAY 18
60's PUNK mid-2AM with COREY
POWER
70's U.S. STUFF THAT ROCKED w/ COREY BARNABY HERE
PISS FACTORY
NEW YORK CITY 1974-76
6AM 9AM
U.S. UNDERGROUND INDEPENDENT IN THE EARLY 70's
GLAM + GLITTER with CURTIS
12:20-2PM PUB + THUG ROCK
RAM-ONES
CRANKED UP REALLY HIGH: ENGLAND 1977
THE ANARCHY TOUR:
SEX PISTOLS
The CLASH
THE HEARTBREAKERS AND (MID-8AM)
The Damned
STRANDED
8AM-11AM AUSTRALIA/NZ '77-'80 w/FRANNY
CLASS WAR
I wanna war, between the rich & the poor
I wanna fight, & I know what I'm fighting for
In a class war
AMERICA 1977 w/ PATRICK 11am 2pm
PUNKARTREVLIGT EUROPE 1977-1980
Stranglers
WIRED
OUT OF VOGUE
'Hands off, you slut. He belongs to me!'
6 10
AMERICA: Mystery Girls '75-80
MISFITS
10PM-MIDNIGHT
PROLE ART THREAT
MIDNIGHT TO 9AM MANCHESTER AND AFTER w/ CONRAD
BUZZCOCKS
BORED TEENAGERS
9AM-2PM
UK 1978-1980 W/ SALLY JACOB
DEMOLITION DANCING with BILL
SCOTLAND
ALTERNATIVE ULSTER NORTHERN IRELAND
SCREAMING AT A WALL
D.C. & THE MIDWEST 1979-1983
GEORGE + PATRICK
OUR FRIENDLY NEIGHBOR TO THE NORTH
CANADUH WITH VIVECUH
NEW YORK HC
5AM 10 PM
AMERICAN WASTE 1980-1983
WEST COAST
BLOOD ON THE ST.s
Oi!
Oi! continues mid-2AM
PEACE LOVE AND ANARCHY
THE CRASS AND PAX LABELS... W/BILL
PUNK'S NOT DEAD
BRITAIN 1980-'83
6AM-1PM W/COREY and staff
TEXAS
I'VE HAD A BAD DAY
2PM-6PM CURTIS AND CONSTANCE
THE KIDS WILL HAVE THEIR SAY
BOSTON
W/CURTIS PATRICK
BOSTON continues mid-2AM
ARTY AGED DON
NOBODY LISTENS ANYMORE
BRITAIN '78-'85
8AM-8PM CURTIS AND PATRICK
ENDLESS BLOCKADE FOR PUSSYFOOTER
INTERNATIONAL HARDCORE....
FROM THE CUT
CHICAGO MINN
CHICAGO AND MINNEAPOLIS continues mid-2AM
PA./NJ.
THRASH 2AM-4 SALLY + COREY
ANYTHING WITH A HOLE
SNUB-CULTURE!
AMERICA 1983-'85 JOE, TIM + CONSTANCE
PUNK ROCK NOW
WITH THE ENTIRE STAFF 6PM-MIDNIGHT
REQUESTS: 495-4818
MIDNIGHT
A PRESENTATION OF WHRB 95.3FM & RECORD HOSPITAL MAY 12-18 1986 COORDINATOR COREY LOOG BRENNAN 617-495-4818

SHE TRADED HER BODY FOR DRUGS— AND KICKS!

Nirvana Girl

N. R. DeMexico

B328
35¢
K

NEVER WAS THERE SO OUTSPOKEN A NOVEL AS THIS... TELLING THE PLAIN, UNCENSORED TRUTH ABOUT TEEN-AGE ADDICTS—AND THEIR DESPERATE SEARCH FOR THRILLS!

Nirvana: Taken at the Green Street Station in Jamaica Plain, in the winter of '89. Note Kurt's dorky pants. (*Debbie Shane*)

THIS TUESDAY THIS TUESDAY THIS TUESDAY THI

R.E.M.

RENEGADES

IFTHENWHY

OLD WALDORF,JUNE 1

R.E.M.: May they live a million years. (*Sandra Lee Phipps*)

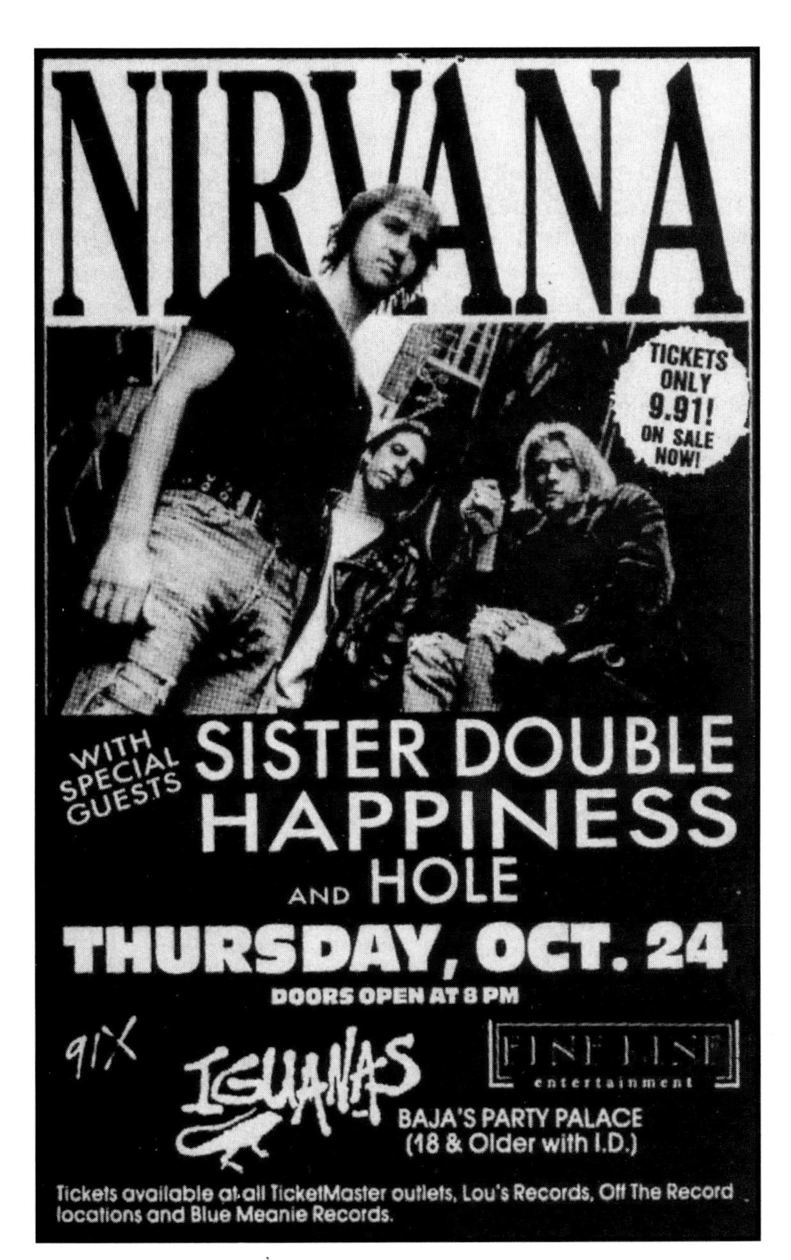

Courtesy of Diane Wright

International Pop Underground Convention

August 20-25, 1991, Olympia, Wash., U.S.A.

As the corporate ogre expands it's creeping influence on the minds of industrialized youth, the time has come for the International Rockers of the World to convene in celebration of our grand independence. Because this society is sick and in desperate need of a little blood-letting; sand, sidewalk and punk pop implosion. Because the corporate ogre has infected the creative community with it's black plague of indentured servitude. Because we are the gravediggers who have buried the grey spectre of rock star myth. Because we are the misfits and we will have our day. We won't go away. Hangman hipsters, new modrockers, sidestreet walkers, scooter mounted dream girls, punks, teds, the instigators of the Love Rock Explosion, the editors of every angry grrrl zine, the plotters of youth rebellion in every form, the midwestern librarians and Scottish ski instructors who live by night, all are setting aside August 20-25, 1991 as the time. Olympia, Washington is the place. A double shot of International Hip Swing is the goal. Barbecues, parades, disco dancing, picnics and wild screaming teenage rock'n'roll are the means. Revolution is the end. Revolution is the beginning. No lackeys to the corporate ogre allowed.

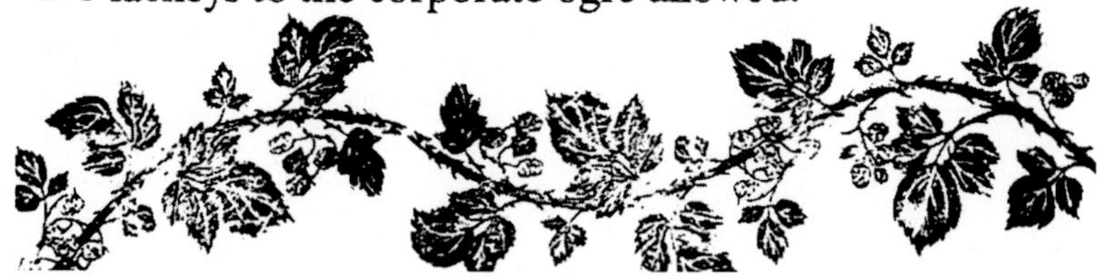

for him by a new Evergreen transfer student named Bruce Pavitt. "I met him the first day I came back to Olympia, and the first thing he said to me was, 'You should write for my fanzine. It's called *Subterranean Pop*.' "

Meanwhile, Foster, David Rauh, and art director Dana Squires had begun *Op* magazine, which verbalized and visualized the musical precepts of the station. Each issue of *Op* was to be devoted to artists whose name began with a single letter of the alphabet, and in the first issue, "A", Calvin contributed the article on Penelope Houston's band the Avengers. "They were one of my favorites because I'd seen them at the Bird in Seattle already."

Other things beside *Op* had happened while Calvin was away as well. A KAOS deejay named Steve Fisk had started a label called Flat, which evolved into one called Mr. Brown. And a bunch of Evergreen students had begun to put on private shows at places on campus. "Evergreen is only seven miles from Olympia, but in those days it was a much more isolated community," Calvin recalls. "The buses only ran till five and never on Sundays, so nobody who lived in town ever knew what was going on there. And downtown was really empty then, a total ghost town. There were no shows at all until 1980–81, and then a guy called Gary May, who was a trusted jazz head, convinced the Gnu Deli to let him put on shows."

The first show, in December 1980, featured Bruce Pavitt's band, Tiny Holes, plus Gary's band, the Breadwinners. It was supposed to include a band with Calvin in it, but the Gnu Deli served liquor, so the show ended up being twenty-one and over, which precluded Calvin from either attending or performing. That was the year that the Canadian hardcore act D.O.A. came and played at Evergreen, which, Calvin claims, was the last time that college has had any involvement in live music. ("At Evergreen there's always only, like, ten or twelve students who are interested in music and the rest are hippies. When I went there they were old hippies and now there's a bunch of young hippies.") After that, the focus moved entirely to downtown Olympia, where by this time, Bruce and Gary had relocated—a radical move for Evergreen students, who normally preferred woodland life.

Slowly a scene of sorts started developing around the Deschutes. In addition to Tiny Holes there was Foster's band, the Pop Philosophers, and a band called the Beakers, and Calvin's band, which was called the Cool Rays, and a band called the Supreme Cool Beings, which featured Heather Lewis, who'd later join with Calvin to form Beat Happening with Bret Lunsford, and one called the West Side Lockers, which was made up of Olympia locals rather than Evergreeners. In the summer of 1981, however, KAOS was under constant fire from Evergreen regarding funding, and many of those formative punk bands broke up. People had a nasty habit of graduating and moving to Seattle.

In 1982 things picked up again. First, the Smithfield Café, which opened on Fourth Street, had performances for all ages. And Gary and Bruce, who lived across the street, were giving performance parties where they'd have an art gallery in one apartment, a live band in another, deejay dancing in a third, and home movies in the laundry room. "That was the first time local teenagers started getting involved," recalls Calvin. "There was a local band called Pet Products that would play those parties. Heather's band, the Supreme Cool Beings, played there too."

The Gnu Deli shows continued, to Calvin's constant chagrin: "I'd always say, 'But it's not fair if people under twenty-one can't go,' and all my friends were all older, and they'd say, 'But no one young *wants* to go to these shows.' But I thought there must be tons of bored teenagers who'd go if they could."

In 1983 Calvin was proven correct when some new Evergreen students from Portland who were in a band called the Young Pioneers rented a downtown storefront and held a concert featuring themselves, Portland's Wipers, and an early version of Calvin's band Beat Happening. Calvin: "And all these teenagers we didn't know showed up with funny haircuts, and we were, like, 'All right, teen punk rock scene, let's *go!*' "

The Wipers' show was a crucial moment in Olympia's punk rock scene. "Those guys just totally blew us away when they set up that show because all this time we'd been complaining and complaining about no place to play, and they just said, 'Let's just rent that empty storefront.' And they did!

"I think up till then there were two things that had been holding us back. One was, we felt like we were so underground, we thought we were practically illegal. It never occurred to us that real people would deal with us or take our money. And then the other thing was, because we'd been used to dealing with KAOS and Evergreen, we thought everything always had to be all nonprofit and cooperative and official. So even when people did try and start something they were always so busy writing their manifesto that they never got anywhere. And then these guys came to town and just called up the building owners and *did* it, and it was great!

"But," he adds, "that space was rented out the next week to a hair salon. It took us a year to find another, which turned out to be the Tropicana."

The Tropicana, which was started by Larry Roberts, Brad Sweek, and Chris Pugh (later the bands Swallow and Creep), opened in March 1984. It was a cooperative of sorts: everyone involved in the downtown Oly scene helped to fix it up and paint it. Some, like Heather Lewis, even lived there. For months, kids worked on the building, all excited because, as Calvin says, "we would finally have our own club."

Calvin and company clearly had high expectations for their all-ages teenage hangout. Did it work out? Calvin pauses a full thirty seconds before answering. "It was . . ." he begins, and then there's another long silence, as he reflects. "It was the most exciting time of my life. I don't know what to say. There has never been a time like that for me, and there never will be again. It was just everything it was supposed to be. It was . . . a teenage revolution.

"It was so important to me," he adds. "Anyone involved in the Tropicana, anyone who was there is special to me. It's funny, I run into Tropicana kids all over the country now, at clubs and things. A lot of them are married and have kids of their own now. But like, I'll go to the movies in Seattle and some kid who was there will go, 'Hey, Calvin,' and let me in free. Because he'd been to the Tropicana."

For the first six months of its existence, the Tropicana tried to be eclectic, like KAOS and *Op*. "One of the things I really like best about Olympia is the way so many ideas get passed down from generation to generation, a generation being, like, about two or three years," comments Calvin. "Everything here is always an event. In early 1984 Bret [Lunsford] and Lois [Maffeo] and I were organizing these alley shows in this alley behind the Martin. We'd just spread the word: 'Alley show in two days!' There was this sort of concrete block for a stage and we'd put lit candles on it and people would jump up and perform. There was no electricity, so it was punk rockers just performing acoustic stuff, which seemed kind of unusual at the time, and there was hardly any division between audience and performer. It was real spontaneous, people would make up stuff on the spot with their friends and stuff.

"The first show, like, that we did was with this rap guy, Whiz Kid, who was in Tommy Boy. His wife had gotten stationed near here in the Air Force, so he was just hanging out. He was a guest on the rap show at KAOS, so we decided to have a dance party with him in the alley and bring our beat boxes. And then we did one a month for four months, and then the Tropicana opened.

"At first the Tropicana tried to present all kinds of events—plays and art and everything—because we knew that there was legitimacy to the idea that there is more to life than rock 'n' roll. And then we got lazy and it was just a rock club. But it was a rock club with great shows—the greatest shows! Black Flag, 54–40, and the U-Men, from Seattle, played their first out-of-town gig there, and the Three O'Clock, from L.A., which was like the biggest show ever, and the Fastbacks, and Green River, and millions of other bands . . . Scratch Acid played there in December of '84. Jody Foster's Army played there. 45 Grave played twice. We [Beat Happening] played there more times than anybody, eleven or twelve times, and that wasn't even our only gigs here! That year we must have played twenty times in Olympia alone, and nowadays we can only play, like, four times a year here."

The Tropicana opened in March 1984, the same month the Metropolis, Seattle's all-ages club, closed. As the only all-ages punk rock club in the state of Washington, kids flocked to it, from Tacoma, from Aberdeen, even from Bellevue. And as the club expanded its clientele, the number of viable punk bands in the area increased accordingly. Suddenly, Aberdeen's Melvins, Calvin's own Beat Happening, and Tacoma's Girl Trouble were all happening at once.

The Tropicana was open for only eleven months, until February 1985, however: "Things move so fast when you're young," says Calvin. The Tropicana was closed down by pressure from local merchants, who bought up the building's lease in order to make way for an indoor mall development next door. "And after that, life really sucked," says Calvin.

During this time, however, Calvin had begun his own label, K Records. (The *K* is for "knowledge.") Originally, the label was intended for cassette-only releases. "We thought that was really punk rock because cassette was the people's medium," he says. "Blasters were really big then, and you could just get a tape and stick it in and play it. We even recorded our stuff on boom boxes, so it seemed like the perfect thing."

K's first release was a Supreme Cool Beings tape culled from a live show on KAOS. Then Calvin released a couple of acoustic compilations: *Danger Is Their Business* and *Dangerous Business International*. The label also released some compilation LPs, *Let's Together* in 1984, and *Let's Kiss* in 1985, and *Let's Sea* in 1986. These tapes had tracks on them by bands like the Melvins, Beat Happening, and the Wimps, a really political Olympia new wave band who made their amps out of cassette players stuck into pizza boxes, as well as some Japanese bands—including Shonen Knife—Beat Happening had hooked up with while in Japan in the summer of 1984. (Most kids go to London to be punk rockers. Beat Happening went to Japan for two months, staying in some abandoned apartments owned by Nippon Steel and playing five gigs, including one at a girls' school, set up through kids met at record stores and gigs there. Incidentally, Calvin got a half semester's worth of credit at Evergreen for the trip.)

K released Best Happening's own cassette recordings, *Beat Happening* and *Three Tea Breakfast*, and John Foster's *Pop Philosophers* too. But the cassette medium was not a thriving one. Calvin says they were lucky if they sold one hundred tapes. "Most people who were doing cassette-only at that time were really experimental and industrial music, so that network didn't really want to have anything to do with our little punk pop stuff."

K went to vinyl in 1985, releasing the LP *Beat Happening*. Around that time K also began collating a mailing list and doing its newsletter. "We were only selling at local stores, because we had no distribution. So we just started making up this mailing list by having people sign it at shows and stuff, and taking names off letters from *Flipside*, and just any way we could."

That list began with five hundred names. It is currently at eight thousand. Meanwhile, Calvin started to add other people's product to his newsletter, in order to help people who were essentially in the same boat as he was. One band who made it onto his distributorship early on was the Melvins. "We loved them immediately because they were from Aberdeen, which is like a sacred place to Olympians. It costs seventy-five cents to get there by bus, and then it's this weird dreary town with great thrift stores. So a band from Aberdeen totally excited us. We thought, 'A band from Aberdeen? It has *got* to be good!' "

Calvin had hooked up with the Melvins' Buzz Osbourne, in fact, as far back as 1983, the day after the Wipers show, when he approached him about getting a gig in Olympia. ("I just found this piece of paper in my desk that says 'Buzz Osbourne, the Nerve'—that was his band name—and the phone number, the other day," laughs Calvin). "And later, when we put together our compilation *Let's Together*, I was, like, 'We must get that band from Aberdeen.' And I remember,

Bret was so impressed by the fact that Buzz's was the only band that got the tape to us on time, and he had to drive all the way in from Aberdeen to do it."

In 1986 Bret began an all-ages club called G.E.S.C.C.O.—Greater Evergreen Students' Community Cooperative Organization—in Olympia. Meanwhile, the Community World Theater started doing all-ages shows in nearby Tacoma. Both clubs spawned scenes of their own. Led by the Melvins, a lot of this music was documented on Deep Six Records, which Calvin was not involved with. "G.E.S.C.C.O. just wasn't like the Tropicana. Something like that only happens once in your life. The right combination of interest and people and places come together. I think the riot grrrl thing is like that right now."

Calvin was totally involved in doing K by that time—and with his band Beat Happening, a trio, made up of Calvin, Heather, and Bret. The band's music, a cross between Jonathan Richman and the Cramps, consists only of drums, guitar, and vocals: two chords played in 4/4 time by three minds with but a single thought. Heather wears shorts and big thick glasses. Calvin has a Dennis the Menace-style cowlick that sticks up behind his head like a permanent Indian feather. Bret's baggy sweatshirt and floppy hair give him the appearance of a naughty twelve-year-old. Onstage, band members trade off various musical duties, switching instruments every three or four songs. When Calvin sings, he stretches like a cat till his tummy shows between his T-shirt and pants. Between verses, he locks his arms behind his head in various fey poses, legs twisting all akimbo. His voice is a deep-daddy growl, but his lyrics are about love and sex as seen through the eyes of a wide-eyed kindergartner, intrigued but frightened, groping for meaning in a sticky-sweet world. He writes songs about candy and kittycats and sleepytime and kisses: "Sea Hunt" and "Bad Seed" and "Hot Chocolate Boy" and "Catwalk": *"I look at them out together/and I see she's wearing my sweater/ah, heck, I should probably let her/I was barely gone/when another boy came along/ I know there's nothing wrong, but I wish he'd leave my sweater alone . . ."*

Heather's songs, however, are (like so many girl things) somewhat more mature. When she comes out from behind the drum set, she rocks back and forth on sneaker-clad heels, humming and droning pretty songs about a girl's own life. "Surprise, surprise, you're my fortune cookie prize," sings Heather. And, "Foggy eyes all looking at your friends, wondering what is to become of them." Those who don't find Beat Happening incredibly affected find it totally disarming, a friendly, lighted candle in a cold cruel world.

Beat Happening's oeuvre always loomed large in my mind, because the Beat Happening record—memorably adorned with a bright yellow cover with a stick-figure cat on a rocket ship—was in high rotation at the Hotel Hell from almost the day it came out. But in the rest of the world, even the underground world, Beat Happening was for a long time socked away behind a wall of noise and indifference. "You have to remember that in 1986 what was really big was really bad hardcore," shrugs Calvin. "And after '86 it was all Scratch Acid and Sonic Youth. So we didn't really fit in with that genre, except super-peripherally. In 1984 we did a few shows in D.C., but we couldn't get a gig in New York. We've toured the U.S. every year since 1986, and went to Europe in '88 and '91, but we were always very unknown until the K Festival. The only person who ever reviewed our records favorably was Gerard at *Conflict*."

Back in Olympia, the G.E.S.C.C.O. was playing host to another Aberdeen band, this one called Skid Row. Calvin was at that band's first show, but can't remember the performance: "I assume because they weren't remarkable." Skid Row soon changed its name to Nirvana. Skid Row's guitarist, Kurt Cobain, soon moved to Olympia from Aberdeen, but, Calvin says, "They were never a significant factor here at all until they became big. I remember him and Chris coming over to my house once with Buzz, they were, like, his entourage. And his girlfriend, Tracy, came up to me one time and said, 'Hey, Calvin, will you put out my boyfriend's band on your label?' and I was, like, 'Send me a tape,' but they never did.

"Later my friend Slim kept saying how great they were, and I believed him, but I didn't hear them for a long time. I remember the first time I heard them, Kurt lived in the same apartment building as my friends Slim and Nicki, and one day I went over there and knocked on the wrong door. Kurt answered the door and said, 'Uh, do you want to come in?' And he'd just recorded 'Love Buzz,' and he was, like, 'Do you want to hear it?' and I was, like, 'OK.' So he played it for me and it totally blew me away. I was really, really surprised. I remember I wrote a review in my fanzine *Sand* where I said, 'This guy's going to make a million bucks.'

"They were carrying around the tape for *Bleach* and it was great too, and there was a brief moment when Nirvana was pissed off at Sub Pop because they weren't putting it out fast enough and they asked me if I'd do it, and I was, like, 'In a minute!' But secretly I was thinking, 'Yeah, right; if I only had the money.' I remember telling them they should put it out themselves, and they were, like, 'Yeah, yeah, right, right.' "

The Tropicana was really so crucial to what we did subsequently. Because it worked so well, it spawned this idea with me that kids were hiding in the woodwork, waiting for stuff to happen to them. A lot of what we did leading up to the [1991 International Pop Underground] Convention was just trying to replicate that spontaneous teenage explosion. We thought that every town would be like Olympia. The whole *Let's* series was about tapping into bands not from Seattle—it was Tacoma, not Seattle; Eugene, not Portland—getting out of the major centers, because Seattle never interested me. That's why later on we did shows in Bellingham, and Ellensburg, and Anacortes, instead of Portland and Seattle. We thought, 'Well, there's an audience for this anywhere. The underground isn't just for a few weirdos—it's culture and music, and anyone will appreciate it if you bring it to their own context.' "

In 1989 Beat Happening arranged just such a cultural outreach program, the Sound Out Northwest Series, playing gigs with Dead Moon and Mudhoney in a bunch of small towns around the Northwest like Astoria and Aberdeen. "I'd go to each town first and look up halls and see how much it cost and put up flyers and stuff," recalls Calvin. "It was a real education."

In 1987 K Records started the International Pop Underground—a singles service that released seven-inches by bands like Mecca Normal and Girl Trouble. Presently, Calvin went into a partnership with Candice Pedersen, who still shares the burden of the business today. In 1988 Rough Trade released Beat Happening's second LP, *Jamboree*. Then 1989 saw the release of *Black Candy* on K only; the band's next two releases, 1991's *Dreamy* and 1992's *You Turn Me On*, would be on Bruce Pavitt's Sub Pop label.

Calvin continues to run K Records and to perform with Beat Happening. The band may be obscure, but it has certainly been influential: bands like Bratmobile, Small Factory, Flying Saucer, Unrest, and Tsunami already owe it a huge debt. Calvin has yet to be commercially vindicated, but his time may well be coming.

John Foster left Olympia in 1984 to do a double stint in the Peace Corps, first in Senegal and then in the Solomon Islands. In 1989, after years of negotiations, Toni Holm and David Rauh started an 85,000-watt FM radio station, KXXO. They made Foster the program director. The format? Soft rock favorites from the sixties, seventies, eighties, and nineties. "They couldn't have gotten either a loan or on the air if they'd said, 'Oh, we plan on pursuing our long-term interest in underground music,' " explains Foster. "So, yeah, I spend most of my time now listening to bad soft rock. But I've gained a lot of respect for the type of people who listen to it. I'm not a snob about it. Radio still touches some of them the way radio used to touch me, it's just not musically. And I knew back when I worked at KAOS that what I liked was totally different from the norm."

The world was a different place back then. For example,

Foster funded the first issue of *Op* with his student loan, which he subsequently paid back from the magazine's profits. "I used all the great social programs of the sixties to finance my way through prep school and college," comments Foster now. "I would not be where I am today without social security, work study, basic grant programs, and the like. And whenever I meet people coming up now in both radio and college, I wonder how they're going to do without it."

ELEVEN

WELL DOWN BLUE HIGHWAY

I found out about Halo of Flies because they have one former member of Otto's Chemical Lounge. I sent 'em a letter asking for a copy of their record and got no reply. So I called directory information and asked for all the J. Agnews in the Minneapolis area, and then I called each one and said, "Hi, are you Jim from Halo of Flies?" But it turned out he'd moved to Seattle.
– Joseph Pope, *Ward Report*, 1987

Come one spring, Francesca and I met each other in New Orleans for a brief vacation. It was during the Jazz and Heritage Festival, so the town was full of rock celebs. One night we went to Tipitina's and persecuted David Byrne and Paul Simon during a Neville Brothers concert. Afterward we went to Jimmie's to see a band called Shot Down in Ecuador, Jr., and we ended up, around three A.M., lying down on the grass strip between the streetcar tracks on Saint Charles Avenue, waiting for the world to stop spinning. Presently, a bunch of scraggly-looking rock dudes walked by, and Francesca lifted her head and moaned boozily, 'Hello, Sun City Girls!" thus probably making the then-unknown Phoenix band's life worth living.

Purged at last, we walked on down the street, till a man who professed to love Eugene Chadbourne—he had a bumper sticker to that effect—invited us to sit in his Galaxie 500. It had been entirely appliquéd inside with thingamajigs. Plastic grapevines draped along its faux fur interior, while toy soldiers and dinosaurs engaged in a horrendous battle on the dash. The car's carpet was all Astroturf, and the seats red velvet. Stalactites and rhinestones and plastic animals and little dollies hung from its ceiling. Francesca and I sat side by side in the backseat for ages, imbibing this wonderland in happy silence till the sun finally came up. In the morning we drove for hours up the river road along the west side of the Mississippi listening to Trotsky Icepick on the car stereo, stopping periodically to draw chalk circles around squashed armadillos and then photograph them for our collection of dead beasts.

That is how I pictured life in a band: night after night of American romance, days spent drinking in the kitschy richness of American life. You see, one of the main tenets of independent rock (initially discovered by the band the Police) is that, given that none of these acts were going to be heard on mainstream radio, the only way to be heard was to cross the country touring, over and over again. Black Flag had perfected the art, years and years past.

The reality of this process was and is a brutal way to (not) make a living: imagine loading yourself into a van, sleeping on people's floors, roadie-ing your own equipment, for about a measly two hundred bucks a night, split five ways—any profit on which you basically owe back to a bunch of rental companies anyway. Often getting stiffed by promoters or thrown out of a club, or getting to the gig and finding out it's been canceled. Having your equipment stolen from back rooms and station wagons, or sitting around dirty warehouses for hours during sound checks in a part of town no one in their right mind would want to frequent. Never seeing an American city by anything but night. Often—especially anywhere west of Denver—bands have to load out their equipment right after their set and drive all night and day to get to the next venue, exhausted—for weeks and weeks on end.

For all the sleeplessness and boredom and hunger of the process, for all the caffeine and Excel, there is also a certain kind of glamour, a glittering infrastructure of the most deeply experienced punk. Picture the highways of America all teeming with bands, pouring secretly across the continent, meeting up and parting, then breaking off again. One time the Dead Milkmen stopped, exhausted, in an all-night truckstop in the South somewhere, and Mojo Nixon walked in the door yelling, "I knew when I saw them they had to be Milkmen!" A few days later Camper Van Beethoven ran into the selfsame Nixon on the steps of the courthouse in Rawlins, Wyoming. Meanwhile, over in Cincinnati, Camper Van Beethoven was unexpectedly backing Tiny Tim as a favor to a club owner whose opening act had canceled out. Glass Eye used to tell me how they liked to leap out of their van occasionally and silk-screen their logo on the pavements of Bumfuck, all across the country. The Cowboy Junkies once drove two days around Lake Superior in the dead of winter, only to arrive at an unadvertised gig where not one person showed up. The Leaving Trains stopped specially to sleep one night on Buddy Holly's grave in Lubbock. And every single band I ever met, however poor, however hurried, always stopped at Graceland on their way through Tennessee.

My friends and I had to live most of our lives on home turf, though: Haight Street and environs, in just the stores and nightclubs where we met only our own. Of course we all had day lives, but they meant so little in comparison to what lay beneath the night. I used to marvel smugly at how well I'd insulated myself from the annoying censoriousness of the real world—except there'd always be the square office co-workers, who'd finger my clothing and talk about my hair and couldn't believe that I went to shows that began at eleven P.M., looking at me all askance. So we lived our real lives in nightclubs, hugged by our bohemian brothers, held safe in its exclusive clutch. We didn't need no stinking door policy: the show time (midnight), the band's obscurity, and the unpleasantness of many of the venues kept away everyone we wanted out.

There used to be this club in San Francisco called the Farm. It was a barnlike dive in the outer Mission District, right under the Army Street off-ramp at somebody's community garden patch. People'd hold punk rock shows there some Saturday nights: Black Flag and Redd Kross and Blue Cheer and the Meat Puppets—for a while there it was also our own Camper Van Beethoven's home away from home. I wish you could have seen Camper then, hunched over their instruments, swaying a little, looking courteously out at the audience as it swirled past their stillness. Camper always had this mannerly detachment. They were too shy to emote, but too talented to avoid moving us, so we'd all be dancing with partners to "Sad Lover's Waltz," leaning into one another during "One of These Days" or "Bad Trip," caught up in the music's mad poignancy, waving our arms around in a parody of hippies space-dancing, beaming up their charms.

The Farm was a funny place, though. If loam could sweat, that's what it smelled like: beery and earthen both; like Kansas grown cement-covered and mountainous on a cold foggy night. The building had the worst toilet situation of all time ever. The whole thing held about five hundred people, but for bathrooms there was only one room with a dirt floor and two stalls in it, and neither stall had a door. This wouldn't have been so bad if it wasn't also co-ed, and half the guys going in there, from some weird male territorial reason, chose instead to piss in a large gulch that had been dug into the corner. Sometimes, if one's personal biology or some other crisis meant one was feeling particularly shy, it was just altogether easier to go out and crouch in the dark recesses of the garden. I'm surprised we didn't all catch typhoid.

Toilets aside—or rather, as the toilets indicate—the Farm was the real thing, punk rock redux, with a dollop of Californi-ate neo-hippieism (represented solely by the members of Camper's hair and the armpits of the girls in the audience) thrown in for good measure. To get there you either had to take about seven buses from the Haight or walk a long way down 24th Street, through a project-ridden combat zone. That's where all the best nightclubs are (and as the eighties progressed, those areas of town grew larger and larger and larger). It's funny, sometimes it feels like I spent my entire twenties sidling through bad neighborhoods, heart pounding furiously, pretending not to see the bums smoking crack on the corner of Bowery and Broadway; casually smashing beer bottles in alleys off Sunset Boulevard to rid the sidewalk of menacing loiterers; walking briskly home down the middle of Lyon Street at two A.M., peering over my shoulder. *Why can't I walk down the street free of suggestion?* Flesh was always buried beneath acres of black fabric, boots, tights, jeans, leotard, leather jacket for good measure. Real life was always like a Henry Rollins rant or Exene Cervenka poem: "Shut up, bitch, like it says on my T-shirt." But I never—knock wood—got into much trouble except for once in Times Square, when one of Tesco Vee's Meatmen providentially came along to my rescue. In my own little Mayberry-esque neighborhood, no self-respecting dirtbag ever preyed on punk rockers: they knew instinctively it wouldn't be all that profitable.

For a while at least, the Hotel Hell was protected from all harm by the fact that our downstairs neighbors were such scary Nazi skinheads. We were as frightened of them as anyone—they used to climb in our windows and steal food from our fridge, and once they scrawled "yuppie scum" on our doorway—but clearly the more criminal element in our neighborhood couldn't tell one set of white kids in combat boots from another. One night when they had band practice till four A.M., Bobbie went downstairs and hit one of them on the head with a hammer—a language they understood. They respected us a lot more after that, but we were still relieved when they got evicted. Furious at being made to leave, on their last night in residence they tore every bit of plaster off the apartment walls and spray-painted epithets all along the bare boards. Before the landlord brought in all the builders, fumigators, and health inspectors necessary to repair the place, we used to take people on guided tours of the damage they'd done.

Another club we liked to frequent was the V.I.S., an old-man bar on Divisidero, which later had its roof raised and became the Kennel Club. In V.I.S. days it was just a big, low-ceilinged room with a six-inch-high stage in one corner, a bar in the center, and a really bad sound system. We saw all the locals there: Faith No More, Camper Van, Spot 1019 and the Donner Party, World of Pooh, American Music Club, Negativland, Game Theory, whoever. Later on, lots of bands from out of town played there, and lots of them ended up staying at our house because it was so nearby. The Dead Milkmen did, for instance, one November, for four or five days: one day I went walking in Golden Gate Park with them and, when we stopped for refreshments at the Japanese Tea Gardens, my fortune said, "You will find yourself surrounded by cultured and autistic people."

Cultured and autistic—that described my household exactly. Flakey band people and other fringe-ophiliacs. I was always meeting total queerbaits in my kitchen who'd later star on MTV. Sex and drugs and rock 'n' roll, man . . . What a totally false impression the outside world has of the inside life, though for a while I did know one woman who generally went for it with whomsoever played guitar in the band. ("Have you ever thought that if she had HIV," an acquaintance sniffed years later, "all the best bands of the mid-eighties would currently be dead?") Later on I used to wonder why more independent bands didn't get AIDS, and I decided it was mere luck. The scene then was small enough, and the number of promiscuous people within it was even smaller, so it remained, thankfully, a closed circle of sorts. If any one of those people had happened to be infected, we'd have been devastated. I suppose we still could be.

I always felt sorry for girls I knew who were going that route, though. They'd meet some great guy while he was on the road, and maybe he'd call or write every now and again, while they, meanwhile, were spoiled for all the nice ordinary guys working at the copy shop or whatever. Meanwhile Mr. Rock Star would be out having the glamorous good time, and they'd be at home living vicariously through a faded tour itinerary pinned to the bedroom wall. Thinking, "Tonight he's at the Nine-Thirty club in D.C." Thinking, "Tomorrow he's at T-T's in Boston."

Having a boyfriend in a band in town was even worse: being ignored in favor of band practice and gigs, usually paying for everything (because they only have money for their rehearsal space and new bass strings), being left alone for weeks on end while the band toured and probably being cheated on. Being, in short, not the center of someone's existence, but the absolute opposite: the very coldest, loneliest satellite in the farthest corner of the solar system. Necessary, perhaps, but not exactly noticed. It never seemed worth it to me.

The American indie scene was not entirely free from groupies and groupiedom, of course. And although it certainly seemed to be less riddled with spandex-clad groupies than other areas of rock, it was always just as misogynistic—more so perhaps than the scenes that came before it, as this kind of misogyny was more a power trip than a sex one. Looking over back issues of *Conflict* and its cohorts, I'm now sickened by the virulent sexism that existed within it. "Why do girls have legs?" asked *Forced Exposure*'s Byron Coley, in a review of Frightwig's album. "So they don't leave a trail." No wonder no woman I knew ever wanted to pick up a guitar! Every female player and audience member—Rebecca Korbet of Pussy Galore, Thalia Zedak of Live Skull, the Throwing Muses, the list just goes on—is belittled in its pages.

Belittlement didn't stop there: Tara Key of Antietam recalls playing a show in Champaign not that long ago at which a member of the Didjits came up to her afterward and asked sneeringly if every time she hit an effects pedal she came.

That was in 1991, and I guess I really didn't realize how bad things were up until then. For the longest time back in the eighties, I was just plain grateful to the band guys I knew for allowing me to listen to them practice, or play acoustic, or just hang out with them while they acted like band guys. I thought that was privilege enough. Back then, it didn't bother me that none of the women I knew (with one single exception) were in bands, and though there was a sense that there were more women in rock at the time—all bassists named Kim, like Kim Gordon of Sonic Youth, Kim Warnick of the Fastbacks, and Kim Deal of the Pixies, as well as drummers, such as Liz Cox of Christmas, Georgia Hubley of Yo La Tengo, and Janet Beveridge Bean of Eleventh Dream Day—I now see that rising figure as having been deceptive. In fact, the indie scene was less welcoming to women than the punk scene before (which, after all, at least gave the world Patti Smith, Chrissie Hynde, Tina Weymouth, and the Cramps' Ivy Rorschach). The indie scene? In all the time I'm talking about, I never heard of any female lead guitarists—not until I met Kathy McCarty of Glass Eye, and later, Tara Key of Antietam. And they were exceptions who only proved the rule: neither band has ever been signed to a major label. "It's like everything that's right now happening politically," shrugged Kim Warnick, in 1991. "Everything liberal is being pushed down, and it carries over to music as well. Twenty-two-year-old girls aren't forming bands because they're being swept up in this whole men-are-stronger/abortion-is-wrong thing. And girls today are raised on MTV. Well, name one woman guitarist you see on MTV."

What you see on MTV, of course, are women squirming around in bustiers. And how come, according to Kathy McCarty, the one time she and Glass Eye's keyboardist Stella Weir wore corsets onstage—as a big joke, Kathy explains, in light of the fact they were playing the Club Lingerie in Los Angeles—the front of the stage was suddenly thronged with fist-thrusting guys? "People really seemed to like us a lot more. That night I was surrounded; guys were pressed up against the stage, and all I could think was, 'God, guys are stupid!' No, I'm not being disparaging, it's a scientific truth!"

So why not wear bustiers all the time?

"Because, you know, wearing your underwear onstage, that's kind of more a cultural statement than an artistic one," Kathy says mildly.

Johnette Napolitano, of the band Concrete Blonde, once

described to me some of the setbacks to being a female in a rock band. "You've got to be able to handle a lot of rejection. Nobody wants to be called a bitch. It hurts like hell and it happens a lot. It's gotten so I'll never tell anyone when I have my period. I hide my tampons even, because I don't want anyone in the road crew saying I hated a sound mix because I'm on the rag.

"Not too many women want to be in a band, because it's a weird thing to want to do," she continued. "It's just easier for men to be on the road and stuff, to sleep on couches, to be up all night, to eat crummy food. And rock 'n' roll is youth oriented. The atmosphere is perpetually adolescent. So many men get in bands to meet girls, but I've never in my life met a woman who started a band to meet men!"

Things are really changing. Just the other day I loaned my apartment to a band called Crackerbash, and another band—one with girls in it—kept leaving messages on the machine about getting together after the gig. It made me realize how, if there's any way I envy the generation after mine, it's this: how much better it must be to be the girls in Calamity Jane, who are Crackerbash's colleagues rather than their hangers-on. How splendid for the women in Calamity Jane that, instead of being left behind, they get to zip off round the country in a van of their very own. That's like one full step better than the axiom someone once propounded to me in regard to *Big Star Third*: a great record is better than a bad boyfriend any day.

But the bandwagon charged on. Picture the pages of a calendar being torn off one by one, and the entire frame of reference simply spinning, spinning, spinning. We knew we were part of a subculture, but somehow, out in medialand, we were being ignored or just confused with the large groups of itinerant Deadheads that were perennially loitering around Telegraph and Haight. And though logically the two groups, post-punks and post-hippies, had much in common—both saw (or see) themselves as critical of their parents and peers, disparaging of consumerism, capitalism, materialism and so on—in our heart of hearts, we were diametrically opposed. Hippie cant always claims that following the Dead is so countercultural, but Dead shows cost twenty bucks minimum to get in, and the band's records come out on Arista. Grubby, hypocritical, self-serving, secretly rich: all the Deadheads grouped with their wretched puppies around Ben and Jerry's remind me of a bunch of expats I met at a garden party in Minorca once, wealthy, Norman Douglas-type characters, who'd strayed a bit too far west, whose refusal to pay taxes had led them to a meaningless, nomadic, and ultimately perfidious existence. Like the Deadheads, they led a life with no attachments, entirely free from responsibility, unwilling to commit or focus or even belong. Even the people I used to know who got SSI by pretending to be crazy and then spent the money on guitars had more pride than that.

One night I came home from aerobics class all hot and sweaty, only to find the doors to both our bathrooms locked and occupied. Typical. The Leaving Trains had been wished on us by their management. The Trains proved themselves to be terrible houseguests, indulging in all the unquestionably verboten band things, such as burning our pots and pans and bringing girls home after the gig. They probably represented the rule in band behavior rather than the exceptions that we'd had staying with us all those years, but even so, Francesca and I devised a punishment for their hapless bass player, Eric: in the dead of night we stole his dorky, Clash-inspired ammunition belt and relieved it of about a foot's worth of ammo. We hoped that when he next put it on, thus discovering it didn't fit, he'd think that his girth had expanded and go on a diet.

Stuff like that was fun to do and to think about later. But how puny a pleasure compared to what the bands were off doing! Whenever a band came to stay, there'd be this kind of hangover for days afterward, a sense of unfulfillment, an emptiness inside. The bands got to flit through life, living out a modern-day *Iliad* or *Odyssey,* driving across America in their beat-up van, one night, perhaps, running smack into Circe, another one steering neatly through some indie-rock version of Scylla and Charybdis, a Cyclops-like club owner or a town full of Furies, but always on the cusp of an evening of utter excitement.

All that time we stayed at home, eagerly waiting for their arrival, fulfilling the drab duties of every day, at the mercy of booking agents who sent us our brief saviors, living hungrily off their exploits. We bought their records and saw all their concerts and spoke and spoke and spoke to our counterparts in each city. We were rapt and wrapped up in a world so very small: there was never a time when I didn't know what record store I'd go to if I ever was in Denver (Wax Trax) or what club to hit to see the God Bullies if I happened to get to Chicago. And we fantasized endlessly about life in Minneapolis and Austin and Athens and Seattle, and discussed endlessly the implications of who was signed to what label. We corresponded, as well: through friends met on the road and inevitably through fanzines: *Motorbooty, Swellsville,* the *Big Takeover, Jersey Beat. Willpower* is still my favorite fanzine of all time ever: a sixteen-page photocopied outlet for Replacements fans around the country. It was literary mayhem, but it somehow managed to exude our collective love. It was the exact visual equivalent of a Replacements song, chaotic and true.

By 1987, though, a lot of this stuff was old hat. First college radio sold itself to a devil called CMJ, and then the once-roilingly internecine wars between indie labels were all winding up in bankruptcy and tragedy, a sullen sort of sad truce, born of greed and the world recession. D. Boon was dead, killed on the highway between Tucson and Pedro. Hüsker Dü was about to split up. Dumptruck was in the midst of a giant lawsuit with RCA. Henry Rollins was allegedly dating television soap stars, and even R.E.M. had passed out of our midst owing to their smash hit single, "The One I Love," off *Document.*

It all happened so fast that we weren't really sure what hit us. There was about a year there, before the San Francisco earthquake ruined the venue, when all our favorite bands were playing the fifteen-hundred-seat Fillmore Auditorium instead of the four-hundred-capacity I Beam. The shows there were invariably great, but it was peculiar seeing the 'mats or the Meat Puppets in such a large place. We'd look around at the anonymous rabid crowd and wonder who the hell everyone was, how they'd found out about the band, where they'd been all our lives. It puzzled and shook us, this invasion of the ordinary people: these were the people who'd hated us to begin with, the ones who'd driven us away. So how could our music appeal to them too? How dare it even try?

We were like horrible kindergartners, unable, unwilling, to share our secret toys with the rest of the world at large. And even if we'd wanted to we were well disturbed by another factor: tickets to shows by our favorite artists were now so much more expensive, about twelve to fifteen dollars per gig instead of six to ten. The world at large had begun to smell money. Major labels started looking to indies for cheap deals on new bands, raiding the rosters of SST and Twin/Tone and Coyote and Db. They'd sign a band—Zeitgeist, say, who left Db for Capitol, or the Replacements, who ditched Twin/Tone for Warners—and press up hundreds of thousands of copies of LPs for the kids, but then those copies would stiff because, although mainstream radio and MTV still had no intention of going near them, college radio's antimajor bias would kick in as well, causing deejays to ostracize a band like the 'mats or the Reivers. I started to feel as if I lived among a bunch of quislings, mean-spirited little people who felt only failure was a meaningful social statement. The cult of loserdom coming right at you. Reject thy favorite rock star, before they can have an opportunity of rejecting unto you.

In retrospect, 1980 to 1992—the whole Republican era—was such a strange time culturally. The corporate ogre notwithstanding, the music our minds were furnished in back then was so lumpy and comfortable, so television blue. We thought we were so radical and outside the norm, but really we were neither fish nor fowl, unable to expand our vocabulary, relying instead on dreamy jangling mush or rehashed metal riffs to speak our tiny thoughts: I hear it all now as a long steady hum. I think now there was a muteness to our era, a mental block of sorts, that intruded into even the most ardent of its music: even Black Flag was just a child's wail of inarticulate anguish, a red-faced, choking scream. For all that time, we were too ashamed of the fate of hippie idealism to recognize our actual allegiance to it. And people without allegiance are like anonymous letter writers: empty, uncommitted, dishonest, and afraid.

Like all the rest of social history, it was probably just something to do with economics. (That and the state of the world's plumbing technology, which they say can explain the entire Western Civ.) But that's not what it felt like at the time. What it felt like was autumn. The summer's green leaves drying up and falling, the sky fading from blue to gray, a crumpled newspaper blowing across the pavement like in an Orson Welles movie, the animals getting all fat and sluggish, the bums on Haight Street getting all tucked up for the long night ahead.

Fin de siècle; or more appropriately perhaps, the between-the-wars period in England, when a generation of upper-class bohemia lovers known as the Bright Young Things, too young to have fought in the Great War and too cynical to believe in its cause, amused themselves by making mischief at debutante parties and otherwise trashing their elders' double standards. Our cause, punk rock, seemed to have suffered a similar ill fate. One night Liz and I were in the Hell's living room laughing sentimentally over the televised *Rock 'n' Roll High School,* when Bobbie wandered in all sneering: "Oh God, I hate the Ramones," she said. We were, like, stunned. We couldn't believe it. Bobbie worshiped Sonic Youth and Wire, the Fall and Big Black, but she couldn't understand the importance or musical greatness of the Clash or even Elvis Costello. She was of the generation for whom dying one's hair or having a mohawk meant absolutely nothing. We'd fought her battle for her . . . and she didn't even care!

In 1936 the Bright Young Things of London stopped nose-thumbing the status quo when fascism and Franco began to loom large on the horizon. Banal as my era's issues may seem in comparison (and especially in this context), I like to think my crowd stopped playing games for a similar sort of reason. My friends and I lived in a bubble. But evil is evil, whatever its guise, and as Peter Buck has said, at some point you just have to sit up and take note. Robert Christgau once suggested that great art only grows out of political oppression, and that's exactly what happened.

Presently the outside world zeroed in on our heretofore poor and unassuming scene. The PMRC (Parents, Music Resource Center) tried to take our albums from us. AIDS began to take its toll. The incipient recession (and other things) caused several huge independent distributing companies to go out of business, thus bankrupting some of our favorite labels. Bush was still president, and the world of our fathers seemed finally beyond repair. Only then did our community finally begin to marshall its puny forces: punk rock, outrage, villainy, and drugs. Violence, empathy, financial cunning, and courage. Be strong, be wrong. *Our little group has always been and always will until the end.* Tiny bands, new bands, angry bands, clarion bands, began to seethe throughout our system, starting up in all new places, places like Stockton and Raleigh and Denver and Aberdeen. The bandwagon planned to keep on keeping on. We would endure.

THREE

ENDLESS NAMELESS

TWELVE

I SAW LUCKY

It's just so gloomy here [in Europe]. The sky is so gray and the architecture is so spiky and torturous. I think it must run into the psyches of the young people. They all walk like they're old. Now in America, there's no strange Christian churches hanging over your head all the time, people don't live on potatoes and walk around frowning. When I'm in California, I feel so embarrassed for all our shitty K Marts and strip malls, but when I'm here, I miss them. Coming to Europe is like going to your grandma's house. It's full of all these pictures and knick-knacks and it's kind of dark and musty smelling. You don't want your grandma ever to die, but you don't want to hang out much at her house, either.

– Perry Farrell, March 1991

I lived in Orange County for six weeks in 1987, and by the end of that time I hated it so much that one afternoon, in a spirit of vengefulness on its residents—the most heinous of which can almost certainly be found of a Saturday at the South Coast Shopping Plaza—Francesca and I walked through the acres and acres of parking lot there and deliberately set off every car alarm we could find. Fran had this theory that if we dressed all nice—in tan nylons and Ellen Tracy work clothes—and carried a large Nordstrom shopping bag, the cops who'd inevitably show up to investigate the cacophony would never think to stop us. "You just *know* they'll be looking for Negroes," she said witheringly when she unfolded to me her plan.

The music of Nirvana reminds me of that momentary defiance and the pleasure of that clamor. Like their music, the action was born of hatred and boredom and misery—a need to insult the entire universe. In the movie of my life, we'll freeze the frame of Fran and me, looking unbelievably dumpy in our Ellen Tracy suits and nylons—why do ladies' suits make everyone look like lesbians?—standing in the middle of an unholy, screaming uproar. A security guard scurries by, looking for a Negro. We grin grimly. And in the movie of my life the song playing in the background will be Nirvana's "Scoff": *Gimme back my, gimme back my, gimme back gimme back GIMME BACK my . . .*

Of course that song hadn't even been written the day that Fran and I went around kicking the bumpers; the day the two of us blew. That incident occurred at the low ebb of the eighties, right after Hüsker Dü broke up, right when it seemed like we'd accomplished nothing. If you'd asked me then, I would have said, yes, punk rock is now, finally, dead. Not only had all my favorite bands—Hüsker Dü, the Minutemen, the Replacements—just gone flat one way or another, but I had myself: coopted, that month, by the *L.A. Times* in some kind of momentary impulse toward hiring more women. (I was fired after four weeks, so the editor could hire his best friend instead.) We all sold out together that year, and none of us made good.

It must have been the very beginning. Unbeknownst to us, in a tiny town in Washington State, Kurt Cobain and Krist Novoselic were putting together Nirvana. Thus, for me and for Francesca and all the rest of us losers, Kurt and company's subsequent rise to the top was more than just the defiant succor of surprise success. It was a victory. It meant that we won. Who were we? We were the outcasts, the crusties, the misfit punk rockers who, after EMI sank the Sex Pistols and the mainstream world turned to the dispassionately goofball world of rancid technopop—Rock of the Eighties! The Cutting Edge of Rock!—had burbled around underground for a decade or so, creating the context for Nirvana to live in and to grow.

That came later. In November 1987 I lived in a corporate

apartment (the Oakwood Arms), originally full to the brim with hideous nautical art, which I stuffed into a closet the minute I got there. The first time Fran came over she opened it by accident and a bunch of pewter anchors and driftwood dolphins and a large pastel photo of a sailboat fell out, and she nearly peed her pants laughing. I'd had to leave behind me my brand-new kitten and my entire record collection, so I went and bought three used ones (records, not kittens): Creedence Clearwater Revival's greatest hits, the Rolling Stones' *High Tide Green Grass*, and the Kinks' *Village Green Preservation Society.* That was all I listened to the entire time I lived there, wolfing down each note, over and over again. I've noticed that when you're lonely and fearful and disgusted with your life, only old music will do. Possibly this has something to do with the popularity of classic rock radio.

Over at the *Times*, I wrote a story a day—about José Feliciano, Waylon Jennings, and Marie Osmond. (Marie was nice. She told me about all the good Mexican restaurants in the area, and commiserated with me about loneliness.) I did a piece on INXS filming their video at Balboa Island (where I met the Huntington Beach gang member) and reviewed an oldies show of Elvis impersonators. One night I went over to a house in Huntington Beach and interviewed some old HB thrashers, the Crowd, whom I'd heard had just got back together. Another day I got to drive to Big Bear to interview a Fixx clone.

But mostly everything was ashes and darkness. There was the night I had to review James Taylor at the Pacific Amphitheater when R.E.M. was playing a mile away at U.C. Irvine, and the afternoon I heard that U2 was playing for free in San Francisco and I put my head down on my desk and cried. Once I accidentally wore a Haight Street junk store dress to work instead of my slick new Nordstrom working-girl miniskirt, and the guy on the copy desk, apparently startled at the shocking looseness of my outerwear, asked me politely when my baby was due. They used to send me into the bathroom to buy nylons from the vending machine when I forgot to wear my own—a machine conveniently provided, I presume, not for me, but because the *Times* clearly felt that being caught with a run in your nylons is a fate worse than death.

The last straw came when my editor sent me out to do a story on the band of Mickey Rooney, Jr. He was appearing at a bar in Huntington Beach called Nightmoves on a Sunday—a night that bar is usually closed. When I got there it turned out that Rooney Jr. had hired it privately, specially for me (me being the physical embodiment of the *L.A. Times*). He and his band played bad covers of Dave Clark Five songs while his wife, seated next to me at the bar, exhorted me to vote for Pat Robertson for president come the next November. Next day, I told my editor to kill the story because, the way I saw it, the Rooneys were just buying copy about themselves. He agreed docilely enough, but, when my review came up a few weeks later, cited this incident as an example of my lack of judgment as a reporter and general intractability as an employee. But he had his own games to play, and it's not like I didn't know about the nastiness of the corporate ogre when I willingly walked into its mouth.

That was in another country, and besides, the wench is dead. Meanwhile, the only new friends I made at that time and in that country were a band called the Pontiac Brothers. They lived in Fullerton and put out records on Frontier. The first day I went to work at the *Times* I called them up, and they very kindly invited me to a party at one of their houses before their gig that night. Oh my God, the thankfulness I felt for that tiny invitation! I called up Francesca and boasted, "I'm invited to party at the Pontiac Brothers'!" acting like I had a life. It was just a party, like any other I'd been to in my own suburban hometown, and yet, just the can of Budweiser yanked from somebody's messy kitchen refrigerator in some low-slung Anaheim bungalow with crabgrass instead of lawn was hospitality enough to appease my poor little starveling punk rock soul.

I told the band members about my situation. "Living in

Newport," I said bitterly to Ward Dotson (who used to be in the Gun Club) "makes me feel like a Negro in 1955."

Ward laughed. "You feel like a Negro? We feel like the Viet Cong!"

The venue that the Po Bros played that night was called Big John's. It burned down a few months later, with somebody still inside it—this didn't surprise me one bit, because the place was already accursed. Little kids lounging around the parking lot used to offer to guard your car for five dollars; if you didn't hand over, they'd slash your tires. Inside, there were about fifty pool tables rammed into an enormous space, with a tiny stage hunched up against one wall. The place was always crammed to the brim with enormous tattooed biker guys in way-too-blue overalls, you know the type I mean? Once I saw Fetchin Bones there and some creepy redneck kept yelling, "Show us your tits!" at lead singer Hope Nicholls. "Only if you show me your little tiny dick," replied Hope, with great dignity.

The guy then got onstage, pantsed himself, and peed, and indeed his dick was little. I personally felt sick.

A couple months later, the Po Bros put out a record called *Johnson* (that means "dick" in slang). Lisa threw a record release party at a bar in way west Hollywood, corner of Sunset and, like, Fontana. It was a total dive, with a neon sign and elderly waitresses and booths made of soft red vinyl. I drove there from my cousin's house in Studio City, west on Cahuenga Boulevard and then straight south. By that time I'd been kicked out on my ass by the *Times*—their plan all along, I realized; I was just a convenient way for them to pretend to fulfill their affirmative action quota without actually hiring me—and was living back in San Francisco again. I used to say being fired by the *L.A. Times* was like being dumped by a bad boyfriend—rejection is rejection, however crummy the guy.

Then it was 1988. Bush had just taken office. College radio airwaves were a mass of strummy jangly whirry bands indistinguishable from one another. Everyone was completely blinded by the sound of Robyn Hitchcock and the Chills. Punk rock? What was that? Back on Haight Street, though, I still walked up Fell Street every Monday night at midnight to see what was happening at the I Beam. Sometime in that winter or spring, I saw the band Big Black, a snot-brained übercool white-noise band on Homestead that was fronted by producer Steve Albini. Albini was the ultimate cutting edge, the sound of fury and metal and motion, cynical, mean, hipper than hip. He spoke big words of integrity and independence and how any band with a day job was a band without morals, because touching corporate money was like touching pitch. His songs—"Il Duce," "Kerosene," "This is Texas"—were pulverizingly harsh. Big Black's lyrics made Sonic Youth's look like nursery rhymes, so very ugly was their assessment of modern life.

Albini himself, in looks, was like your basic indie rock nerd: bespectacled, blue-jeaned, T-shirted, like every band we liked. That's probably why we were so appalled at our first sight of the opening band. Dressed in Guns N' Roses-esque black leather pants and spandex, glammy makeup, silver boots and frills, they were the exact opposite of what we'd come to expect from indie bands at the I Beam. The lead singer's head was all covered in bleached-blond ringletlike dreadlocks: he looked like no one so much as Romeo's pal Mercutio. The guitarist had fishnets on under his torn jeans. The band's music sounded just like Led Zeppelin. We stomped out of the main room of the I Beam, disgusted . . . until suddenly, inexplicably, about fifteen minutes into the set, we were hooked somewhere through the midsection and reeled back into the room by nothing at all but the sound emanating from the stage. I remember standing furtively next to it and staring up at that lead singer as he bent the notes in the upper registers and the band whirled along in tribelike unison, away down way beneath his voice. The singer was called Perry Farrell and the band was Jane's Addiction.

Jane's legend has it that the band was born in a slutty cavern off Hollywood Boulevard, where the band members were introduced to one another and subsequently funded in their quest for world domination by the proceeds of a prostitute named Jane. This is probably a highly embroidered rock 'n' roll myth, but what is true is that Jane's Addiction comes from a California the Beach Boys never knew, where the ocean is oil-polluted and girls in orange neoprene bikinis are afraid to walk alone at dusk. Singer Perry Farrell (a play on the word *peripheral;* his real name is Simon Bernstein) was once a waiter at a Newport Beach fern bar, which led to a gig lipsynching in drag to David Bowie and Mick Jagger songs. After moving up to Hollywood, Perry busted up his first band, Psi-Com, when the other members tried to get him to become a Hare Krishna. "It made me start to sing about anything that was debauchery, just to get back at them," he told *Creem* years later.

Farrell, then in his late twenties, decided to find younger musicians to work with, ones who were more open to suggestion. His search led him to Eric Avery, Stephen Perkins, and David Navarro, three kids whose musical sensibilities were steeped in Led Zeppisms and Dead shit. Farrell—older, charming, and single-mindedly articulate—practically forced them to sow that barren ground with the fertile seed of punk and rhythm. No doubt the actual mating process was cruel and difficult, a rape of sorts, but it resulted in music that sounded good over the din of crazed children howling over the constant wail of car alarms and police sirens and the deadening strains of classic rock radio. "The thing about being from America," Farrell once told me, "is that instead of being haunted by history, you can deal with the present and invent the new. Our music deals with things they just don't have in Europe: gangs and the ocean and a funky beat."

Jane's Addiction began playing around L.A. in late 1986. From the first, they made quite an impression: Farrell, clad in black leather bustier and chiffon skirts, his head all feathers and dreadlocks; the rest of the band, equally striking-looking, pounding away behind him. They were like a Culture Club gone Butthole Surfing, and the result was tremendously appealing. By 1987, the band had signed a million-dollar deal with Warner Brothers. In the interim, they released a self-titled live album on Triple X records. In 1988 their major-label debut, *Nothing's Shocking*, was released. It sold moderately well and was nominated for a Grammy, but was hardly a best-seller; Great White and bands like that did much better with none of the street cred, critical acclaim, or ability. Why? Because they got played on the radio, a circumstance that for some reason (we could say that program directors didn't have the ears to tap it as a potential hit and leave it at that) continued to elude Jane's Addiction to the end.

Jane's signing was in actuality the result of a wave of a bunch of hard rock/metal band signings instigated by the success of Guns N' Roses, Poison, and Motley Crue. But their enormous cult following remained something of a secret to the powers that be. The mainstream industry saw their record sales as merely mediocre compared to, say, those of Def Leppard, while members of the underground world despised them for their major-label status and the visual glamour that was read as a harking back to the bad old days of bloated behemoth rock.

Additionally, many rock critics dismissed them as aurally retrogressive as well, though that was an erroneous take on them: Jane's music may bear at first listen a slight resemblance to Led Zeppelin, but it's hard to imagine that amoral band writing a song like "Ted, Just Admit It," a condemnation of serial killer Ted Bundy, or "Nothing's Shocking," a searing indictment of television news, or Jane's' signature song, "Jane says," which was a compassionate look at the life of junkies, pimps, and prostitutes, sung from the perspective of a bewigged whore named Jane, whose sad refrain (between verses consisting of begging for dope) is "I'm gonna kick tomorrow." In short, Jane's' whole ethos—the combination of Sonic Youth's trash culture aesthetic with the speedy, hardcore punkfunk assault of the Red Hot Chili Peppers and their ilk—was tempered by an unlikely compassion. The band may have originally culled its inspiration from the soulless malls of SoCal, but the unwitting result was a harsh, prismatic comment on modern America's cultural blackout, something new and timely, risen from the ash of elsewhere.

Jane's' advent was thus a pivotal moment in the underground. The band's triumph was that it managed to singlehandedly graft the unelitist stance of suburban youth to the economic values of the underground, thus carving a larger piece of audience out of America than had previously been thought possible.

In spite of the magnificence of their new aesthetic, like so many bands before them, Jane's' music continued to go completely unheard on any form of radio, while their live popularity just increased and increased. By the time their second record, *Ritual De Lo Habitual*, was released in 1989, they were a major touring act, playing to audiences of five thousand to ten thousand in venues nationwide, and to larger ones in Europe. They had succeeded on a level far greater than that of any of the more critically acclaimed alternative bands—Sonic Youth, the Pixies, Hüsker Dü, or the Replacements. And, unlike Great White, they were just as beloved by their audience . . . whoever that was.

Jane's' mainstream success still wouldn't be important if it wasn't for an oft-forgotten factor, which is that at heart Perry Farrell was pure L.A. punk rocker. Though he grew up in Miami, a city not noted for its happening underground scene, he'd been a figure kicking around the fringes of L.A. hardcore for years. "There were no bands coming out of Miami, just clubs with recorded music and concert hall things. So I wasn't into punk rock music until I moved to Hollywood, and that was right when the indie scene was really flourishing. I was into hardcore at its best and so on—I hung out with SST people, with the Minutemen, X, Social D, Savage Republic—that's where I cut my teeth and that's why I still have such a concern for having control over my product."

Farrell's first band was called Psi-Com, which he describes as "Cure, Siouxsie, Cocteau Twins stuff." Presently, in keeping with lots of people who had bands in those days, he decided to release a single on his own label. "And, like a lot of kids who do that, I just got ripped off. There are, like, a thousand copies of that record in existence. That's how many I pressed. I mailed off five hundred and put five hundred in stores, but I lost five hundred just getting the records between the record plant and my house, because a friend of mine I'd given the money to pay for the wax ripped off five hundred bucks to pay his rent.

"I guess what I found out was that doing things without the help of a major label doesn't necessarily mean purity. Indies can be just as corrupt as majors. Because the thing is, guys like that are hanging around on every level, and in fact, at the bottom of the ladder you meet more of the scummier people. They're at the bottom because that's where they belong. Warner Brothers is less likely to behave that way, because they don't need my money as much. So long as I'm working hard, so long as I make any money at all, they're happy.

"So, yeah, there's a modern way to make it in this business, and we have avoided a lot of sellout things. I feel like we earned our success because we did come from the streets and we only played with good bands along the way. I haven't changed my approach to art at all—I did the Ice T single on a two-track for less money than an SST band spends on a record; all the fetishes I put onstage cost less than a thousand dollars to build because it's all secondhand thrift store stuff. It's all totally homegrown, because I can't stand a corporate rock band either."

Farrell's punk rock roots manifested themselves in another way as well, which was that as soon as he had some economic power, he decided to use it. Not, like so many bands before or after him, by starting a vanity label, or signing other bands to his own, but by reshaping a market that, at that time in particular, was riddled with poor promotion, overly high ticket costs, and unsellable tour packages.

That fall I was lucky enough to spend a week with the Pixies on tour in Mittel Europe—in 1990, European politics and borders were changing so quickly that no other term seemed appropriate—as they opened for David Bowie at some large German festivals, and then went on to play gigs of their own.

The Pixies were a Boston-based band whose large new sound—strange broken phrases parsed through hugely amplified snippets of guitar licks and a roaringly loud beat—would become an eerily liberating force in popular music around about that year. The band had come up through a route somewhat different from that of most other punk bands, getting signed in their first six months of existence to 4AD in England, but, alongside Jane's Addiction, they were one of several U.S. bands whose mind-altering music was immediately more popular in Europe than in the United States. (Indeed, their popularity in the States still lags far behind their relative importance.) That fall the Pixies released their fourth record, *Bossanova*, and every song on it solidified their place in my mind as the best band on the planet at the time. Crossing Alp upon Alp in a driving rainstorm, there I was merrily singing (for some reason) "March of the Oompa Loompas" with Kim and periodically thumb-wrestling for control of the tape deck. David only wanted to hear Rhino Records' *Disco Hits of the '70s*. Kim only wanted to hear *Bohemian Rhapsody.* I only wanted to hear the Replacements' *All Shook Down*, which everyone in the band hated beyond all reason: "No, no, we can hear it again if you want to," said Kim good-naturedly, "just to make sure we hate it as much as we think we do." The bus kept breaking down on the inclines, and Neil, the bus driver, eventually had to tie a piece of string to the windshield wipers, which he pulled through the side window just to get them to wipe. We were in such a hurry that for sustenance we were reduced to subsistence level: bad German biscuits, beer, and candy. And I'd just lost my passport, so I lived in total fear at every border stopping.

Still, those enormous Eurofestivals were a real eye opener, especially to an American raised on Summer Jams featuring REO, Boston, Saxxon, and the like. Here, what we in the United States called "alternative music" was really coming into its own. There was a sense in the tents behind the jerry-built stage in Ulm that the Pixies had some secret hold over the entire proceedings, a sort of artistic superiority that was acknowledged by all. I certainly gained a measure of respect for David

Bowie, a surprisingly puny man in a sweatsuit, as I listened to him eagerly discussing the records of the Legendary Stardust Cowboy with a polite but unenthused Pixie, Charles Thompson; and as I heard him, standing surreptitiously behind me in the wings, singing the words to "Is She Weird" at the top of his famous lungs. (Later that year, his band Tin Machine would cover the Pixies' "Debaser.")

A few hours later, when Bowie appeared transformed, all coiffed and *maquillé* in a black tuxedo, and took the stage by moonlight, we finally did become suitably awed. Someone served us drinks as we sat placidly on Bowie's anvil cases, watching sixty-five thousand German fans sing "Starman" to the sky. And afterward, the promoters threw a party in a marquee out on the fairgrounds, with huge haunches of meat, steins of beer and an oompah band in lederhosen that played Bavarian melodies while the Americans in the room guffawed. "Now be nice," I admonished. "Jeez, we're in Bavaria, after all. It's like having a mariachi band in California!" Everyone nods sagely, all serious for a second. Then someone can't suppress a mutter of "Hans und Franz," at which everyone busts out laughing uncontrollably. It really was very like the Schmenge Brothers on SCTV. Presently someone tossed a roll into a tuba, and before you knew what was happening, a food fight was in progress: in about two minutes, every scrap of manna was strewn about the grass. "That was so rock 'n' roll," howled Kim Deal delightedly, in the bus. "That was the most rock 'n' roll thing that's happened to us yet!" We sang "Rock 'n' Roll" by Gary Glitter all the way back to the hotel.

Jane's Addiction was scheduled to headline at the Reading Festival, an annual three-day mud bath thirty miles outside London, as all this was occurring. The festival, which began in 1970, had just changed its format from dinosaur rock to alternative bands. Jane's Addiction, unbeknownst to the public, was in the midst of personal turmoil—the usual band breakup threats, augmented by rumored drug problems and roadwear. The band ended up canceling its appearance at Reading owing to Farrell's throat problems. But one day of the festival was to be headlined by the Pixies, and on that day, Jane's booking agent, Marc Geiger, went to the festival anyway, taking drummer Stephen Perkins with him. Together, Geiger and Perkins dreamed up a similar festival, to take place in America and travel from venue to venue.

I know all about what happened that day, because I ran into Marc a couple days later. He was seated next to me in a large orange double-decker bus that was crossing the Austrian Alps, traveling with the Pixies. What I didn't know was that he was gathering information for putting together similar festivals in the United States. On that rainy afternoon, as the bus meandered its way between Munich and Vienna, Geiger expounded his theory to me of how a Reading Festival—or a festival like the ones Bowie and the Pixies were doing here in Germany—could work in the States. He was going to book it, he said. It was going to feature Siouxsie and the Banshees, the Pixies, Jane's Addiction, and the Butthole Surfers.

"But that'll never work," I said indignantly. "You'll never make any money."

"Sure I will," he said, all confident. "It works in England, and California is the size of two Englands. You've got a bigger rock market in every state in America than you can get in all of Germany. And besides, the venues are all in place. You don't have to build them up from scratch in a field somewhere the way they do here."

Geiger obligingly worked out the finances on a little piece of paper for me, proving how if you did more than five dates selling seven to ten thousand tickets each, you'd break even. Anything over that was pure profit. I shrugged. That was all very well: my own opinion was that, unlike Germany, America didn't want to know from Jane's, the Buttholes, and the Pixies. Not in Bumfuck, Idaho, they didn't.

Also I secretly thought the whole thing wouldn't be any fun to go to. I thought back to Days on the Green, long ago: Kansas, Fleetwood Mac, Boston, and Gary Wright, at the

Oakland Coliseum Stadium, July 1975. My girlfriends Kelly and Lori and Annette and I running, running, running, across the field for the best spot, all set for a day of sun and fun, lying flat out on some itchy blanket flirting with the boys near us. Wearing halter tops, I'll have you know! And up onstage—a stage flanked by this colossal mural illustration of a Union Jack or something—teeny-tiny figures, cavorting and gesticulating and singing "My Love Is Alive."

That's what punk rock was getting away from. Six months, eight months later, I was at Winterland grooving to Patti Smith, and oh, God, how I reviled Days on the Green! Sure, it seems unfair in retrospect that the Undertones and the Buzzcocks and even the Ramones were never big enough to support such a concept—that, thanks to disco's debilitating effect on radio promotion, the eighties flashed by without ever creating any new bands large enough to support the concert season. The exceptions prove the rule, and they are the Police, who broke up in 1985; Wham, who broke up even sooner; and U2, who are the Led Zeppelin of the nineties. No, punk rock never got its due: instead, the airwaves and the concert venues are flooded with re-formed Pink Floyds and Genesis, resuscitated Eric Claptons and Stevie Winwoods, staid old Dire Straitses and Bruce Springsteens and John Cougars and the Grateful Dead. It always made me mad, in a way, that we'd got such short shrift. But on the other hand, we always had more fun down in the trenches.

And now Geiger was telling me that he was going to create a concert world for alternative rock in that selfsame image? Even at the time, the idea made me thoughtful. At that time the Pixies were on the cusp of some kind of small success: in Europe, they headlined to two thousand, but in the United States, it was still Monday nights at the I Beam. I wondered, if my favorite bands had gotten all large and satisfied, would it have made their music any better? Would they have stayed together longer? Been happier people? Still interested me at all?

For all these thirteen years there's been so much good

music. The unheard music. And people, just everyday people, could have been listening to it all along instead of to crap. In the end, it comes down to whether you believed that people really wanted to hear Bruce Springsteen instead of the Replacements, or whether you thought they were being deprived of that choice by the powers that be. You can't have it both ways, and if you believe the latter thing, as I have always intrinsically believed, then you have to rejoice when those powers change hands.

We dropped Geiger off at the airport in Vienna. That night the Pixies played a Quonset hut on the banks of the Danube called CA-Zelt (which someone told me translates to "Bank-Owned Tent"). I can see them now, all bathed in orange light, music roaring round me as the band detachedly studies their shoes and Charles, veins bulging out, his face all red, bellows, "I am the son of a motherfucker!" into the startled and rain-soaked September night. Caught up in the zenith of the Pixies that week in concert, I forgot all about Marc Geiger's crazy notions for the next six months—until one day in 1991 an editor called me up and said the word *Lollapalooza*.

THIRTEEN

DID THE RIGHT THING

We owe you nothing.
– Fugazi

To get to Compton Terrace, a fifteen-thousand-seat concert venue owned in part by Stevie Nicks's father and located smack in the center of the Gila River Indian Reservation in Arizona, one has to drive by a route called, I'm not kidding you, the Superstition Highway. It's well down Interstate 10 beyond Phoenix, where the road leaves Tempe for Tucson; where the dust begins to rise. Out there you can see for miles: brown scrub desert and hot blue sky, the occasional mesa popping up over the rim of the world.

I drove down the Superstition Highway on my way to the opening night of the first Lollapalooza tour, sandwiched all the way between an eighteen-wheeler and a beat-up Honda Civic with a Hüsker Dü bumper sticker and the words "Punish Me" scratched on its dirty back windshield. It was July 18, ten months after that rainy bus ride in Europe, and it was 110 degrees outside and no shade anywhere; so hot that they had to run showers along the back of the venue for concertgoers to stand beneath, so hot that the bathrooms stood empty the entire time, since every drop of moisture in every person's body was being absorbed or evaporated by other means. It was so hot that only the Butthole Surfers, who, after all, are crazy, from Texas, and well known for setting themselves on fire at concerts, were cool enough to wear pants. When Ice T took the stage, he said, "I feel like I just landed on the surface of the sun." It was so hot that by ten o'clock in the evening, during Jane's Addiction's set, fifteen thousand once-drunk revelers lay flat out in heat prostration on the lawn, listening to raucous songs like "Been Caught Stealing" and "Had a Dad," rendered motionless and at peace. They listened to it as if it were chamber music, which it actually sounded like within the hugeness of that Arizona night.

That was the finale of the first show of the first Lollapalooza. Some stuff had gone wrong that day—Nine Inch Nails had their juice cut off by accident and threw an onstage tantrum; the members of Jane's Addiction got into a little fight during one number, I forget which—but all in all, the package tour could only be called an unmitigated success. Despite the weather, the first show sold three thousand tickets more than its promoters had expected, paving the way for one of the most successful concert tours of the summer of 1991. That afternoon I found myself giving Marc Geiger, last seen exiting the Pixies' bus in Wien, an exaggerated look of amazement across the asphalt, and then, reluctantly, the thumbs-up signal. And him? He's shaking his head at me, positively smirking.

Ever since it began, I'd had my doubts about the righteousness of the Lollapalooza phenomenon. And yet, when I saw Henry Rollins—you remember Henry, formerly in Dischord's SOA and later on in Black Flag—face down the Compton Terrace crowd of some nine thousand early in the day, I felt a very personal sense of achievement. When I heard the selfsame crowd cheering my beloved Buttholes, I shook my head in disbelief. And by the time I saw them, later in the day, chanting, "Want to be a cop killer, cop killer, cop killer" along with Ice T's new band Body Count, I knew for a fact something momentous was occurring. It was the first whisper, a ghostly sigh of success, a rumor whistling across the plain, that the old guard was changing. Forget mainstream radio and the color-bound gridlock of the rest of the industry: the ecstatic reception of Ice T's new band by fifteen thousand unbriefed Arizona teenagers said that there might be room in the real world after all for challenging music. At least there was a place, now, for the population to hear it.

*

The day after the Lollapalooza show in Arizona, I drove from San Diego to Los Angeles to interview Nirvana. Their manager, John Silva, had just Fed Exed me a package containing four songs from their upcoming release, at that time not yet titled *Nevermind*, but my rental car didn't have a tape deck, so I had to play it by dangling my tape recorder, on full blast, in front of my ear while I drove up Highway 405.

So I drove, and I listened, again and again, all the way through, then I hit rewind and listened again. I remember thinking, when I heard the first number—the words went *"Love myself better than you/know it's wrong, but what can I do?"*—that if the world was a different sort of place, it'd be a huge hit single. Then the next number began. *"One baby to another said, 'I'm lucky I met you'/I don't care what you think unless it is about me"*—and I got kind of excited. The next number, "Lithium," was one long lurch in the pit of my stomach, a disturbance in my physical self, a sensation somewhat akin to fright.

Then "Teen Spirit" began. You know those opening chords? You know the gas pedal? You know the first line, *"Load up on drugs and bring your friends/it's fun to lose and to pretend"*? When I first heard "Smells Like Teen Spirit," I didn't think, "Why, this will be a monster hit that will transform the record industry and subsequently my life." I just felt afraid. Oh, rock 'n' roll beguiles but it betrays as well. When I heard "Teen Spirit," I felt sick with love for that song, sick with the thought that other people might dare to criticize it. Here, I knew, was one more thing to go to bat for, one more band by which I'd measure truth, one more life-changing, attitude-shaping, bigger-than-its-parts song of surrender. I felt sick because it was a battle call, and battles are always bloody. Somebody always loses.

I listened to those four songs for two and a half hours. At the end of them, I reached my destination—the Beverly Garland Hotel—and saw, in the parking lot, the three people who'd sung them, standing around idly, waiting for me to show up. Krist was lurching around in the parking lot, all goofily, while he gestured me into a parking space. And I couldn't help thinking back to when I'd first met Nirvana. It was in another kind of parking lot: the DMZish asphalt area of a McDonald's in San Ysidro (rebuilt on a new site since the famous sniper massacre of several years ago). It was a parking lot full of sullen teens in beat-up Mavericks, a ton of screaming children and the inevitable Baptist church choir on its way to a sing-off or something equally improbable out in the sticks. Saturday afternoons at McDonald's are the same the world over, and that Saturday at the Dairy Mart Road McDonald's in San Ysidro was no exception.

Nirvana was on its way across the U.S. border for weekend gigs at a nightclub called Iguana's in Tijuana. Trailed by a square yellow truck that was serving as the equipment van for the headliner, Dinosaur Jr., the band pulled into the lot one afternoon in June. They were an hour late, owing to traffic in Orange County, and still looked half asleep. When their manager pushed me unceremoniously into one of the dirtiest, smelliest vans I've even been in, no one even looked up to ask who I was. I looked around disconsolately. Pizza crusts, candy wrappers, a cooler full of warm water and crushed cans; graffiti all over the inside of the van and a pair of grotty hightop sneakers tied so that they hung out the crack of a window (presumably because they smelled so bad). The seats of the van had been ripped out and replaced by the kind of torn plaid sofas that you sometimes see out on street corners in San Francisco that even halfway houses have already rejected.

I sat down gingerly on one, surrounded by baleful stares. The atmosphere was positively foreboding. The only person who wasn't nearly comatose was David Grohl, Nirvana's drummer, who (typically, I soon discovered) managed to utter a semifriendly "Hi!" Then, as we pulled out of the parking lot, I reached up nervously and turned my black baseball cap, with its K Records logo on it, back to front, Sub Pop style. There was the slightest stir from the back seat, as Kurt Cobain sat straight up. "Where'd you get that cap?" he asked.

"Made it myself with liquid paper," I replied. Kurt didn't answer. Then suddenly, shyly, he thrust his arm out under my nose. On the back of it was a tattoo of the exact same symbol. "Dave did it with a pin," Kurt said proudly, glancing over at him.

"You didn't just get it 'cause your name begins with K, did you?" I asked suspiciously.

"No!" Kurt exclaimed at once. "That's not it at all. I like the K label a lot and what Calvin's doing, and I wanted a tattoo and I couldn't think of anything else. Besides, [K] exposed me to so much good music, like the Vaselines, who are my favorite band ever. They didn't influence me, it was just a reminder of how much I really value innocence and children and my youth. Beat Happening had a lot to do with reminding me of how precious that whole childlike world is. I have great memories of what it was like to be a little kid. It was a really good time, and I see a lot of beauty in it. I was happiest then. I didn't have to worry about anything."

That was my first meeting with Nirvana. Back when I'd first heard *Bleach*, I had thought, "This band is kind of like the Pixies crossed with Soul Asylum." When I saw them play that gig in TJ, I realized that what Nirvana actually equalled was the Pixies *times* Soul Asylum. ("Thanks," said Kurt. "That's very close, I'd say. I never liked Soul Asylum, but I went to see them once, and I think we're closely related in our live shows. The Pixies, I've felt a real musical bond with them. I was blown away by them. That's very close to what we were doing and are doing more so now.") Live that night, Nirvana threw off sheer power in enormous bursts, leaning over their guitars with the weight of their fury, smashing them down on the ground, sometimes hurling them at each other; its members leaping, guitars and all, onto a surface of human flesh, Kurt held upright, clutched by each leg, howling "Teen Spirit" to an enthralled cabal, bodies plunging literally over the chicken wire-encased third-tier balcony and then bouncing off the skin below. Sometimes it was as if the guitars themselves had become possessed by the music and, poltergeist style, were seizing their owners like the brooms in *Fantasia* or something, hurling them around so many stages I stopped counting. Once I saw Kurt leap on Krist's shoulders, forcing him to the floor with his unexpected burden, both still playing notes all ripped apart from impact.

All this brilliance couldn't come from a more unlikely set of guys. Nirvana's founders—bassist Krist Novoselic and guitarist Kurt Cobain (Grohl, from Washington, D.C., joined the group in 1990; he was their fifth drummer in as many years)—are the embodiment of small-town stoners, the American equivalent of the kids in England who angrily declared that they had No Future back in 1977. They are the type of self-described "negative creeps"—shy, weasel-faced, introverted—that it's practically impossible to imagine copping any of the classic rock poses of stardom. When they turn on like light bulbs onstage, there's an unfeigned freedom, an intuitiveness so inarticulate there's almost no point in interviewing them. They are a little hard to get to know. Kurt did once tell me his favorite books are by philosophers—"Bukowski, Beckett, anyone beginning with a *B*"—and that he once tackled Nietzsche, but didn't understand a word of it. But you can't tell me that the guy who wrote the words "*Love myself better than you/know it's wrong but what can I do?*" didn't absorb the tenets of Man and Superman, even if Novoselic does jeer at the idea.

"Oh yeah, we're pocket philosophers," Krist says, laughing.

"Well, blue-collar ones, maybe," Kurt adds defensively.

One thing I do know about Nirvana's talent and music: it comes of obsessiveness and determination—the kind of determination that saw the band, in its early days, traveling up to Seattle time and again in a Volkswagen with all its seats torn out, packed up with tiny amps, an old Sears trap drum set, cymbal stands that were originally music stands from high school, basically equipment that was the Melvins' scraps—not to mention the three band members themselves, one of whom is six foot seven. And it comes of a genuine love of the misfit status that growing up on the outside in Aberdeen, Washington, will give a kid with a brain, a craziness that can't be faked by anyone. If there is one single thread that holds all of their banal observations together, it is that of eccentricity. Nirvana has learned to love the feeling of not belonging, to the point where the very idea of actually belonging scares them. "I just can't believe," says Kurt, "that anyone would start a band just to make the scene and be cool and have chicks. I just can't believe it."

Unlike many grungy white-boy college rock bands today, Kurt Cobain and Krist Novoselic take great pride in the fact that they even graduated from high school. They met in Aberdeen, the way people in high school do: they just kind of knew each other. They say they were always attracted to people on the outside—misfits, outcasts, strangers with candy.

"The first concert I ever went to," recalls Krist, "was the Scorpions. I went with these gay guys 'cause I was the only one with a car. One guy was my age and the other was older. And we were driving up to Seattle, and I looked in the back seat and they were making out and I'm, like, 'Jeepers creepers.' I was seventeen. They didn't bug me or anything. I kind of laughed. I thought it was funny 'cause I never saw gay people before. So we went to the show, it was the Scorpions, and it was totally boring. I stood up front and threw my shirt on the stage. And afterwards I couldn't find the other guys, so I just left without 'em."

Kurt interrupts. "Hey, I was friends with that guy! Randall [not his real name], he was my best friend in tenth grade and everyone else assumed I was gay too. I didn't even know he was gay but everyone else did, so there was all these gay-bashing rumors going on, like they were going to beat me up, there were really bad vibes going on in my P.E. class and then my mom forbid me to hang out with him anymore because he was gay. Randall! He's a great guy. I was always attracted to him 'cause he was really different. He had a really different perspective."

But wasn't it odd that a gay guy would like the Scorpions?

"No. Everybody liked the Scorpions in Aberdeen. It's a small hick town, those are the only records you can buy there," Kurt says. "Scorpions or Ozzy Osbourne."

"Not me," says Krist. "I didn't like 'em. I liked 'em when I was way younger, but then they started coming out with—well, all their records were crappy, but *Blackout* was the crappiest. Then I liked prog rock, and then I discovered punk rock. In 1983. I heard a compilation tape made by a friend. And then I listened to *Generic Flipper* and it was a revelation. It was art. It made me realize it was art. It was valid, it was beautiful. 'Cause I gave things validity by going, like 'Is it as good as *Physical Graffiti*?' And Flipper was suddenly, like, 'Sure it is! If not better. Well, they both have their moments.' It was a revelation!

"My friend Buzz gave the tape to me. He's in the Melvins. He was the punk rock guru of Aberdeen. He's the guy who discovered punk rock and spread the good news around town. But he only told it to the most deserving, 'cause a lot of people would discount it. And then I tried to turn people on to it, and they'd be, like . . . one guy I know, I remember he goes, 'Ah, that punk rock stuff . . . all it is is, "Want to fuck my mom! want to fuck my mom!" ' "

Kurt: "He probably wanted to fuck *his* mom. He probably wanted to fuck Randall!" (He and Krist collapse in giggles.)

Luckily for Krist, one of the deserving people to whom Buzz gave a tape was Kurt, who kind of knew Krist from around town. "I'd met Buzz probably around the same time you met Buzz," recalls Kurt. "And one night I went over to hear the Melvins practice before they were the Melvins and they were playing, like, Jimi Hendrix and Cream and stuff like that. And I was really drunk and I thought they were the greatest band I'd ever seen, it was really awesome, and right around that time Buzz started getting into punk rock. Then they started playing punk rock music and they had a free concert right behind Thriftways supermarket where Buzz worked, and they plugged into the city power supply and played punk rock music for about fifty redneck kids. And when I saw them play, it just blew me away, I was instantly a punk rocker. I abandoned all my friends, 'cause they didn't like any of the music. And then I asked Buzz to make me a compilation tape of punk rock songs and I got a spiky haircut."

Krist reflects on this information for a moment. "You know what happened is, punk rock kind of galvanized people in Aberdeen. It brought us together and we got our own little scene after a while, and we all hung out. Everybody realized—all the misfits realized—that rednecks weren't just dicks, they were *total* dicks. And punk rock had all this cool political, personal message, you know what I mean? It was a lot more cerebral than just stupid cock rock, you know? Dead Kennedys. MDC, remember? Dead Cops! Corporate Death Burger! We were never exposed to any radical ideas, all the ideas came from, like, San Francisco, or Berkeley."

"My first rock experience was Sammy Hagar in seventh grade," Kurt says. "My friend and I were taken by his sister to the show in Seattle. And on the way there we drank a case of beer and we were stuck in traffic and I had to go so bad I peed my pants! And when we got into the concert people were passing pipes around, marijuana, and I'd never smoked pot before, and I got really high, and I had a Bic lighter in my sweatshirt, inside the pocket, and I was tripping out and I lit myself on fire. So I stunk of pee and I caught on fire . . . and I didn't really like the concert at all. It just wasn't the right type of music for me. I didn't understand it. I liked rock 'n' roll but not that concert, it didn't thrill me. He [Sammy] seemed really fake.

"When I was a little kid I had a guitar and I'd run around the house with it and sing Beatles songs and I'd have concerts for my family when they came over, on Christmas, and I'd play my guitar and play Beatles songs. I always wanted to be a rock star when I was a little kid. Then when I was a teenager, it was just different. . . . I still liked music a lot, but it wasn't what everyone else liked. I hated Kiss, I hated Boston, it was so fake . . . and at the time I couldn't understand why people liked it. I never thought about rock when I was a teenager.

"But when I saw the Melvins play that show and I started getting into punk rock, it really changed me. I wanted to start a band really bad, and I got an electric guitar and I was really into it, but I couldn't find anyone in Aberdeen to be in a band with. I was lucky to find Krist at the time. A few years after we'd been hanging out, I made a tape of some punk rock songs I'd written with Dale, the Melvins' drummer, and I played it for Krist at my aunt's house and he really liked it, and he suggested we start a band. It sounded *exactly* like Black Flag. Totally abrasive, fast, punk music. There were some Nirvana elements, some slower songs, even then. And some heavy, Black Sabbath-influenced stuff. I can't deny Black Sabbath. Or Black Flag."

For a while, the band was called Skid Row. "Our drummer," Kurt recalls, "was this stoner guy, but he had a drum set and we kind of coaxed him into joining the band, coming to practice. But we got really serious and he wasn't that serious. He'd get drunk, miss a lot of practices. So we had a lot of trouble starting out. It didn't seem like a real legitimate band, or as legitimate as we wanted it to be. We didn't even have enough money to buy records, and there were no stores in Aberdeen.

"The closest place to see shows was Olympia or Tacoma. Tacoma is seventy miles. Seattle was one hundred miles. We didn't get up there very often, just for the major punk rock shows, Black Flag and stuff. When I first started playing guitar, I just started writing songs right away. I knew one Cars song and 'Back in Black' and after that I just started writing. I didn't think it was important to learn other songs because I just knew I wanted to start a band.

"At the time the Community World Theater was a really good place for new bands to start out 'cause they'd let you play. But you know what?" he adds, "it was pretty easy to get booked. That was the thing about it. There weren't a lot of really popular bands coming into town. So it was mostly local bands that played. Olympia and Tacoma were kind of more punk rock that way—it was easier to play there than in Seattle."

"But did anyone come see you?"

"Oh no. Maybe twenty people. There was one show in Seattle where nobody came. We didn't even play. We loaded up our stuff and left."

Dave, who's been lying completely silent, soaking up the rays for the last hour, suddenly looks up. "Really, nobody came at all?"

Kurt grins. "Not one single person, except for Jon and Bruce. It was at the Central Tavern."

Jon, of course, is Jonathan Poneman. Bruce is Bruce Pavitt, who by that time had started Sub Pop Records. During that year, 1987, Nirvana got some money together, kicked their drummer out of the band, hired Dale Crover of the Melvins, and recorded a demo at Jack Endino's studio in Seattle in a single day. Poneman heard it and liked it, eventually offering to put it out.

"Jon put out our single about six months after talking to him," Krist recalls. "We didn't know anything about Sub Pop at the time. We just loved playing. It's just so totally *fun*. It was the most important thing in my life at the time. It was awesome!"

Still, for a tiny podunk band like Nirvana to put a record out must have been a pretty big deal.

Kurt shrugs. "We were excited, yeah, but after a while the excitement kind of left because it took over a year for our album to come out, 'cause we were waiting for Sub Pop to get enough money to put it out, and we ended up paying for the recording ourselves. It cost six hundred and six dollars. That's cheap. And still," he adds, "when we went on tour, kids would come up to us in flocks, going, 'Where can we get the record? We can't find it.' That's the only reason we decided to go with a major, is just the assurance of getting our records into small towns like Aberdeen."

Kurt still feels sort of bad about being on a major label. "But what were we going to do, stay on Sub Pop? You couldn't even find our last record! And we were under contract to them, and somebody had to have the money to get us out of the deal."

Nirvana's not ungrateful to Sub Pop. "The Sub Pop hype thing helped a lot, the Seattle Sound thing. We just kind of got caught up in it," says Krist.

Kurt adds, "In England we were always very popular. I mean, it's kind of an unusual thing for a band that's as young as us to have gone over there so soon, and Sub Pop did that for us. But going to Europe that soon [in 1988], it was exciting but it was hell at the same time. We didn't eat very much, it was a very low-budget thing. We were touring with Tad in the same van and three extra people. Eleven people. It was really grueling, 'cause we had three days off in seven and a half weeks. We were playing a lot and not eating too much."

What was the highlight?

Kurt (without even stopping to think): "Oh! that place in Austria! Up in the mountains, with all the trolls? The troll village!"

Krist: "Oh yeah! A bunch of inbred villagers going, 'Play some rock and roll, bay-bee!' There was a guy who looked like Mick Fleetwood with a big huge knife scar down the side of his face. And there was a guy with a machete in his hand, and it was some huge holiday and everyone was all wasted, people were passed out on the floor! There was this really fat troll, saying, 'Come on, bay-bee, play something hea-veee.' And there was this guy playing the blues machine. He rented himself out to, like, the Austrian version of bar mitzvahs. Oh God, I would love to rent him for our record release party. The guys in Mudhoney would go crazy."

Kurt adds, "We also played one of our best shows in this town called Redmond. It was just a party. And all these rednecks were there . . ."

Krist: "But they moved into the kitchen, they didn't like us at all. They were scared of us."

"We were really drunk," Kurt laughs, "so we started making spectacles of ourselves. Playing off of the bad vibes we were giving to the rednecks, you know—jumping off tables and pretending we were rock stars. And Krist jumped through a window. Then we started playing 'Sex Bomb' for about an hour, and our girlfriends were hanging on us and grabbing our legs and doing a mock lesbian scene, and that really started freaking out the rednecks!"

"But why was this the best show ever?"

Kurt thinks for a sec. "Oh, just because it was such a great vibe, I mean, we were totally wigging the rednecks out! And that was the idea of punk rock to us in the first place, was to abuse your audience. And what better audience to have than a redneck audience?"

By that time, Kurt had lived in Olympia for about a year, and Krist lived in nearby Tacoma, about twenty miles away. As Krist explains, at that time Sub Pop was talking about signing a big distribution deal with Sony (which eventually fell through). Nirvana got their own lawyer, who shopped them to various labels in Los Angeles. Eventually Geffen Records paid Sub Pop Records seventy thousand plus points for the privilege of licensing Nirvana.

Nirvana had initially recorded the songs for *Nevermind* as demos for Sub Pop. When they signed to Geffen, they re-recorded much of it— as well as adding tracks—at Butch Vig's studio in the spring of 1991. The band had two weeks of studio time booked, but it only took them a week and a half to lay it down. Kurt was still writing lyrics in the studio. "Endless Nameless," the buried track on the CD version (it begins ten minutes after "Something in the Way" ends) was a bunch of experimental shit they laid down in the studio at that time. The cello part on "Something" was added at the last minute, when Kirk Canning, a member of the band Spoon, happened to stop by the apartment the band was staying at in Madison.

Thus, *Nevermind* was initially conceived and marketed by the major label as just another relatively low-budget alternative band project. Kurt shrugs. "The level of success we're on doesn't really matter to us. It's a fine thing, a flattering thing to have major labels want you, but it doesn't matter. We could be dropped in two years and go back to putting out records ourselves and it wouldn't matter, 'cause it's not what we were looking for. We didn't want to be staying at the Beverly Garland Hotel, we just wanted people to get the records. And we did do it on an independent level. That's the beauty of it."

Krist: "We should make a made-for-TV movie. 'The Nirvana Story.' Who will play you?"

Kurt: "Ernest Borgnine. Who'll be you?"

"Someone tall—Kareem Abdul Jabbar? We'll have these intense scenes. 'I'm in this band, and what I say *goes!*' We'll be throwing our wine goblets through the window. Then there'll be the love part: 'Baby, I'm sorry, I've got to go out with the band.' And she'll be, like, 'Don't you love me?' And I'm, like, 'Hasta la vista!' The love! The camaraderie! (That'll be in the van with Tad in Europe.) The triumph! Us onstage. The letdowns: *'Booo!'* We're getting shit thrown at us. And it'll be directed just like an ABC After School Special. 'You know I love you, baby, but I've got to put the band before anything.' 'Yes, I understand.' 'But you'll live in my heart forever.' 'Go, love of mine.' "

Kurt grins. "And then the end. Our manager will come by and go, 'You guys have been dropped. You're broke.' And the last line is, Krist picks up the phone and goes, 'Hello, operator? Give me Sub Pop!' "

FOURTEEN

LOUDER THAN LOVE

The weirdest thing that's happened to me recently is some kid that was in line in front of me turned around. He got on his hands and knees and started bowing. *No*. I wanted to kick him in the teeth. It was really embarrassing.
– Mark Arm, 1992

There's a place in the stairwell of the Terminal Sales building in downtown Seattle where, on a clear day, you can see Mount Rainier. It's on the stairwell up to the penthouse suite that houses Sub Pop Records. Midway to the top, if you crouch down and peer through the window bars in the corner, you'll find you have the most splendid view. Spread out below you will be downtown Seattle, Pike's Place Market, the Kingdome, and Puget Sound. Lights wink on in the late haze of November, and you can almost smell the salmon as they slap up against the vendors' stalls. And looming far off in the drizzly distance to the southeast is the peak itself: purple and white, a Technicolor backdrop of a draggy old lug of a mountain. In the twilight, it looks like it's being embraced by the entire sky.

Then you continue on up the steps and into Sub Pop, where the walls have been decorated by local cartoonists and the view from the picture windows is toward the less picturesque north. It's a crazy day at Sub Pop today, because there are so many bands in town tonight: Royal Trux, the Laughing Hyenas, Love Battery, Sloan. Some members of these have stopped by for a chat with Bruce and Jon, leaving the rest of the staff behind to cope as best they can, which they do by alternating between extreme business and the giggles. Periodically, the fax machine spews forth yet another article on Seattle: a preview look at *Vogue*'s December grunge issue, with a story in it by Jonathan Poneman, a copy of *New York Newsday* that roasts Mudhoney, an irate fashion article in the *San Francisco Chronicle* headed "It Makes You Look Like Scum." Each fax makes everyone laugh even harder—and they've been getting them nonstop for the last seven months.

Tonight Bruce is giving an all-night disco party (in grand Evergreen-Olympia tradition). Tomorrow is the Portland Lame Fest, featuring the Sub Pop bands Sprinkler, Pond, and Love Battery, and much of the staff is planning on road-tripping it down there for an all-night binge. Meanwhile, it's Friday, and by five P.M. they're blasting a new Dutch act on Matador, which is treated to a vicious set of orals. "Does it sound like teen spirit?" comes the inevitable question. "No, it sounds like 10,000 Maniacs!"

Over in the conference room, which looks out on the Olympic Mountains to the west, I watch videos of Sub Pop acts both past and future, from Tokyo's SuperSnazz—four perky Japanese girls doing by-the-book grunge—to Mudhoney, whose major-label video debut of "Suck You Dry" is set ten years in the future at a club that is holding a fictitious grunge anniversary. The joke, of course, is that no one is there. The band plays to the bartender (played by Bruce Pavitt), the doorman (Jon Poneman), and one crazy Australian dude (in actuality Ed, the artist who drew the *Every Good Boy Deserves Fudge* cover).

This is the kind of acerbic wit that's characterized Sub Pop from its beginning: a wry-dry pride in assumed loserdom that masks a lot of true Seattlans' fiercely independent nature. A year ago, despite a seventy-thousand-dollar check from Geffen for the rights to the next record by Nirvana, Sub Pop was in serious trouble, nearly bankrupt, owing money to merchants all over the country. Bruce and Jon were forced to fire all their employees. Then they manufactured T-shirts that read, "Sub Pop: What part of 'we don't have any money' don't you understand?"

Then *Nevermind* came out, and within months the company

was solvent again. The agreement with Geffen had happened to include points on the record after sales of 200,000—a stipulation that at the time seemed hardly lucrative, since the record had an initial shipment of only 40,000. But Sub Pop started accruing income on that part of the contract within months of the record's release, as well as collecting monies for the precious back catalog: *Bleach,* Nirvana's first album, went gold in May.

Sub Pop T-shirts still have the word "loser" emblazoned on the back. Sub Popsters wear that word proudly. Originally, they called themselves losers because they had chosen of their own volition not to compete in the mainstream market. So it's hard not to rejoice in the fact that anyone associated with Sub Pop can now call themselves a loser only in an ironic sense.

Four years after its inception, Sub Pop is one of the healthiest independent labels in the country—and certainly the most celebrated. It is the brainchild of Bruce Pavitt and his partner, Jonathan Poneman, longtime Seattle scenesters who worked previously in college radio, alternative record stores, underground media, and food service before scraping together the money to start Sub Pop proper in 1986.

Because of Sub Pop and its antecedents—the fanzine, K Records, and bands like Green River and the U-Men—Seattle was being touted in the underground as the next Minneapolis as far back as that year. Seattle, thanks to Nirvana (who aren't even really from Seattle), became known as the rock capital of the world. And the world took note. In early 1992 *Rolling Stone* ran a feature on it—as did the *New Yorker. Newsweek* and *Time* were quick to note the ensuing A & R frenzy; *Entertainment Weekly* and *Women's Wear Daily* were only a little bit later for the train. By October 1992 fashion runways of Milan, Paris, and New York featured "the grunge look" as their theme. And around the same time, Seattle cable ran a public-access comedy skit depicting an A & R person standing on a corner, trying to hand out recording contracts to passersby. But each likely looking rock guy he stops says, "Sorry, I already have one."

Seattle wasn't always like this though. Twenty years ago, Seattle was known to the rest of the world as the home of Boeing and not much else: poor white factory workers living in trailer parks and everyone depressed all the time because of the rain. But since that time, the Pacific Northwest has accrued more than its fair share of liberal white people, who moved there to escape the high crime, high rent, and high smog rates of everywhere else: post-commune hippies, living out near Spokane in teepees pitched on someone else's land, and small businessmen following the lead of Bill Gates, who began Microsoft software company in the Bellevue environs.

Gates is now one of the richest men in the United States, and he has cast a long, long shadow over the new people of the Northwest. Now microbreweries and coffee-roasting plants abound. Espresso is the drug of choice. But once upon a time, Seattle was a barren and sickly wasteland of suburban-feeling middle America, the kind of place where Camaros and metal music ruled the pleasant green side streets of Greater Puget Sound. There was no good radio, no good nightclubs, and the kind of cops who hated even the least little hint of youth culture.

In short, it was exactly the sort of place that abounds with kids to whom punk rock would appeal. So by 1978 Seattle had a small but thriving punk rock scene. Kids who grew up in the inner city mingled with kids from nearby suburban Bellevue and Renton, driving into downtown to see shows at all-ages clubs like the Bird and the Vogue and Roscoe Louie. The world at large knew only about Quarterflash, but in fact there were lots of local punk rock bands, too, the Blackouts and the Fartz and the U-Men, and Ten Minute Warning and the Cheaters (which would later evolve into the Fastbacks).

As befits a city that's chock full of well-stocked newsstands, the Seattle scene was media-driven, almost from the start. The *Rocket* was a monthly music magazine devoted to Seattle music that, in addition to providing media support, nurtured a number of talented staff members. Many of its early art directors went on to bigger publications, such as the *Voice, Metropolis,* and Fox TV (Matt Groening).

In addition, the *Rocket* did a nice job covering what musical talent was at hand. "Other than music sections in local alternative papers, like the *Voice* or the *L.A. Weekly*," says Bruce Pavitt, "there really aren't that many magazines devoted to regional rock scenes, and those out there, like *BAM* in California and *Illinois Entertainer*, are incredibly mediocre because they're ad-driven instead of editorial-driven. The *Rocket* was the best free, well-distributed music magazine to come out reliably every month."

From 1982 to nearly the end of the decade, Seattle had a good college station as well: KCMU, the University of Washington station (which word on the street says has recently become yuppified beyond recognition). Before that year, KCMU had been primarily a Top 40–style training ground for university students. But a change in the power structure there opened it to more and more deejays with a bent toward local music. Some, like Kim Thayil, Mark Arm, and Bruce Fairweather, were in local bands (the first-named in Soundgarden, the second two in Green River). Others, like Bruce Pavitt, Charles Peterson, and Jonathan Poneman, were fans and friends, eager to play local music on their shifts, willing to focus their shows entirely on American independents.

"Yeah," says Nils Bernstein, "there's always been good radio, and good clubs, and good publications, but they've never really lasted. The laws were such that a good club didn't really exist for long. The police would be really harsh on punk rockers and underground shows and stuff. It was a surprisingly not great climate in the beginning to support a scene.

"And yet everyone lived together, everyone jammed together, everyone hung out and went to the same shows and had the same record collections. And there were so many good bands and good shows all the time to go see, and even the opening bands would be great. Feast would play and draw four hundred people, and they didn't have any records out or anything. No one really had any records out at that time except the Fastbacks."

*

That changed when Bruce Pavitt began Sub Pop. Pavitt grew up in Illinois, where he attended an alternative high school. After two years at Blackburn College in central Illinois, however, he decided he wanted to transfer to a looser environment, where classes had less than thirty people and the curriculum was less formalized. In his researches, he hit upon Evergreen State College in Olympia, Washington. Evergreen was doubly appealing because it was the only state-funded alternative school in the country, and thus the cheapest. "Even out of state it was, like, two thousand a year tuition," he recalls now, "so there were lots of out-of-state students, and that was good too."

The summer before he was going to transfer, Pavitt was shown an issue of John Foster's *Op* magazine. Pavitt recalls that KAOS, the Evergreen college station, gave U.S. independent label releases top priority "in a political as opposed to an aesthetic way. People wanted to play their Dead bootlegs on the airwaves and call that 'free format,' as opposed to having a policy supporting independent labels. Up till then, there were a lot of good regional punk publications like *Slash* and *Search and Destroy*, but no one was really championing the politics and economics of independent labels. So it [*Op*] really conceptualized what I was interested in at the time. And then I noticed at the bottom it was based in Olympia, and that was it," Pavitt says now. "It was like this really coincidental coming together of forces in my life."

Pavitt moved to Olympia in 1979 and began working both at KAOS and as an intern at *Op*. "Because *Op* was the only magazine in the world doing that at the time, every independent label in the U.S. sent stuff to review. So it was this amazing resource. I'd spend tons of time just riffling through the singles and cassettes in John's library, and Evergreen had a loose enough curriculum that I even got credit for it."

Another thing Pavitt got credit for—for a degree he says is in punk rock—was his fanzine, *Subterranean Pop*. It alternated between print and cassette, which he distributed to about five hundred people throughout the country, via various protodeveloping channels. The cassette version of Sub Pop was sort of his first foray into labeldom, and it was, Pavitt now recalls, "kind of a conscious exercise in marketing and 'networking.' I figured, if I could get a tape together featuring a lot of cool underground bands from cities outside of New York and L.A. where there was no media attention at all, then a handful of people in each city would buy it. And it worked! The first cassette sold two thousand, which was pretty good for that time."

The first cassette featured tracks ranging from artists like Jad Fair (Maryland) to Jason and the Scorchers (Nashville). (The latter-named band went almost immediately to sign to a major, A & M, where they were molded, hyped as roots rock, and instantly dropped.) Even at that time, Pavitt's main emphasis was regional scenes: "It was like sociology or something, just a passionate curiosity I had as to what makes one scene take off when another dies. See, I was from Chicago, where there were tons of great bands but nobody cared about 'em because they weren't from England. The UK has a sophisticated hype machine so that a band that's been together one week can instantly get more famous than the Wipers, who had been the best band in Oregon for years."

Pavitt continued living in Olympia and doing his fanzine and KAOS radio show for a couple of years after graduating in 1981. "Going to Olympia was a lot like becoming a Moonie," Pavitt recalls now. "My parents really lost me to punk rock for a while there."

Like the church of Mr. Moon, Evergreen has always been a haven for serious hippiedom. But that didn't bother Pavitt: "I listened to my share of the Dead, so that was OK. I mean, the Ramones totally changed my life, but that said, I could still relate to yurt people or whatever. I could always see that the real essence of the punk work was Dead Kennedys' putting stuff out themselves and the homegrown nature of *Search and Destroy* and people taking control of their own culture, and when I was going through my romantic idealistic hippie phase, what I was into was the self-sufficiency aspect of it, like growing your own food and using solar energy and stuff, so it was just a logical jump to apply that to music."

After four years of Olympia, Pavitt moved to Seattle, where he started doing a column once a month in the *Rocket* (called "Sub Pop U.S.A.") and a show by the same name on KCMU once a week as well. Both Sub Pops featured only U.S. indie releases. From 1983 to 1986 Pavitt worked tons of shitty jobs in all aspects of the industry. In 1985 he opened a record store called Bomb Shelter, which folded in six months; his next co-venture, Fallout Records, was more successful, because it stocked both records and skateboards.

"People laughed in my face when I suggested the idea," recalls Pavitt, "but I saw it as a synthesizing, a merging of trends, and it pretty much worked. The skateboard sales always went better than the record sales, though—they still do—and then I had a falling-out with the people who I started it with, and I cashed out. It was a super-depressing time for me, and then I got this job at Yesco Corporation, which was soon bought by Muzak—it was like the closest music industry job as you could get in Seattle!"

Pavitt's title was Tape Returns Coordinator, which meant that he did total gruntwork in the warehouse. Pretty soon he got jobs there for his friends in bands: Mark Arm, and Tad Doyle, and members of Swallow and the Walkabouts. "For us, it was a step up from food service: a way to scrub little pieces of plastic and get health insurance at the same time."

Pavitt wasn't too crazy about life at Muzak at the time, but in retrospect, he credits that job as helping to shape his future endeavor. "It ended up being another real think tank environment. It was all these local musicians plus me, and I'd listened to millions of hours of tapes and had some perspective on things. We'd sit around and drink coffee at break time and discuss music. It was a lot like school, because we *had* to be there. Through constant interaction, we developed some of our opinions and theories about music there. They just kept flowing out of us.

"We had this ghetto blaster there, and I remember that's where I first heard. 'Touch Me, I'm Sick.' Mark brought it in at break one day and I was, like, 'This is pretty good, Mark!' So much of that music—the early years that people mythologize now of Mudhoney and Tad and Nirvana—was all unveiled at coffee break at Muzak!

"I remember Jack Endino, who recorded a lot of bands' demos, brought Jon a tape of Nirvana, and Jon thought the guy in the band had a good voice, so I brought it into Muzak. And we were playing it at coffee break and Mark Arm goes, 'This band sucks!' "

That was later. In 1986, while still working at Muzak, Pavitt released *Sub Pop 100* with money borrowed from his father. It was a collection of bands from around the country (including Sonic Youth from New York, Steve Albini from Chicago, Savage Republic from Los Angeles, and the U-Men, the Wipers, and Green River more locally). The LP expanded on the original cassette idea of attracting listeners around the country, but Pavitt added yet another marketing concept to the release. This time, along with promo copies of *Sub Pop 100*, he included a free copy of a single by Green River, as a sort of preview of what he intended to be his next release. Pavitt used to do all the mailings out of Muzak's warehouse, and distributors who called up to order copies were often startled when the receptionist answered, "Muzak Corporation." "Really you could say Muzak was Sub Pop's first headquarters," he says now.

Pavitt's main ambition was having a label that would document his own scene, however—a goal that presupposes that there was scene to document. But by then there actually was, led by the bands Soundgarden, Green River, Bundle of Hiss, and Feast. Then Green River broke up and mutated into, on the one hand, Mother Love Bone (Stone Gossard and Jeff Ament, now of Pearl Jam) and on the other (Mark Arm and Steve Turner) Mudhoney, which also included Danny Blossom from Bundle of Hiss and Matt Lukin from the Melvins. The Melvins were always on the outskirts because they didn't live in Seattle, they just played there sometimes. (And in 1988 they moved to San Francisco.)

H Hour then moved to Seattle from Boise, Idaho, with Tad

Doyle on drums. Tad recorded a demo in his bedroom that everyone was all excited about and that turned into his first single. Then he formed a band with Kurt from Bundle of Hiss. And in 1987 Sub Pop released Green River's *Dry As a Bone* EP, this time including with promos a single by Soundgarden, the next band slated up. Then he went into partnership with Poneman and released Soundgarden's *Screaming Life* and *Fopp* EPs. Those releases, visually augmented by Charles Peterson's distinctive black-and-white in-motion photography style, combined with Mudhoney's *Touch Me, I'm Sick* and *Superfuzz Bigmuff* EP to create Seattle's much-vaunted grunge rock sound.

We know now that the type of music called grunge was developed elsewhere by Hüsker Dü and the Butthole Surfers. Seattle's special twist on the genre was an unusually laissez-faire attitude to all kinds of unhip musical sources, an attitude that sometimes gets translated as "suburban" but is in fact probably more due to Seattle's liberal hippie parentage. "It was always very nice and communal and let's-all-swap-records-and-be-into-music-together here," explains Nils. "It wasn't like we were bonding against all the fascists or rednecks in town. It seems like everywhere else punk and metal were such diametric opposites, and there were fights and stuff between metal heads and punk rockers. But in Seattle they kind of coexisted all peacefully. There were a lot of punk rockers and metal heads and hippies, and there were a lot of punk rock hippies and metal punk rockers. Everyone lived together, everyone jammed together, everyone hung out and went to the same shows and had the same record collections. And when one person bought the first Big Black record, everyone did."

Pavitt agrees. "There was a lot of early-seventies rock—like Sabbath—playing alongside a lot of great underground stuff: Scratch Acid, Soul Asylum, Pussy Galore, the great indie bands of the time. People didn't feel as much guilt for listening to records that weren't cool here—there was no *Maximum Rock 'n' Roll* articulating some perfect hardcore vision here, no stylistic dogma. It was all totally unself-conscious."

"Big Black, Scratch Acid, and Killdozer," agrees Nils.

"Those were the bands that got everyone turned on to having a lot heavier sound."

Another aspect of Sub Pop acts that is often left unmentioned is a certain—for lack of a better word—homoeroticism that permeated many of its early acts, a physical undercurrent of sexual tension that suffused the very being of early Sub Pop—associated bands like Soundgarden, the Fluid (from Denver), and the Afghan Whigs (from Cincinnati). Those three acts in particular feature singers whose stage personae go well beyond the usual limits of guy-on-guy empathy. They stare their audience right in the eye, accosting their psyches with a visible twinge of desire, their highly suggestive voices menacing and teasing, the slow, churning music building up to a sudden violent leap into the crowd, their hair mingling with other people's mouths, their hands and bellies on taut, sweaty flesh. Watching guys watch the Fluid's vocalist, John Robinson, or the Whigs' Greg Dulli, slack-jawed and tense, willing the singers to sweat on their very brows, is an enlightening experience: there's such an obvious difference between that and the sight of, say, your usual guitar god or hammy singer, or even a more traditional alternative guy singing love songs about girls or beer. The Sub Pop dude-fans don't want to *be* Robinson or Dulli: they want to be *with* him. Whether they admit it or not (and I think many of them might even cop to it if you asked them), these fans are turned on by them. In terms of actual sexual fulfillment, it is probably entirely innocent—just as, for most girls, watching David Cassidy or Neil Diamond (or Mick Jagger or Chris Cornell) is innocent of any real need for sexual liaison. But it is this highly compelling aspect of Sub Pop's sound and character that has popularized it beyond the equally musically excellent but more traditionally gender-oriented sound of, say, Minneapolis or Austin.

"I think that's true," comments Nils. "A lot of Sub Pop's original appeal was seeing guys respond to the sexiness of these other guys. It was guys being very sweaty and sensual and playing very sexy music. None of these people were gay or bi, but a lot of people around here are very tolerant and supportive of stuff like that.

"I don't know about other cities. I mean, in other cities do all the big dude rockers hug each other when they see each other? Do they kiss each other on the lips like they do here at parties? There's just a lot of physical closeness between guys here, and it's not sexual or anything, it's just generational. I don't necessarily think that stuff's confined to Seattle."

Perhaps not. But it was in Seattle where the new ethos got its most approval; where it bred. "You can't ever go to a city and say, 'There's nothing happening here,'" agrees Pavitt. "There's potential everywhere. It just comes down to having someone organize it, and, also, to the nuances of personal relationships. Just the right group of people inspiring each other.

"We had our share of bad luck, but I think one reason the whole thing worked was because we'd all worked together. We had war stories because we'd been buddies at Muzak and we each knew how horrible and terrible it was there. We had this infinite faith in each other's talents. There's three things a label should be able to give a band: financial support, intellectual support, and emotional support. Even if you have no money, at least you can discuss their ideas and their music, and sympathize with their problems. When a band's on tour and their van breaks down in Minnesota and they call you up all sad at two A.M., you go, 'Well, I can't send you any money, 'cause I don't have any, but gee, I really feel sorry for you!' Sometimes, early on, that kind of thing really carries people through."

Because of Sub Pop's chronic insolvency, some of its flagship bands, including Nirvana and Mudhoney, had phases of bitterness about their alliance with the label. But nothing succeeds like success, and now that Sub Pop's solvent again, no one feels the least bit bad at all. The label has yet to be allied to a major, and thus has managed to remain true to many of the independent ideals Pavitt theorized about back in Olympia.

"People think Nirvana saved our ass," he says now, "and that's true to a certain extent, but Jon and I had a pretty articulate business vision all along. Even at first, when we had no money at all, we put bands on stipends and got them to tour Europe. We just always thought people should be able to make a living at music. And Jon and I knew that if we could get Tad to Europe, they'd go crazy for him, because he embodies every European's image of the ugly American. Then we got in over our heads because we didn't have the computers or the expertise to juggle with so many commitments like that, but our motives were always cool: empowering the artists.

"I believe that business should reinvest in their own community. I really see our company as a small community bank or arts organization. My big criticism of the American business climate is that it really turned its back on the business community. As an independent record label, we just couldn't get a loan. And the whole reason the American economy went down the tubes in the eighties is because access to capital was so fucked up.

"I truly believe that if every small business in America could just get a reasonable loan, then the economy of the U.S. would be in much better shape. So I take a lot of pride in the fact that we give small loans to musicians—albeit in a conservative, responsible manner. Right now an amazing amount of musicians make a lot of money off our label, and that makes me feel really good. Because throughout the eighties when I was working at all these shitty jobs, I was really, really angry. I was, like, 'I have a college degree, and the guy next to me, he's incredibly talented, and he has a college degree too, and we're both chopping carrots! This is fucked! It pisses me off!' The doors were shut unless you wanted to work for a large organization."

One of the criticisms of the Seattle sound from the start has always been its apolitical stance. Bands like Mudhoney and the Fluid were never remotely issue-oriented, and in fact somehow seemed to embody the fuck-it-all nevermindhood of white surburban kids in the late eighties. Controversy continues to swirl around the Dwarves LP *Blood, Guts, and Pussy,* which portrays some serious sexist shit on the cover. But Pavitt and Poneman are anything but apolitical. Except for First Amendment rights (which they are especially vocal about, as the Dwarves LP proves), they confine most of their ideology to business rather than music.

"I guess I'm a democratic capitalist," says Pavitt. "I think it [politics] comes down to empowering people financially. That's where we borrowed a little from the majors. They'd say, 'Here's some money,' you have a right to make a living; but they rarely understand what makes music important. They never fail to strip it of its context and just look at haircuts or ties or something. My thinking is, the one thing that gives music its potency is its context. You have to look at the artists' community at large, where they're coming from, who they were speaking to in the first place. Look at San Francisco in the sixties: Haight Ashbury, Owlsley, Ginsberg. That's what made the Grateful Dead and the Jefferson Airplane more than just bands: that's what made them resonant and important. Or a better example is Dischord in D.C.: teenagers making records, and their whole antidrug philosophy, putting huge *X*s on their hands to mark their solidarity with people underage. The context is the whole story.

"We were always very conscious that people need to be liking something more than just the band—that to understand it, they need to understand the community it comes from. That's why our photos always, from the very start, showed the fans as well as the bands: so people could see the real intimacy between the two, so that they could feel, 'Yes! I could be a part of it!' In our world, the fans were celebrated as much as the bands.

"In the eighties there was so much selfishness and such a lack of community. History will confirm that the eighties were a selfish era. And so, especially at that time, people really needed to tap into a sense of community, and we wanted to show that there was one, somewhere out there, one they could tap into."

The rest of this tale I think you know. "They," says Bruce, meaning you-know-who, "were a total phenomenon in the

Northwest right from the start. When they played around here, it was like no other band had their magic. I mean, it was just three chords and three guys with shaggy hair, but I remember really early on Calvin going, 'They're like the *Beatles!*' All those people who'd never go to indie shows went to see them, like your girlfriend's brother's girlfriend's sister. You could see early on people who had absolutely no historical appreciation of indie rock at all being just moved by it."

The first time Bruce saw them himself was at the Central, on a Sunday night. The band, having driven the 110 miles from Aberdeen that afternoon, was the first of three bands playing that night, and there was literally no one in the audience except the sound man, Bruce, and Jon. "I remember they played 'Blew' and that was a good song, but their drummer had a mustache, and I was, like, 'I don't know if that will cut it, Jon,' because I'm kind of symbol-oriented, and that mustache . . . I was only half serious, though."

Bruce and Jon signed them anyway (despite the advice of Mark Arm, who had nixed their demo at coffee break at Muzak) and released the seven-inch single "Love Buzz" in late 1987. Nirvana then paid to record *Bleach* at Endino's studios, for a total of $606.17. After a lengthy delay, Sub Pop put it out in 1988 and sent the band to Europe, right on the cusp of England's obsession with all things Seattlan—which was engineered by Sub Pop itself, by flying a critic, Everett True, over to hype the scene, a circumstance that stems from Pavitt's aforementioned long-held resentment of and admiration for the British hype machine.

Still, by 1990, Nirvana, along with Sub Pop staples the Fluid and Mudhoney, were disturbed by Sub Pop's lack of funds and began talking to majors. (So too, did Sub Pop, which had numerous aborted negotiations with Columbia—now Sony—regarding a distribution deal around the same time.) The balloon would have gone up for Sub Pop once and for all if it hadn't been for one fortuitous night in 1990, directly after a Babes in Toyland show.

"Up till then we'd gone on handshake deals with all our

acts alone," Pavitt says. "And then one night I had this disco party with Babes in Toyland, and Krist came over at two A.M. all drunk, and he had this huge jug of wine in his hand, and he was demanding a contract. So I called up Jon and I was going, 'Look, Novoselic is over here all drunk and he's going to kill me. Get over here with something!'

"We actually had had a lawyer draw up some contracts at that time, but we had no money whatsoever, we were like bottom of the barrel, so they hadn't gotten around to sending them out to us. So Jon just sort of cut and pasted together a contract out of a 'write your own record contract' book, and they signed it, and it was a damn lucky break for us. I don't even want to think about what would have happened if it hadn't been for that night!"

Now it's two years later and we're back at the Sub Pop offices, and today's the day the Velocity Girl single "Creepy" just came out, and shipping reports are excellent. The album's due in a week, and Sub Pop's retail guy is waxing all enthusiastic. "This is the easiest day I ever had! It's all back-ordered, with no problems at all! This LP, I predict, will be up to six figures."

In his cubicle nearby, Nils is madly constructing guest lists for Sub Pop shows all over the country, faxing out amended memos to clubs from Florida to Maine. "Hey, Nils, there was a Led Zeppelin show in 1974 that I missed, can you get me on the list?" Kim yells over to him sarcastically, when it seems like he's going to lose his mind. "Set the wayback machine, please . . ."

Down in the warehouse, Sub Pop's grunt workers, Kevin, Ian, and Scott, are packing up Beat Happening and Sprinkler CDs in boxes in a room packed with stacks of Rein Sanction photos, Pond posters, Fastbacks advance cassettes, and Dwarves T-shirts. One entire wall of the warehouse is covered in weird mail, ranging from a crayoned picture of Mark Arm to a childishly handwritten request for back catalogs to ruled-paper pleas for Kurt Cobain's home address. It looks uncannily like the burlap-covered bulletin board of a grade school, but it's not all hearts and roses: there's one letter signed "Michelle" that claims Nirvana's sold out: "Let's just hope our own Sonic Youth don't do the same!" she sneers in purple felt tip.

I laughingly tell Kevin and company about Sonic Youth's dreadful new movie, *1991: The Year That Punk Broke*, which (fortunate for Sonic Youth) also features a lot of footage of Nirvana in Europe: ". . . and it sounds like it was all recorded through the camera mike, plus a lot of it is long shots, so it's exactly like being at the very back of a mud field watching them play Reading," I wind up disparagingly. My audience is silent. Longing looks flit across their teenaged faces. "But we'll never see them from *any* vantage point at Reading," says Kevin, wistfully.

Kevin and company have all seen Nirvana in situations the rest of us would covet: at the Central and the Off Ramp and the Seattle of the past, when boys all body-swam in slow motion on the top of the warm loving shoulders of the crowd; when Kurt and Krist would continually thrust themselves into it, flesh on flesh: when no one mean or cruel or stupid was allowed into that magic circle. Back when there was a sense of community. Oh, Nils? How 'bout setting the wayback machine and taking us back to 1988?

"Nineteen eighty-eight," sighs Pavitt, flicking aside *Vogue* and *Newsday*, "was a great year. *Touch Me, I'm Sick* came out, and so did *Love Buzz*. Ninety-two is a great year too: because sales equals money and money equals power, and there's no denying it's nice to have both. But '88 was really innocent and special. I miss it a lot, but I'm glad everybody here's got a computer on their desk too."

FIFTEEN

US UNTAMED

And then, and then, the devastatingly metaphorical part. Here he comes: this tiny little kid lugging a red Radio Flyer wagon and on it he's got a goldfish bowl with water in it and a goldfish—love in a goldfish bowl—and he's got this hand-lettered sign on a piece of cardboard attached to the wagon that identifies this goldfish as none other than BUBBLES THE INCREDIBLY BEAUTIFUL GOLDFISH—which makes me want to grin like an idiot and which breaks my heart too because—oh!—this kid wants to show the world his incredibly beautiful goldfish and if I've learned anything at all, I've learned that it's sometimes a risky thing to show the world the things you really, truly love, because pretty soon the world swoops down like a vulture to look at what you love, and to put a price on what you love, and to think of marketing schemes, and men in suits soon show up with fountain pens and contracts . . .

– Simon Dumenco, *Baltimore City Paper*, October 4, 1991

About a month and a half after Nirvana played TJ, the band was in Europe, opening for Sonic Youth and Nick Cave at a bunch of large festivals and anticipating the release of the now-completed *Nevermind* in September. Meanwhile, Fran and I were stumbling around State Street in a condition of total shock. It was the last night of the International Pop Underground Convention in Olympia, Washington, and we had accidentally come upon the saddest sight in the entire state of Washington. Just two blocks west of the Capitol Theater, between sets by L7 and Some Velvet Sidewalk, we ran into an enclave of drunken, bored teenagers cruising in their parents' cars.

There they were, in all their hot August Saturday-night glory, blasting Lynyrd Skynyrd from the windows of their trucks and yelling out their phone numbers to one another. It was a classic scene of the boringness of small-town summer life—with one tragic twist. Because even as they acted out the age-old rituals of wasted American youth, the newest, coolest youth rock revolution ever was occurring right around the corner.

The shame of it! Imagine being sixteen and listening to bad classic rock on your Blaupunkt when Fugazi is about to take the stage on the very next block. You may as well have grown up in Woodstock, New York, in 1969 and spent the entire weekend of the fateful concert there watching television, wishing it would stop raining—only Olympia's kids didn't even have the weather as an excuse. In years to come, those kids are going to have to face the fact that during the last week of August 1991, every single one of them could have seen Fugazi, Thee Headcoats, the Pastels, Beat Happening, the Melvins, the Fastbacks, and over forty other bands take part in the International Pop Underground Convention's five days of fun. They could have, as the convention's manifesto, prominently displayed on the walls and windows of O-Town everywhere, so eloquently put it, "hit the streets to the motorbike beat of the cranked and crush crash-pop." They could, as the IPU entreated them, have pulled on their slacks and Mexican army boots, gotten ready for some sonic pop pogo action, and taken part in a love rock revolution, all for the four- or five-dollar price of admission that each all-ages show cost.

They could have, but they didn't.

Oops.

Francesca and I, however, had planned our entire summer around the convention, ever since we received our invitation (thanks to the K label mailing list) back in April. We sent our thirty-five dollars and passport-sized photos for laminates that would admit us to every show early. And when we first arrived in Olympia on the afternoon of Wednesday, the twenty-first, and found ourselves tooling down Capitol Avenue at five o'clock in our rental car past an entire block of tattooed love boys and body-pierced hippy chicks, we instantly became two minds with but a single thought. "Paradise found!"

Or, as the cutest member of the Nation of Ulysses' posse, who tried to sell us their record after the band's blistering set of crush crash pop, put it: "Word."

Natives of Olympia, however, clearly fearful that some of the attendees (the New York natives in particular) might suddenly undergo weird *crises du coeur,* quit their jobs, and move to O-Town, and thus drive Olympia rents up from the going rate of seventy-five to ninety dollars or something, hastened to assure us out-of-town conventioneers that it wasn't usually like this in Olympia. "It's usually forty degrees and drizzling," they said anxiously—though not without a touch of smugness.

Yeah, right. And Washington State is filled with crazed woodsmen, environmental terrorists, brown recluse spiders, damp fog, and unstable volcanos—I've seen those "Californians, Go Home" T-shirts. Lies, all lies. During the convention, it was eighty degrees and incredibly sunny. Most days, you could see Mount Rainier, Mount St. Helens, and Mount Hood, all in the Cascade Range to the east; to the west, the craggy Olympic Mountains; and to the north, beautiful Puget Sound.

"Make Love Rock, Not War" was the motto of the IPU Convention. The phrase appeared, bat signal-like, on the side of the City of Olympia Performing Arts Center every night. But the International Pop Underground Convention wasn't merely about cutesy-pie hearts and flowers, acoustic duets, and twenty-five-cent candy. Organized by the leader of Beat Happening and the K label, Calvin Johnson, and his partner, Candice Pedersen, the convention was a brief recapitulation of Olympia's punk rock history, compressed and encapsulated in

120 hours, and open to the public. It encompassed all the alley shows and all-night disco parties, Stella Mars's Girl City studio fashion show and cakewalks, and all the nights when Bruce Pavitt and Gary May showed filmstrips in their laundry rooms and girls and boys invented acoustic punk songs (like Lois Maffeo's now-legendary song "Bikini Kill") at salons in the Angeles and the Martin Arms. It was a serious public séance, beseeching the spirit of the Tropicana, Calvin's eleven-month-long period of punk rock dream come true, to preside over a party in its retrospective honor. Only this time the rest of us non-Olympians were invited along for the ride.

The main attraction of course was twelve shows in five days at three different venues. Most shows featured four bands and were held either at the two-hundred-person capacity North Shore Surf Club, for afternoon gigs from five to nine, or the six-hundredish-seat Capitol Theater, where the concerts began at nine. There was one gig held on Friday morning at ten A.M., which featured Bratmobile and Jad Fair, and one Saturday afternoon concert sponsored by the city of Olympia at Capitol Lake Park. There was one night—"girly night"—devoted entirely to women artists, a well-meaning gesture that ended up seeming needless when one considered that almost 90 percent of all the acts performing contained at least one woman. There was a spoken-word reading at the Smithfield Café, a Sub Pop-sponsored barbeque at Evergreen State College, a five-film *Planet of the Apes* festival, and a cakewalk (featuring cakes judged in categories such as Most Playfully Bewitching Cake, the Heftiest Cake, the Least Cakey Cake, and the Cake with the Most Boyfriends). The first winner was Bruce Pavitt, whose record company, Sub Pop, was at that time nearing Chapter Eleven, making him the unwitting butt of most convention jokes: when he won a confection-covered rock (the Cake Most Likely to Cause Sharp and Prolonged Discomfort) someone yelled, "Why don't you sell it?"

Additionally, the convention included a Pet Parade featuring 855 children and their pets, over half of whom were dressed as that year's big kid trend, dalmatians. The Pet Parade is an

Olympian tradition, but Calvin intentionally timed the convention to coincide with its occurrence.

The result of all these activities was that, if you had wanted to, you could have spent all five days in the four-block area that bounded the two nightclubs, the K offices, Sylvester Park, and Calvin's apartment building, and never once have gotten bored. You can't say that about five days at the New Music Seminar—or even five days in Tahiti. Whether we were walking around Capitol Lake between afternoon sets by Olive Lawn and Courtney Love (the band featuring Lois Maffeo, not the person married to Kurt), sitting in our hotel room watching "Ladies and Gentlemen, the Fabulous Stains" on cable, or rocking out to the Mummies, Fran and I felt, the entire time, this ridiculously heart-felt sensation of having found our proper place. For me and Fran, the convention was the culmination of our ten years as part of the American underground community. I remember Shelli Novoselic (whose husband, Krist, was in Europe at the time) throwing her arm round my shoulder during Beat Happening's version of "Redhead Walking," and the two of us leaning over the balcony together, bellowing the lyrics down into the pit. We were like a couple of boozing high school girls singing Free's "All Right Now" at a football game: an all-American activity neither of us experienced with any degree of comfort back when we had the chance.

Four hundred and fifty people bought laminates to the IPU Convention. In a town the size of Olympia, that meant that the vegetarian falafel place ran out of ingredients the first day, and the bars ran out of microbrewery beer before the weekend. There were times—generally at breakfast at the silly old Spar Bar when, to Olympia's dismay, the counter became packed—when the entire situation seemed like a cross between your high school cafeteria and CBGB's, in the sense that although, as was the case in high school, you knew everybody present, you also knew (unlike in high school) that they were all totally cool. One morning during the convention, my friend Debbie Shane recalled walking up to her motel room just as another guest, beloved indie-rock guy Jad Fair, had stepped on to his balcony to stretch. "The entire parking lot just spontaneously started clapping for him," she recalls.

The way the convention had been organized eliminated most of the attendant problems of big conventions or concert festivals I'd been to. It wasn't anything like the New Music Seminar, South by Southwest, or even Lollapalooza. First of all, its selective obscurity managed to bring together just the right mix of people—mostly from Portland, Seattle, San Francisco, and, for some reason, New York. The Pastels flew in from Scotland, Kreviss and Mecca Normal came from Canada, and Thee Headcoats are from England, making it truly international. Originally, Johnson and Pedersen had not intended for the thirty-five-dollar full-festival laminated passes to be sold at the festival itself, only preordered by mail. "But when these two girls showed up Wednesday afternoon straight from New Zealand," Pedersen said, "we made an exception."

Calvin is still pretty disingenuous on the political aspects of the IPU Convention: he likes to claim that he held it just for his own amusement. When pressed, he admits that the time was right for such an event. "I liked the idea of giving people who were doing similar music a chance to spend some time together. I mean, usually you see a cool band in a city and maybe hang out for a couple of hours after the show and that's all. Also, there's a lot of fans and people who write letters to each other and never get to meet."

Later, my friend Ira Robbins, who long ago began *Trouser Press* magazine and who was covering the convention for *Rolling Stone*, commented that the convention was also proof that interest among alternative/indie music extends beyond the college radio ranks. "Not to get too sociological about it, but clearly there is an audience out there for the underground that isn't college radio-oriented," he said. "It's more radical than that. They simply aren't satisfied with what passes for alternative on the radio these days. To them, Beat Happening and Fugazi are as commercial as they're willing to go. These are people who are no more interested in Big Dipper than they are in C & C Music Factory.

"That they exist is pretty great," he added. "What was incredible was how Calvin created an uncompetitive atmosphere for them to perform in, [one] that dismantled all the traditional precepts of rock 'n' roll, where people are competing with each other. K's atmosphere was without any critical stupidity."

That audience didn't lack critical acumen, however. I heard every possible opinion ranging from great to horrid about the events of Tuesday, August 20 (Grrrly Night). But there was also a lack of attitude, a kind of broadmindedness that's extremely rare in fanzine-indie circles. People were positively tolerant. It was eerie. Some of the bands whose merits and demerits were hotly debated by festival-goers included Mecca Normal, Girl Trouble, and the Melvins, who played Saturday afternoon at Capitol Lake Park, thus scaring off the entire native population of Olympia, who might have been sincerely charmed by other acts. The latter band's sludgy set, however, was enlivened by the sight of their parents and grandparents, who'd driven into town from the coastal town of Aberdeen, where they and Nirvana hail from, all dressed in Melvins T-shirts, serenely rocking out.

Judging purely on T-shirts, the Melvins and Nirvana get the Most Beloved Band award for Olympia proper, even though the former has relocated to San Francisco and the latter had just signed to Geffen, thus rendering them, to their own chagrin, officially "too large" to play the convention. (L7, who had recently signed to Slash, was the only major-label band at the convention; another band, Solomon Grundy, is a side project of major-label contract holder Van Conner of the Screaming Trees.) The backs of Nirvana's new Geffen-made T-shirts read, "Flower-sniffin' kitty-pettin' baby-kissin' corporate rock whores" (a play on their *Bleach* T-shirts, which read, "Crack-smokin' satan-worshipin' fudge-packin' motherfucks"), but that didn't stop Nirvana from contributing an unreleased track to the local label Kill Rock Stars' compilation LF, on sale at the K store. And in fact, Olympia citizen Kurt Cobain was going to play at K as a duo with his girlfriend, till his management *insisted* that Nirvana play the Reading Festival in England instead.

Other bands that won unanimous approval at the convention were San Jose's cornier than corny, bandage-wrapped Mummies, who played covers of songs by Devo and Dave Clark, Olympia's own grrrl-style revolutionaries Bikini Kill, Pop Llama's eternally punky Fastbacks (whose fans got the award for best moshers and stage divers) and a rap group called High Performance, who drew the unenviable task of going on just before Fugazi and, dauntless, succeeded.

Even musicians were infected with the general mood of acceptance and approval. Fugazi's Guy Picciotto announced he was undergoing some kind of psychological disease: "Like, I'll be watching Jad Fair and I'll be thinking, 'There's no *way* I'm ever plugging into an amplifier again.' And then I'll be watching the Mummies and I'll be thinking, 'There's just no *way* I'm ever stepping onstage unless it's in a mummy suit.' And then I'll be watching Bratmobile thinking, 'There's no way unless I undergo some kind of gender transformation. . . .' "

There was the great and powerful Beat Happening, who were most humbly scheduled to perform second on Thursday night, just after a one-time/one-song-only reunion of John Foster's Pop Philosophers. For the rest of the week after their set, you could see at any time thirty or forty fans on the lawn at Sylvester Park practicing their Calvin-sthenics—especially a new move whereby Calvin rocks over onto his stomach by way of his ankles and knees. We who tried it later found it a bit painful, but he pulled it off with ease.

Numerous fanzine and alternative types declared themselves most eager to see the two foreign bands, the Pastels and Thee Headcoats. But the apex of the entire week was the transcendent set by D.C.'s Fugazi. Even though the band members had been hanging out K-ing all week—on Friday night, in fact, Ian MacKaye worked taking tickets at the door of the Capitol for six hours—their advent late Saturday night was still enshrouded with intense excitement, a kind of starlike atmosphere that was foreign to the rest of the festival. A hush fell over the entire arena before they took the stage, but when they did, nothing could have topped them. The band's warmth and strength were totally transforming, playing as they did off an audience vibe that, after five days of festivities, had coalesced into pure perfection. Ian: "This is a song called 'Suggestion,' and if anyone feels like they should be the one who should sing it, please feel free." Immediately, a woman from the audience leaps onstage and sings: *"Is my body the only trait, in the eyes of men?"* By the end of the song, the entire female portion of the convention was virtually seething the chorus, *"She did nothing to deserve it,"* over and over and over again, while the band turned into a kind of musical volcano, pouring hot licks like lava onto our souls. By the time the band got to "Reprovisional," the auditorium felt as if it had lifted off the planet and been beamed to some far better place—a place where K rules, of course.

Months later, I met a guy from Portland—Sean Croghan, the singer for Crackerbash—who told me he'd gone to Olympia only to see Fugazi, but was so impressed at the sight of Ian taking tickets at the door the night before that he volunteered to do security for Fugazi's gig, didn't even see their show, and still went home totally thrilled. Another guy I met just a few weeks later, Pearl Jam's Eddie Vedder, said that particular show made him want to quit his band and start a new record label. In March I was in the basement of a castle in the heart of East Berlin when I ran into a German woman named Anna who'd K'd alongside me all that week. And while driving across the bleak Dutch countryside in a rented Volvo six months hence, Rebecca Gates, from the Spinanes, confided to me that only after the convention did she have the courage to call herself a musician.

Of course, the convention wasn't entirely perfect. Some of the younger people I met later, especially ones in bands, complained that Olympia citizens were cliquish and unwelcoming to outsiders, and that was probably true: Fran and I didn't meet a lot of natives there, but we were perfectly happy just to stand around observing all the riot grrrls and motorcycle boys living out the new future. Then, poor little Jarvis, the Capitol Theater house cat, who spent much of his time purring on people's laps—well, OK, my lap—during loud punk rock sets, wound up in disgrace after being caught peeing on a box of medium-size Beat Happening T-shirts. More importantly, the sound at the North Shore Surf Club shows was invariably terrible, with "Can we have some more guitars in the monitors?" eventually overtaking "We'd like to thank Calvin and Candice" as the most-uttered phrase. Thee Headcoats solved the sound problem by plugging into the amps, not the p.a., which made them sound as if they were in mono (obviously intentionally), but their set was marred by their drunken jibes at the straightedge nature of the gig (which, I found out later, had more to do with the Olympia police department's intense strictness about liquor laws than with Calvin's own personal beliefs). This was especially irritating, since playing at an all-ages show clearly hadn't stopped Thee Headcoats from getting tanked.

The convention was a monument to the blissed-out love rock atmosphere that Calvin has created within the confines of his town—once again, the do-it-yourself attitude taken to its logical utopian extreme. In the end, what separated the IPU Convention from the real world of alternative rock and the music industry as a whole wasn't just Candice and Calvin's ideals, music, and lifestyle, but their adeptness at converting the best things about their scene—its insularity and geniality, its breathtakingly unforced acceptance of all types of music and people, and its occasional flashes of musical genius—into a public show-and-tell for their friends. Faults and all, the International Pop Underground Convention simply couldn't, to my mind, have been improved upon. At the moment, there are no plans for a second one.

After the convention, everything was different. It was like falling in love, or seeing the Sex Pistols concert, all over again: I couldn't regard anything in quite the same light ever again. It was as if I'd been climbing an icy mountain and had almost reached the top when suddenly I looked backward and saw, way down in the valley below, the world I'd left behind. In the crevasse they were dancing and singing the best, the only, music that mattered: in that valley was a joyous mosh pit, and I was barred forever from its confines unless I chose to slide all the way down the mountain on my stomach, giving up my ground, forgoing forever the top of the fucking heap.

So that's exactly what I did. I didn't have a moment's hesitation. I pulled up my T-shirt and let fly, toboggan-style, all the way to the bottom of the hill. The K Festival may have had no quarter outside its own ridiculously tiny sphere, and the negative backlash among those who didn't attend (and even some who did) was tremendous. But it was like the French Revolution or something: just the fact that it had happened at all somehow affected everything around it. Three weeks after it was over, Geffen released *Nevermind,* and from the moment it hit the stores it behaved in the manner that all the albums before it—from the Circle Jerks' *Group Sex* through Jane's Addiction's *Ritual De Lo Habitual*—didn't. Unlike *Pleased to Meet Me* and *Goo,* it flew off the shelves like it was possessed of the devil. The jewel cases were so determined to walk away from the stores that contained them, popping into people's pockets all of their own accord.

All the people on the bandwagon bought the record as a matter of course. Those people account for only a small portion of the vast quantities of *Nevermind* that got carried out into the streets—removed by way of the shopping bags of metal kids and college freshmen, people who seemingly sniffed out its sincerity without so much as hearing a word. "Smells Like Teen Spirit" wasn't even a rumor on radio yet; the video wasn't pushed on MTV until well into October (after which album sales started going right through the roof). But in the first three weeks of release, *Nevermind* sold 200,000 copies—more than two years' worth of total sales for Sonic Youth's *Goo.*

Meanwhile, Nirvana was touring midsize halls, first in Europe—they did Reading (playing early in the day's bill) during the K Festival—and then in America. My friend Wendy and I drove down to Mexico to see them headline Iguana's in Tijuana: it was the first time I ever saw boys jump headlong onto the dance floor from the third-floor balcony, like lemmings or Icarus, maddened by the sound of art. In late October, Nirvana reached San Francisco's Warfield Theater, supported by L7 and Sister Double Happiness, and the pandemonium level was similarly awesome. It was the night after the death of San Francisco's premiere promoter, Bill Graham, in a freak helicopter accident, and I remember all the Bill Graham Presents employees were crying in the aisles. From the opening chords of "Rape Me," a new song Kurt was opening sets with, the audience was roiling: shook by the pleasure so lightly called physical, by the innate recognition that they'd come upon their own kind.

After the show, I went backstage to say hi. The band was all jazzed because they'd been given huge white terry-cloth bathrobes, with their names—Dave, Krist, and Kurt—stitched over the breast pockets. The robes were some of the last posthumous gifts of Bill Graham himself. Nirvana was just on its way back to Los Angeles (to do a prochoice benefit for the Fund for the Feminist Majority, their second that year), and John was assuring Kurt that if he would only be good and not dawdle in the morning, they'd all get back to Los Angeles early enough to take a quick side trip up the Grapevine, to see Christo's golden umbrella project. (Kurt, however, did dawdle—and it didn't matter, because the umbrellas were tragically shut the next day in the aftermath of a freak wind that resulted in art death.)

Presently, Kurt and I held a desultory conversation, in which I gushed about the K Festival and he gushed about Reading. ("And we met Sonic Youth and they were *so cool* to us!") Next morning, my phone machine was positively flooded with phone calls from acquaintances: "I saw you talking to Kurt Cobain." They'd say the name in hushed tones—*Kurt*

Cobain—like that. It occurred to me that there was suddenly some kind of aura of celebrity around Kurt that surpassed anyone else from my scene.

In November "Teen Spirit" was MTV's number-one video, and *Nevermind* was absolutely charging up the charts. On the eighteenth of that month—the same day MTV banned Michael Jackson's "Black or White" video—Nirvana was already at number seven on the album charts. Ahead of them was a phalanx of records by impossibly famous superstars and super-respected cult heroes: Michael Jackson, Garth Brooks, U2, Metallica, Ice Cube, and both LPs by Guns N' Roses. In December Nirvana rose to number four, passing the three metal LPs and one alternative artist, but the other three LPs, which represented the three other obsessions of mainstream America (country, rap, and pop) were clearly invincible.

At Christmastime, every kid on earth went to the record store with his Chanukah or Christmas bucks, and there was only one record anyone wanted, and that was *Nevermind*. That month, Nirvana did some precontracted dates at large arenas, opening for the Red Hot Chili Peppers, whose October release *Blood Sugar Sex Magik* was at that time (pre "Under the Bridge") doing disappointing sells, selling one copy for every four by their opening act. At the first concert, in Los Angeles, Nirvana got onstage and ripped immediately into "Baba O'Reilly." (Kurt: "I'm, like, 'Krist, I feel like we're in *The Who*,' and he says, 'Hey, let's play "Teenage Wasteland!" ' We didn't know how to play it, but the chords to 'Louie Louie' worked out.")

On New Year's Eve the band played the Cow Palace in San Francisco, sandwiched between comers Pearl Jam and the Red Hot Chili Peppers. That show is, I fear, almost indescribable. From the moment it began—with Eddie Vedder of Pearl Jam singing the middle section of Fugazi's "Suggestion" a cappella—it was a madhouse. By the time Nirvana took the stage, members of the mosh pit, which stretched from the stage to the back of the arena, were being thrown up in the air like tufts of dirt out of a live minefield. The crowd kept rising up and rolling forward on a relentless wave of motion, folding over onto the photo pit, meeting up with itself midair. Even members of each band's own entourage were losing their composure in the glory of the moment. Some crazed bystander was flailing around so badly he kept hitting my sister in the face with his moppy head of long hair, and she's swiping at him going, "Get off me! get off me!" and I'm, like, going, "But Viv! That's Keanu Reeves you're trying to hush!"

The Nirvana guys all hopped in a cab immediately afterward in order to see their friends the Melvins play the Kennel Club. I stuck around for the Chili Peppers' set, which was made worthwhile when Eddie stage-dove into the crowd during "Yertle that Turtle." Then it was over and I was shivering in the ice cold night. Eddie had just given me a bunch of Pearl Jam stickers that said things like "Why go home?" and I was sifting through them as I walked along an endless row of motionless cars in the traffic-jammed parking lot, trying to reach my own. Some kids in a Jeep looked down at me and started begging. "Can we have one, can we have one?"

"Only if you can prove you love Pearl Jam as much as I do."

"We do, we do! We just drove two hundred miles here to see them!"

"Well, sing a song!"

There was a pause and then, I swear to God, the whole Jeep full of kids simultaneously busts into the same strange line: "*Gnashed his teeth and bit the recess lady's breast . . .*"

I gave 'em the whole handful.

There are two schools of thought about the rampant success of *Nevermind*. One school argues simply that it succeeded because it was a great record, great enough to break through the crusted and rigid structure of an industry that had been impenetrable to countless other great records for years. The other school agrees, but believes as well that the record fell by good luck into a right time-right place scenario ten years in the making: a sort of secret hole scratched painstakingly through the aforementioned wall of conformity, eked into being while no one was looking by prisoners of the underground with the pinlike persistence of the Birdman of Alcatraz.

Nevermind succeeded because the music on it spoke, finally, in a language that millions of people oblivious to most nuances understood at last. The record said such important things, whispering them intimately from guts to ears, seizing kids' imaginations, and their crises, and of course their hearts and minds. *Let It Be* was a great album, *The Good Son* a more menacing one, *Our Beloved Revolutionary Sweetheart* more accomplished, *Out of Step* more exciting, *Green* more beautiful, and *Ten* much more universally popular. But *Nevermind* captured the actual time. It imprisoned ten years of zeitgeist on a solitary slice of vinyl; it sloughed off age-old skin and invented something entirely new.

Nirvana's music is just endlessly inventive, entirely in touch with so many aspects of punk and beyond, from the brittle quickness of hardcore, to the slow thudding bass of metal, from Beatles-y melodies to Replacements-y gut singing, all poignant and shit, to the R.E.M.-like poetic obfuscation of the words. There's absolutely nothing simple about the rhythms of "Aneurysm." "Hairspray Queen" shifts between noisefest to baying nonsense without ever losing the thread of melody. "Been a Son" somehow manages to describe the systematic belittlement of women in Western society without ever even mentioning anything about the topic beyond the chorus.

Those songs are just Nirvana outtakes, each one a showcase of only one of the band's strengths. Sometimes it's the band that roars to the fore: the bass falling up and down the scale, the guitar screeching, both thudding away together on top of Dave Grohl's drumming, which manages to be simultaneously supple and yet sound like he's holding his sticks with his fists. More often than not, what catches at your psyche is the sound of Kurt's voice, a perfect-pitched tenor with a strangely breaking, husky twist to it.

Lastly there are his lyrics, fragmentary, evocative, deep. "*A mulatto, an albino, a mosquito, my libido . . .*" may look like inarticulate gibberish in print, but that song's lovers know exactly what he means even if they could never say so: a mulatto *puny outcast* an albino *freaks like me* a mosquito *carrying diseased thoughts throughout my system* my libido *makes up my mind for me.* Kurt's just named the enemy, and having named it, turned and faced his fear. Who am I? I am no man. Isn't that a quote from the Koran? And "Teen Spirit" is just as true. Have you never felt like that? Hoarse, sweaty, desperate, helpless—and then having felt it, felt just like Kurt . . . *a denial a denial a denial!*

In that chorus, at that peak moment of truth, millions of kids heard the words of power. Until now, the chorus says, you have been nothing. Now you need never be nothing again. *Kids don't follow?* How 'bout kids don't crow? Between the end of the IPU Convention and the beginning of Nirvana's success, some strange wind began to blow through the big bad brains of the country at large. It was as if the band had one huge cloak on, and as they swiftly turned their backs on loserdom forever, it was sweeping back the waves of doubt that lurk unceasingly within the cautious breasts of the mainstream. Knocking out all phony contenders. Causing a stiff breeze to whistle up the corridors of fame. Casting a black shadow over corporate America. *Whoosh.*

SIXTEEN

COMES BEFORE SWINE

Ninety percent of underground bands are as shitty as major-label ones, but if there was only one set of ovens, I know which set I'd eradicate from the face of the planet.

– Steve Albini

No less glamorous locale on the face of the planet Earth exists than that of the Los Angeles Airport Marriott Hotel. Even confirmed Americana lovers would shun its beige contours for more picturesque pieces of shit: gang-torn South Central, say, or the Mojave Desert, or a tacky miniature golf course well outside Bakersfield, or downtown Tijuana. But Century Boulevard at Airport? Wim Wenders could do nothing with it. Tom Wolfe would drop his pen.

The day I was there was the right time, right place. For what it was, anyway: the site of the Concrete Foundation Forum's New Metal Seminar. Like the LAX Marriott, there's something so basic about metal machine music. That's what I was thinking as I headed into its cement confines, about two minutes after deplaning off runway 12, and greeted by the sound of some hard-working heavy metal band—either Atunga, or Flesh, or Electric Mayhem, or Impetigo, I never found out which. They were busy filling the air with thick slabs of white noise. The Marriott was using the loading dock for band showcases all day long, which was appropriate—though even from that distance the internal damage could be considerable. At one point I stepped into one of the ballrooms just as several acoustic tiles fell out of the ceiling in a puff of gray dust. Plonk.

Just as I went through the doors of the hotel my arm was seized by a harried-looking Julie. "I've lost Lemmy Kilmister!" she wailed, looking this way and that at a lobby packed with hoary-looking Lemmy clones. "Now, if you were Lemmy Kilmister, where would you be?"

I gave her a withering look and we turned smartly on our heels, bee-lining it for the bar, where we were immediately confronted with this Lemster, snug inside his lair. He was surrounded by well-wishers, but deigned to give me a friendly little wink over the contents of his glass. "Whoa!" thought I. "Guess I can go home now!"

Unfortunately, the conference had barely begun, and my presence was necessary in order to chronicle the uncharted depths to which a struggling new band called Pearl Jam was willing to plummet in order to help their just-released LP *Ten* go gold. Pearl Jam is not really a metal band such as the world knows it. They don't wear spandex and tennies or have big foofy hair or sing songs about the joy of bad sex and hard drugs. They don't play music with a lot of high diddle-diddle guitar solos, but from Epic Records' point of view, marketing them as a new metal band made more sense that slotting them into the more limited college radio alternative music world or even attempting to forge them a place in the tight AOR world, where the very few slots for new records are always sewn up by older comeback artists such as the Allman Brothers, Procol Harum, Eric Clapton, or the Stones.

In the wake of Nirvana's success—or, rather, in its shadow, as it were: the wave was still swelling when these events took place—the metal world had suddenly become the only viable place to market alternative bands to the mainstream. Many of the panels and a lot of the award ceremonies were consumed by the question, Why doesn't the public take heavy metal more seriously?—especially this year, when four of the top ten LPs in the country that week—Guns N' Roses I and II, Queensryche, and Metallica—were metal. But the answer was self-evident from the entire proceedings: People don't take metal seriously because it's not serious.

There is an up side to both the Concrete Convention and the metal world in general, and it is this: youth culture. "I originally went in [to the convention] with a lot of apprehension," said Ron Coleman of SST Records. "But I found that the heavy-metal world is currently embracing a far wider range of music than, say, the alternative or commercial radio world. It's a lot more accommodating to our more radical acts. And the people seem a lot more genuine."

That didn't stop Coleman from giving me a black T-shirt with the slogan "Don't Suck Corporate Cock" emblazoned on the front. Despite the evidence of the rock logo panty booth—the one attended by the girl clad only in AC/DC panties ("Go ahead, ask her how much she's being paid hourly to degrade us all," fumed Julie)—Coleman is right. Metal music is the final frontier, the only popular and successful area of rock music left where the fans are genuinely involved in the making of its stars.

Thus, in the nineties the metal world brought success to bands like Jane's Addiction, Public Enemy, and NWA. Its aegis happily included bands as divergent as the Red Hot Chili Peppers and Body Count, Living Colour and Coleman's own Skinyard. And its embrace is much warmer than the one greeting bands in the snootier echelons of pop. In the metal world, as in the rap world, new bands are sought out and valued by fans. Debut albums have a tendency to go gold. It is an oddly unpretentious place: like war and babies, it still enjoys itself, unself-consciously, and for no good reason. There were no TVs heaved out of windows, but I did keep seeing wet pot-bellied long-haired metal types, leaping into the pool from their balconies, and fire alarms were kept going every hour on the hour all night long.

I tried to take the pranks in the spirit in which they were meant during my three-day incarceration at the Marriott: not so much inconsiderateness as a hallowed heavy-metal tradition of hotel behavior. Certainly the spirit of Led Zeppelin's legendary hotel mayhem was invoked—a fact that seemed doubly poignant when I stepped into an elevator one day alongside Jason Bonham, son of John "Bonzo" Bonham and the leader of the band Bonham. As we rode downward together silently, I couldn't help thinking Snoopy-like, "Here I am riding in an elevator with a man whose father is revered for suffocating in his own vomit and who allegedly once made a woman fuck a live shark. What's more," I added to myself before we hit bottom, "I am now riding in an elevator with a man who *knows* I know his father is revered for suffocating in his own vomit and who once allegedly made a woman fuck a live shark."

Yes, the elevators were a constant source of interest to any reporter with his or her ears open. One time I was waiting with a bunch of people to get in an elevator. But when the doors finally opened, a bimbo in spandex came out and haughtily blocked anyone from getting in. Behind her all-too-buxom frame we caught a glimpse of a sullen Paul Stanley (formerly of Kiss), now makeupless, old, and hair-extended, huddling in the corner.

On another ride, I overheard two metal band members looking through the contents of their freebie bags. One said to the other, "Hey, I bet I can get some cash for these CDs over at Arons." "I don't need to do that," replied the other, with a touch of smugness in his voice. "*My* wife has a *job*."

The panels at the conference weren't half as edifying. Take the sound-plagued press panel. Moderator: "Heavy metal is the bratty child of rock 'n' roll, which has long been shunted aside by the media as not worthy of coverage. Lauren Spencer of *Spin* magazine, do you think this is changing, and if so, why?"

Spencer (after long attempting to speak between an ear-splitting buzz in the monitor): "Yes."

Moderator: "Kim Thayil of Soundgarden, what do you think?"

Thayil (also after long attempting to speak between an ear-splitting buzz in the monitor): "Uh, what was the question?"

The longest period of unrelenting silliness was probably during Thursday evening's Concrete Foundation Awards Ceremony, a two-hundred-dollars-a-seat fundraiser for the T. J. Martell Foundation, a music-run charity that raises money for AIDS, leukemia, and other cancer research. The entire thing was a laugh riot: almost every video that could break broke, while presenters such as Penelope Spheeris, Rich Rubin, the actor Anthony Michael Hall, and the guy who plays the Terminator II read stilted, nonsensical speeches, each with seemingly less aplomb than the last. Only our pal Lemmy came off well, reading his monologue for Best Thrash Band complete with cockney asides. " 'Thrash is the dark side of metal,' " read Lemmy. "Well, that's a contradiction in terms, wot? 'It is pure angst.' What a load of rubbish, eh?" And so on.

Tension wasn't exactly mounting, since most of the night's big winners—Jane's Addiction, Queensryche, and Slayer—were absent from the proceedings, so a veil of boredom rent with occasional gusts of giggle (generally beginning in my vicinity) enveloped the audience. By the end of the night, the series of technical and organizational disasters had become so severe that I actually started to pity emcee Riki Rachtman (the second most obnoxious MTV deejay ever). I think it was when he announced presenters Dweezil Zappa and George Lynch, and they didn't appear, so Riki had to read each guy's dialogue off the teleprompter, prefacing each remark with a comment like, "then George says," and "to which Dweezil replies," and so on.

Reporters in a nearby press room were attempting to watch the proceedings on a closed-circuit television set. When I dropped by for a sound bite, the television was broken, and everyone in there was jeering at the screen. Periodically, a Concrete rep would lead someone in—Ronnie James Dio, say, or Ozzy Osbourne—and the photographers would leap on their chairs to take pictures while yelling, "Ozzy, baby! Over here, over here!"

The reporters were allowed to ask questions as well, but nobody had any to ask. I could only think of rude things, about face-lifts (Ozzy), hair extensions (Kiss) or the lack thereof (Dio), and I managed to refrain.

On the final evening of the convention there was a

star-studded gala concert, open to the public, at the six-thousand-seat Palladium Theater in Hollywood. It was headlined by Spinal Tap. During the opening act, Seattle's Soundgarden, San Diego native surfer and number-one Soundgarden fan Eddie Vedder and his three younger brothers swarmed the mosh pit, leaping repeatedly onstage and throwing themselves off again, till their wild and abandoned stage-diving caught the attention of the guards. Eddie was dragged out of the arena by the scruff of his neck and ejected unceremoniously into the parking lot.

A few minutes later, Eddie took to the stage again, this time from the top, as co-lead singer for the next band up, a temporary outfit called Temple of the Dog. "And," he recollects smugly, "the first thing I did was, I gathered all the spittle together in my mouth before I started singing and then accidentally on purpose let it gob all over the head of the very guard who had just tossed me out of the arena!"

Like most success stories, the rise of Eddie Vedder is a bit complex. To begin with, the band Eddie was singing with that night, Temple of the Dog, is a temporary combo, formed by members of Soundgarden and Mother Love Bone in a tribute to Love Bone's late lead singer Andrew Wood, who died of a heroin o.d. on the eve of the release of MLB's debut LP, *Apple*, in March 1989.

Mother Love Bone was a band made up of one half of Green River. The other half formed Mudhoney. But after Wood's death, Love Bone's core members, Jeff Ament, Stone Gossard, and Mike McCready, had to find a new singer or disband. So they put the word out, along with a tape of some instrumental music. Eventually, the tape made its way, hand to hand, to Vedder via Jack Irons, a former Red Hot Chili Pepper now in the band Eleven. (And there's a quiz in fifteen minutes.)

When he received the tape, Vedder was working nights as a glorified night watchman at a gas station in San Diego. He'd work the midnight shift ("It gave me time to read and write"), get off at eight A.M., go surfing near Encinitas, go home, and then play his music while his roommates were out of the house. Eddie had his own band, Bad Radio, and helped his girlfriend run shows at a club called Winter's, for which he made the flyers.

In the spring of 1990 Vedder got Mother Love Bone's tape, listened to it one night, and then purportedly wrote the lyrics to three songs while surfing the next morning. The Love Bones heard his lyrics and hired him on the spot. Two weeks later he was resettled, living in the basement of an art gallery in downtown Seattle. Within a few months, he was touring with them under the temporary band name Mookie Blaylock.

The band was renamed Pearl Jam and signed to Epic Records. They recorded an album called *Ten*, which was released in September 1991. *Ten* had a hit, "Alive"; thanks to the metal marketing strategy, it started selling fifty-five thousand copies a week almost instantly. Gold and platinum were no sweat. Then the record *Temple of the Dog* was re-released. So was *Apple*. Finally, the soundtrack to the movie *Singles*, which featured Eddie, Stony, and Jeff alongside Matt Dillon, plus two songs by Pearl Jam, was released. Everything charted. High.

Thus the story of Pearl Jam is a lot like that of Nirvana, only more so; only different. Because for Eddie and Pearl Jam the last year has been one of incredible creativity and a load of hard work.

When all this happened, it had only been a little over a year since Eddie's band Bad Radio had played a benefit for Amnesty International at San Diego State. Eddie helped organize it, and it wasn't easy. "You know, working with an organization and playing for free, and then the gig didn't go all that great, and I remember after it was all over, I walked out into the parking lot and someone had stolen my car stereo. My little piece-of-shit car stereo! And just then someone I know walked up to me and goes, 'Hey I just called your house, man, and your phone's been turned off.'

"And at that moment I was, like, 'What the fuck am I doing? My life's falling apart, and I can't see any results. I have no money and no time to have a relationship or a family or just be normal . . .' " Eddie pauses. "But then I remember this thing I once heard Edward Albee say at a lecture. He said that he was so thankful that he enjoyed playing [the role of] a playwright, because that's what he was, a playwright. I feel the same about being a musician. I've always been obsessed with it, since back before I even have memory.

"The other night," confides Eddie, "it was, like, two A.M. and I was riding in the bus, watching the world go by and listening to the new Neil Young record, and all of a sudden I went, 'Oh my God! I'm in a tour bus and tomorrow we're going to open for the Chili Peppers.' And it was like, 'How did I get here?' I spent my life getting here!

"But really, everything I've ever done has led to this. Like, I used to go help out at the Bacchanal, be a kind of unpaid roadie there. I remember I did that once for a Joe Strummer gig; I forwent my twenty-dollar paycheck that night to just go hang out at sound check, because to me, just to look at Joe Strummer's guitar was cool. I'd get chills just looking at it. And that night the power went off and I sat in a tiny room with Joe Strummer for, like, an hour with just this big mag light on his face. It was a totally surreal experience. I remember he gave me a hit off his cigarette and it was half pot and half tobacco, and I nearly puked, but of course you can't puke in front of your hero.

"Anyway, that was the same night that I met Jack Irons, who later became my best friend. And not only has he been hugely inspirational in my life, but he also hooked me up with these guys."

In October, Nirvana's out on tour in America, and here in L.A., somewhere along Pico Boulevard in one of those nondescript flat-front buildings you see only in L.A., Pearl Jam was filming a video for the song "Jeremy." I walked into the studio to a burst of applause: the crew is spontaneously acclaiming Eddie's thirteenth lipsynched take. *Clearly I remember pickin' on the boy, seemed a harmless little fuck* . . . Take number fourteen proceeds directly: Eddie, perched on a revolving platform, singing "Jeremy" while the platform turns slowly, causing his face to dive in and out of shadows. The effect is achieved by a stagehand who lies flat on the ground out of sight of the camera, spinning the platform by hand at a slow and even rate for the entire six-minute song. Whenever he fucks up—speeds up or slows down—they have to do it again. *Ooh, but we unleashed a lion, gnashed his teeth and bit the recess lady's breast, how can I forget?*

Anyone who's ever been to a video or movie shoot knows it's no substitute for the real thing. And yet, as Eddie, clad in undershirt, shorts, and combat boots, with a strip of black duct tape picturesquely encircling his arm, began to sing, I was amazed at the level of his conviction. He looked positively epic up there—one leg thrust forward, his arms crossed in front of him, his eyes closed. He was giving it up for the camera, utterly, religiously, for the fourteenth time that day. *Time to erase me, time to erase me from the blackboard . . . Jeremy spoke in class today.*

A couple of takes later, the director, Chris Cuffaro, says Eddie's done. It's now Stony's turn to mount the platform and fake play. Eddie hops off and we immediately go into a private huddle, prompted by my baby bracelet with the word "Fugazi" on it. It seems we'd both attended the show in Olympia, which is now generally acknowledged as the band's best show ever. We start reciting our favorite moments to one another: "Remember when Ian said, 'This song is *not* cool?' " "And when the girl sang, 'She did nothing to deserve it?' "

"It's weird," Eddie says. "Just the night before that show, we'd played our own record-release party at the Space Needle for three thousand people for free. And afterwards, they thrust us into this disco with all these pink Pearl Jam posters up and made us shake all these people named, like, Barney and Mike's hands. I guess I just wasn't prepared for it. I guess I thought it'd be, like, they'd play the record and I'd sit in a corner and eat free slices of cantaloupe with my friends. And it wasn't like that at all. It was so weird. And the only thing that really saved my sanity was getting into my truck and going down to Olympia to see Fugazi the next day.

"Of course, afterwards I went back to band rehearsal and I go, 'OK, that's it, I'm quitting the band and starting my own label!' But when I thought about it, I realized, that's what's right for Ian, but for us, well, the relationship we have with the people in the business is pretty good. I've only been in it a year, but Stony and Jeff have worked with the same people for four years, and we have a rapport with them. Our A & R person and the vice president of the company, they listen to us, and they have influence. If I don't want to do something, then I don't do it. At least, I talk to them first. They like to see how dedicated we are to an idea, they're just checking. But you know what? When we talk it all out, I usually get my own way."

One argument Eddie lost with Epic was one about going on MTV's "Headbanger's Ball." He didn't want to, but the record company convinced him he had to do it. So Eddie went on armed with a felt-tip Sharpie, and while Riki Rachtman interviewed him, he busied himself writing on his arm. Near the end of their chat, he lifted his arm up to the camera. In large letters, he'd scrawled the word FUGAZI.

The night after the video shoot, Pearl Jam is playing at Winter's, the tiny club on El Cajon Boulevard where Eddie used to work. Given the rapid success of *Ten*, Pearl Jam could have booked into a bigger place. But Eddie felt he owed this club something. Unfortunately, the venue only holds about 125 people, and by ten P.M. it's completely sold out. The scene outside is growing ugly: girls begging to be allowed in, guys insisting they were on the guest list. "I guess I forgot how many friends I have," Eddie says ruefully.

Pearl Jam is only the second band I've ever seen in a

nightclub that I wished was in a stadium. (The other one was Jane's Addiction.) Their music is a big item: vast, majestic, arena rock—not metal, but groovy, anthemic, sensitive-boy stuff. Just the day before, the *L.A. Times* had compared the band to the Who, declaring that "Alive" was the ultimate celebration of the death of nihilism, a display of "pure existential joy."

It was a great show, a swan song of sorts; a bid farewell to smoky nightclubs forever. But the moment I valued most wasn't when Eddie sang my favorite line in "Alive"—"But do I deserve to be?"—or when a member of the audience gave him a soft tap on the jaw when he sang the part in "Jeremy" where Jeremy "hit me with a surprise left" or even when he stood up on the amplifiers and the entire crowd beckoned him down, down, down, till he finally flung himself outstretched on their waiting arms.

No, the best part was when the band stopped for a minute to refuel and guitarist McCready began quietly strumming the opening chords to Nirvana's "Smells Like Teen Spirit." Within seconds, an exhausted Vedder and the entire audience began singing at the top of their lungs: "With the lights out, it's less dangerous/here we are now, entertain us/we're so stupid, and contagious . . ."

Later I said to Eddie, "It's been a great year for records. You know, Fugazi, Nirvana, Pearl Jam."

Eddie gasped. "Don't even put our name in the same *sentence* with them. I can't deal with that at all!"

Months later, Kurt Cobain starts ragging on Pearl Jam in the pages of various magazines—*Musician, Rolling Stone*—lumping them in with Nirvana-bes, calling them totally fake. This is unfair, especially since Pearl Jam is both personally and musically totally unlike Nirvana, nice where the one band is crabby, acquiescent where the other is trouble, classic where the other is punky, major where the other is indie. But there is a sense, to those in the scene, that Pearl Jam's massive success is at least partly due to Nirvana's. And in and around Seattle, a lot of jealous people resent Pearl Jam for purely monetary reasons. It's just the age-old indie–major battle, the bloody cry of "sell-out" cleaving the heavens the minute somebody makes good.

By May 1992, it's clear that Pearl Jam's success, however coddled it has been by time and circumstances, is entirely genuine. Even Kurt makes up with Eddie, which is fortunate, since by that time there is probably no one else on the planet situated quite as peculiarly as he in terms of fame. Long before that, back in October 1991, I spoke to Eddie about the possibility of that kind of success, as he sat in his hotel room in Ames, Iowa, sewing up a torn Butthole Surfers T-shirt and getting ready to shoot some baskets with some of the Red Hot Chili Peppers. At the time, Pearl Jam was completing a U.S. tour, opening for the Smashing Pumpkins and the Peppers, two bands that Eddie professes to love. "Every night," he says, "right after I leave the stage, I leap into the front of the audience for the Pumpkins' set and I don't go until the Peppers leave the stage."

His own sets are going well too. "We still feel like we're giving it up every night. I can't just sing 'em. I feel 'em.

"Last night," he adds, "I leapt from the stage to the speakers to the box thing on the side where the king and queen would sit, if they happened to show up that night, and then I ran as fast as I could across the balcony and back into the king-and-queen thing on the other side of the stage, and then back down onstage, where four guards immediately attacked me. They got me into this headlock, and everybody's yelling, 'Let go! Let go! He's the singer,' and then I go away, and just as I was running off, this guard made a swipe at me and totally missed and fell right smack on his face."

That night, Eddie admits, was the first time that leaping into the audience started to seem dangerous. "They nearly tore me to pieces. Out of sheer love, I think. I got in the shower later and had all these bloody open wounds.

"The audiences," he sighs, "are suddenly getting bigger. And when they get bigger, I get smaller."

SEVENTEEN

NEW DAY RISING

Shadowy plaid flannel shirts—a grunge staple—were rendered in silk chiffon and tied around the waist, over pants, for a skirtlike effect. Whether the women who dress in this style, in all its deliberate sloppiness, want it delivered to them as a package look, put together by a designer, strikes me as open to question, but perhaps in the long run it doesn't matter: on an individual basis, these clothes, taken out of the context in which Jacobs presents them, could be made to signify any number of things. . . . The message encoded in the clothes is . . . that the person wearing them doesn't care too much about fashion, that this is someone who doesn't work too hard at his or her self-presentation, that there is a virtue in looking, if not poor, then, at the very least, unconcerned with money.

– Holly Brubach, *The New Yorker*

You wake—if you ever slept—when you feel the bus stop rolling. Uncramp yourself from the crouch position the bunk's dimensions demand and shiver for a solid hour or so from the blast of air conditioning that pours on you from the slats. When you finally emerge from the bus's confines into the painful white sunshine of early morning, the catering camp is clattering away with cups of coffee and eggs and bacon. An army of huge riggers is already hard at work pouring out the contents of the eight sixteen-wheel trucks onto the stage. You blink. Rub crap out of your eyes and hair. Adjust your slept-in clothes and go sit by the banks of the muddy and mighty Ohio River, mosquitoes buzzing madly along its swampy edge. You feel, you think, like you're at a pioneer railway camp in 1860, like Laura and Mary in the little house on the prairie, like Huckleberry Finn, like the cat on the Oregon Trail. In fact, if it's Tuesday, this must be the Riverbend Amphitheater on the outskirts of Cincinnati, seventh stop on the Lollapalooza II whistle-stop rock 'n' roll tour.

Once the word was Three Stooges slang for a huge sucker of an event. Now Lollapalooza is just another term for a gargantuan rock concert, featuring a concourse packed with games, clothing, and food vendors, political groups distributing free information, and two stages presenting what passes these days for alternative rock. Last year, in the midst of one of the worst concert seasons ever, the seventeen-city package—featuring Jane's Addiction, Siouxsie and the Banshees, Living Colour, Nine Inch Nails, Ice T and Body Count, Butthole Surfers, and Rollins Band—grossed an average of $397,625 per date, nearly leading concert revenues for the entire summer. Its popularity helped to boost the profile of "alternative" music, thus aiding Nirvana's subsequent success and the feeding frenzy for bands like Helmet. This year's Lollapalooza—now featuring the Red Hot Chili Peppers, Ice Cube, Soundgarden, Ministry, Pearl Jam, Lush, and the Jesus and Mary Chain—won't be as groundbreaking as last year's was. It can't be, because the ground's already been broken, trampled, in fact, under a stampede of industry people and kids who all saw the green light. But Lollapalooza II raises the question: is the tour pushing the envelope of artistic license out to the cornfields of America, or is it perhaps merely licking it shut again with the same old, same old, arena rock shtick: white males, long hair, loud guitars, love?

Hoping desperately for the sincerity of last year's Lollapalooza, but surrounded by the circuslike atmosphere on the banks of the Ohio River that morning, I couldn't help recalling a famous big-top maxim: the one about fooling all of the people some of the time.

In *Humbug: The Art of P. T. Barnum* Neil Harris says that early circuses in America in the 1850s traveled by riverboat instead of tent and wagon, floating from one town to the next without having to reconstruct facilities in each place they visited. Lollapalooza is not nearly so efficient. (Though give them time, man, give them time. For all we know, hundreds of workmen in some warehouse in New Orleans are busy constructing floating Forums even as we speak.) As it is, even in the venues where there are facilities for a giant rock concert, the stage needs to be loaded in and out each day—an almost twenty-four-hour process.

Unlike Barnum and Bailey's, which used the smack-new U.S. railway service to its utmost, this circus travels by bus and truck between venues. Sometimes, however, the buses break. Pearl Jam's busted between Cincinnati and Cleveland last summer, forcing drummer Dave Abruzzese to run across Interstate 75 like a madman, in an attempt to flag down Soundgarden for a hitch. Another night, somewhere between Denver and the Mississippi River, singer Eddie Vedder was left behind in Bumfuck, Kansas, at a truckstop at three A.M. He had to hitch the next three hundred miles to Saint Louis. And then he claimed he liked doing it.

Like Perry Farrell last year, Vedder is the physical embodiment of this year's Lollapalooza, the heart and soul of the event. It's not just that the presence of his band, Pearl Jam, on the Lollapalooza tour (a presence that was decided on long before their debut album, *Ten*, began leaping up the charts) has sold untold numbers of tickets to the extravaganza. It's not just that their predetermined time slot—they go on second—brings everyone with a ticket into Lollapalooza early, there to experience the entire kit and caboodle. It's that Eddie himself is the quintessential Lollapaloozer, exuding aerobic intensity, embodying emotional and physical courageousness during every day's performance.

This is Eddie at Lollapalooza, throwing his head back, his stringy brown hair blown backward by the wet summer breeze, while directly in front of him a vast green hillside on the banks of the Cuyahoga River in Ohio is fast turning to mud. Vast sheets of rain, swept across the seated portion of the arena like a transparent gauze curtain, drench a crowd of twenty thousand that smothers in its grip. Eddie smiles beatifically, stretching his arms outward, in layout position, and as he does so the audience moves in unison closer, thrusting its bosom hard toward the band. Their faces shine in jubilance. Bodies surf on the crowd's crest. Boys leap upward, beckoning to Eddie, stammering out welcoming phrases at the top of their lungs, unheard above the music and the wind. They beckon to him pleadingly with mammoth gestures, reaching out their long skinny arms, then slamming fists emphatically against their chests. But Eddie waits. Tension mounts. He ranges round the stage in circles, heaving and singing, his voice booming through the weather, the crowd bearing down the hillside, closer and closer, completely rapt. And then, at the perfect psychological moment, he does it. Climbing the side of the speaker stacks, he leaps into their midst, a fifteen-foot drop, again in slo-mo, his body twisting all the way down.

Sometimes Eddie does even crazier things. At St. Louis's Riverport Amphitheater (best known as the shed where Axl Rose got in twubble), Eddie started climbing the scaffolding in the middle of the song "Why Go" and didn't stop until he'd reached the roof. There, high above the audience, snug inside the rafters of the covered portion of the arena, Eddie walked along the inside of a giant steel beam to the very back of the seven-thousand-seat bowl while the band continued jamming. Can you even imagine what it was like when he poked his head out directly above the lawn area? Can you see the pandemonium of the minions down below, when, James Bond-like, he leapt from the *roof* directly into the mosh pit on the grass?

"I wept," a fat kid named Todd from Delano, Kansas, told me afterward, his expression exuding that this was only the simple truth.

"I," said Eddie, wryly, about an hour later, "threw up."

Clearly Eddie is Lollapalooza's hero—a cross between young Springsteen and Henry Rollins, a neo-punk rock icon raised on Minor Threat and SST, and one of the few people here who attended the IPU Convention. (OK, so I'm the other.) And Eddie's own personal quandary—he feels guilty about the size and lack of intimacy of his own artistic success—mirrors the essential quandary of Lollapalooza. That is, whether it is a genuine outgrowth and expression of the underground, or is merely exploitative of it, a kind of K Mart-ization of the Amer-indie world.

In fact, it is neither—or at worst, it is both. These bands are, after all, punk rock's revenge—not to mention punk rock's victory, thirteen years late. From Ministry's pointedly frightening "N.W.O." through Ice Cube's confrontational performance style, punk rock attitude stands out a mile. Jesus and Mary Chain's Jim Reid will wax eloquent about his favorite band, Subway Sect. Soundgarden's Ben Shepherd will tell you about his collection of set lists from his favorite shows ever: MDC, Dirty Rotten Imbeciles, Dead Kennedys. Every band here has played a forty-watt club. Every band here has made their own flyers. Every band here has toured the entire country, slept on floors, crammed six to a van. Punk rock? "I loved that era," sighs Anthony Kiedis. "To me, that type of hardcore, fuck-everything energy was just the ultimate fuel to express that. But it'll never be the same. That was just a completely wonderful era that'll probably never happen again, and it shouldn't."

Personally, I wish it would. But Lollapalooza is not a bad legacy for a bunch of baby busters trying to relive their elders' glory. This year, Farrell's role in Lollapalooza is smaller than last year: he had some input in ideas for the festival, and he is also involved financially, as one of three partners in Lollapalooza, Inc., a joint venture with Ted Gardner and with Don Muller of Triad Artists. That means he and his partners will gain fiscally from any profits made on the thirty-six-date tour. But it also means he'll take a loss, if a loss there be. Where's the risk involved? Most of it was taken last year, when taking seven bands on the road, not one of which was headlining status in arenas of those sizes, in a season when literally every tour was bombing big-time, was about as risky a business venture as you can get.

Today, Geiger downplays the first Lollapalooza's stunning

success. "It was so obvious," he says. "The Cure was selling out Irvine Meadows in a day. Depeche Mode had done stadiums. We just couldn't have gone wrong. Jane's was gigantic, Nine Inch Nails were huge, Ice T had just come off *New Jack City* and *O.G.*, Siouxsie had a sizeable MTV video hit. It didn't take a brain surgeon to recognize this. If you knew anything about the concert business, you knew we had a product that'd work."

Part of the surprise of last year's success had to do with the underground nature of Jane's Addiction's popularity. Prior to the soundscan change in Billboard charts, no one seemed to realize how popular that band was. This year—post-Nirvana—the underground is both larger and less . . . well, less underground than last year. This year, thanks to last year's success, there was fierce competition for the gig among American venues. Every date sold out in hours. The Los Angeles dates, at Irvine Meadows on September 11, 12, and 13, sold out in four hours. After each show that I attended, promoters toasted the producers with expensive champagnes. One pair in particular, after obsequiously glad-handing the entire crew, anxiously offered to change the loading dock of their venue in order to entice Lollapalooza back next year.

Clearly, this year, financial risk is not a problem, although a couple of bands, notably Lush and Jesus and Mary Chain, are taking a loss for the privilege of being on the tour. "The only way to make money on the road in America," comments Jim Reid of the Chain, "is to tour in a minivan and lift your own amps. And that's impossible in venues of this size."

Profit is, of course, the main motive of any concert promotion: no one at Lollapalooza is doing anybody any favors, and Lollapalooza seems to be grossing an average of about $500,000 a night. But when you see the tour in action—seven crew trucks, 160 crew members, ten buses, countless telephone lines, fax machines, a masseuse named Flano, and the entire traveling concourse area, the expense for which is the burden of Lollapalooza, Inc. (who contracted it to Bill Graham Presents), and not the promoter—it seems unlikely that profit is as mammoth as the industry sources like to think it is. Instead, Lollapalooza is spreading money around the country at an alarming rate. One night the tour commandeered 150 rooms in a hotel outside St. Louis. When the buses arrived, the lot was filled with kids' cars with the words "Welcome Lollapaloozers" soaped onto all the windows.

Why spend so much on it? "Because," explains Peter Barsotti, who's in charge of the concourse area, "Lollapalooza is trying to establish itself as an annual show. They want to deliver the goods. They want, when kids hear Lollapalooza's on sale, for them to go, 'Oh, Lollapalooza, I'm going. By the way, who's playing?' And that takes some doing. It's important they establish that when you buy a ticket to Lollapalooza it'll be an affair to remember, something you don't want to miss."

Why do the venues admit outside vendors that cut into their profits? "A nine-hour show means the kids have to eat twice," says Barsotti. "The concessionaire for the arena will sell as much as they're going to sell anyway. Plus," he adds, "they have the beer."

Every venue looks alike. McRock Concert, USA. Every audience looks the same too. "White kids in white T-shirts," describes Soundgarden's Kim Thayil. "Every audience is replaceable." In that case, where is the genuine underground? Haight Street and Telegraph Avenue, Melrose, Capitol Hill, and B and Second streets in the deep East Village seem to live in every state now, twenty thousand strong, from town to town to town. You can get Doc Martens anywhere. It's a Lollapalooza nation.

One morning, tour accountant Stuart Ross and I, cups of coffee in hand, take a walk through the Riverbend concourse, where, though it's only nine A.M., San Francisco's Sharkbait is already busily setting up its rhythmic best and the vendors are wearily setting up their booths of food, clothes, and trinkets. We think we're tired: the traveling food and clothing vendors are doing the exact same journeys and distances, only in rental cars. No bus equals no sleep. First to arrive, last to tear down, no catering, and no rest. "The bands have it easy," sneers smart-drink salesperson Joanna Sweett. "They have it cush."

Stuart takes me over to inspect the political-awareness and information tent, where workers are setting up tables with brochures on AIDS awareness, PETA, Young Democrats and (a group that was strong in the Midwest, though not, I was told, elsewhere) the Young Libertarians. Lollapalooza invited more right-wing groups along as well—the Republicans, the National Rifle Association, and antiabortion groups—but at most venues those groups chose not to show. Do they consider this crowd a lost cause? Do these enormous groups of Lollapaloozers—eighteen- to twenty-four-year-old white males, for the most part—have such a decidedly liberal bent that conservatives are right in thinking there's no point in proselytizing to them? Or do the right-wingers just assume they don't vote?

Stuart approaches the workers at a table for the Bethany House Homeless Shelter. They look up alarmed. "Are we taking up too much room?" the leader asks anxiously. "We can condense ourselves, really."

"That's not the problem," Stuart says seriously. "I was just wondering. Who should I deliver the check we have for you to this evening?"

The check is probably the crux of Lollapalooza. Mr. Lifto, the man who lifts heavy weights by attaching a hook through the hole in his penis, gets more media attention, but the real nub of the matter is here. The festival is earning money for local charities in two separate ways. One is by adding a fifty-cent surcharge to the ticket, to be devoted to a local homeless shelter in that venue's area. The other is by means of the Wheel of Safe Sex and the "Wake Up Mr. President, What about the Homeless?" game. Concertgoers can buy tickets to play each game for a dollar, the proceeds of which go to the same local charity as the surcharge.

"Our agenda will change every year," explains Ted Gardner. "This year it was homelessness, particularly homeless families, particularly with the proviso that we wished to concentrate on shelters and charities aimed toward families and women. Next year, we'll go after something different.

"Leave it to Bono to save the world, but if you throw a thousand bucks or whatever from the Wheel of Safe Sex to the homeless coalition of that local community and context, then you've done something. It's not a big gesture or anything, but it's something. It's like microeconomics. And I prefer that because then you can make tangible differences."

One of the most-heard criticisms of this year's Lollapalooza III in the media has been that its seven-band lineup is "too safe." The accusation is meant both commercially and artistically; it's also relative. Lollapalooza isn't a safe bill compared to, say, Summer Jam featuring Hammer, MC Lyte and TLC, or compared to Guns N' Roses and Metallica, but it does seem safe (to those who criticize it as such) compared to last year's lineup, which featured three bands on independent labels—Rollins Band, the Butthole Surfers, and Nine Inch Nails—as well as Ice T and Body Count, whose inclusion was considered radical even though his oeuvre was a good deal less edgy than Ice Cube's stance.

What these critics aren't taking into account is that, when Lollapalooza II was booked back in October, the Chili Peppers' *Blood Sex Sugar Magik* had just been released. A crossover hit on the level of "Under the Bridge" wasn't even dreamed of. The same thing goes for Pearl Jam's inclusion: they were asked to join the tour early on, which is why they're still featured second on the bill, directly after Lush.

Opinion is still divided as to whether L2 would have done the sales it's done without the Chili Peppers—or without "Under the Bridge"—on the bill. Another factor naysayers aren't considering is that the whole reason Lollapalooza seems like a safe lineup is entirely because of last year's festival. The effect of that tour's overwhelming success in a season when every other tour except the Grateful Dead's did poorly cannot be overstated. Because of last year's Lollapalooza, radio formats changed. MTV added hours of "alternative" programming.

British critics credit Lollapalooza with influencing the Reading Festival to feature its first black headline act—Public Enemy—ever, while a recent issue of *The Rap Sheet* magazine credits T and Cube's successful inclusion on this rock tour as one reason bigger venues in New York (notably the Garden and the Ritz) were booking rap artists again.

In the wake of Nirvana's success (a success that Lollapalooza paved the way for), record companies started signing and pushing alternative bands. Since last year, all three independent bands on last year's lineup have been signed to majors, as have many others, such as Helmet, Urge Overkill, and Babes in Toyland, whose inclusion on this tour would *not* have been considered "safe."

Ted Gardner, who in his former role as Jane's Addiction's manager was instrumental in putting together Lollapalooza I, agrees. "I love to think," says Gardner, "that we were a catalyst for those bands happening. Radio will tell you it was their idea. Record companies will say it was their hard work. I believe it was us."

His belief is well founded. In December 1992 the *L.A. Daily News* reported that the success of Lollapalooza I had prompted MTV to add new-music programming in the shape of a weekly feature entitled "Breaking Out of Bounds." "We have a lot of genre-specific shows like 'Yo, MTV Raps' and 'Headbanger's Ball,' " said Rick Krim, vice president of MTV talent and artists, "but thanks to Lollapalooza, we know new-music listeners are not limited. People who like Ice T and Body Count also like Jane's Addiction and the Pixies."

Record companies now know that too. Just being associated with Lollapalooza is already considered an important coup for a new band. "When we found out the lineup last fall, we were running around the office going, 'Pearl Jam got Lollapalooza, Pearl Jam got Lollapalooza!' " recalls John Doelp, vice president of Epic Records. Doelp, whose act Living Colour was on last year's bill, knows firsthand how the tour can help his artists, and he says the success of last year's tour cannot be overestimated. "It opened up a lot of people's eyes," he says. "It gave people in the industry an awareness of the total viability of alternative music in the mass market. More importantly, there's now a more informed consumer out there. Without [last year's] Lollapalooza, I don't think the Chili Peppers' fall tour would have done so well, which in turn helped Pearl Jam, because they were the openers."

MTV and the record industry may be willing to give Lollapalooza credit for breaking ground, but commercial radio—always slow to follow, much less lead—is less forthcoming in its praise. Phyllis Stark, radio columnist at *Billboard,* denies Lollapalooza's influence on the industry in the past year. Radio play of new alternative acts "is just a cyclical thing, based on what's out there," she says. "I'd say Jesus Jones's crossover success was far more influential [than Lollapalooza was] to radio programming, and that came about in the same old way, with SBK practically naming their first-born children after programming directors in order to get it on the air."

Stark adds that although twenty-one radio stations changed their format to modern rock last year, that figure is relative. In the same period, she explains, eighty-six changed to country, and ninety-eight to news and talk formats.

The figure still concedes that a modern rock format is pretty healthy for stations right now. Harder to quantify—and possibly more significant—are the new crossover hits, so-called alternative cuts now being played on classic rock stations. Despite Stark's disclaimer, songs like "Alive," "Under the Bridge," and "Teen Angst" by Cracker probably had significantly less chance of being heard on AOR radio before Lollapalooza's success.

Doelp believes that their profile on this year's tour will help push Pearl Jam to number one. But he adds that the band that will really benefit on the tour is Ministry. "The whole thing used to be only for the very hip, but now it's hitting the edge of the K Mart crowd. In this economy, that's great. Whether a kid gets a record at K Mart or Newbury Comix is totally irrelevant if the music is good."

Ted Mico agrees. "Lollapalooza didn't create this new

underground. There is a thirst for adventure still, and it's a diet that hasn't been fed by MTV or anybody else around. It was certainly there, and that's why Lollapalooza I happened and was successful and stuff. I don't think Lollapalooza created that market, it just fed that market. Nirvana cashed in as well. That happened at the right time. Last year Lollapalooza played to over half a million people, and that's a market that business just can't ignore. I don't think it will have that kind of impact again because it had it. You can't smash a wall in twice. The wall doesn't exist now."

"The underground," shrugs Emma Anderson of Lush, "is dead." Band mate Chris Acland: "Long live the underground."

That night, mud-spattered and greasy-haired, I braved the shower situation, a locker-size place in some upstairs nook or cranny of the facility. Down below I could hear the echoey bellowing of the Red Hot Chili Peppers—from this angle, they're all bass—and the screams of the collected children of the corn as they sing along. It's probably the eeriest shower I've ever taken: there's no hot water and about an inch of murky gray slime in the stall I have to step gingerly into, but I succeed in getting myself tolerably clean. When I get out I notice a ghostly silence from the beyond, but I wrap a towel around my midsection and step into the hallway. There, at the end of a darkened corridor, the brawny silhouette of Anthony Kiedis is lurching slowly on toward me, in some kind of post-show trance. It was like the end of some bad movie, and the scene played out forever, Anthony limping lamely past me, his eyes burnt out with pure fatigue, and me, clutching my puny towel, wondering desperately if I ought to say something. Like "Hi." Like "Great show, Anthony!" (despite my not having seen it). Or like "Jeez, I'm sorry there's no hot water left."

Back in the tour bus, I settle onto the front couch, to wait patiently for accounts to be settled. Every time I try to watch any portion of the Olympics coverage on television, everyone throws things at the screen and jeers at me. Load-out doesn't end till, like, two A.M., after which the two Teds and Nicki and Stuart and I all sit up in the bus for hours, watching the road meet the night sky, drinking Dom that a pleased promoter gave us and roaring with laughter. Outside the bus, signs for places occasionally loom across the windshield; giddily I think how the road, like time itself, is slippin', slippin', slippin' into the future. I emerge in the morning again into the confines of another nameless field of green, my hair more crunkled up than ever. In Cleveland, we are told, it's rained nonstop for the last three weeks, and there's more expected tomorrow. There's a flood warning out on the Ohio River, which banks itself right up on the backstage area: it's risen fifteen feet in the last twenty-four hours. "But the sun shines on the righteous," our informant says happily. Today we're righteous.

For the public the day begins when the powers that be put *Ritual De Lo Habitual* on the loudspeaker and let the kids all in. The contents of a thousand cars with Mudhoney stickers on their butts and plates from all over empty into the arena. In Missouri, there's cars from Illinois, Kansas, Iowa, Nebraska, and Tennessee. In Ohio, there's plates from Indiana, Pennsylvania, and Kentucky, states not lucky enough to get their own Lollapalooza. Brightly colored banners greet the Lollapaloozers, who run frantically across the hay-covered lawn for good spots. The hay is to sop up yesterday's rain. I remember running like that once, across a stadium field with my girlfriends to see Kansas, Fleetwood Mac, and Gary Wright at the Oakland Coliseum Arena. Lollapalooza is the modern-day version of that day. Sure, Beat Happening's not on the bill; sure, it costs you thirty dollars and not five. That doesn't mean that certain aspects of seventies and eighties arena rock haven't been entirely eliminated from the mix.

Not everyone here is having a great time today, though. Indiana's Vulgar Boatmen are scheduled for the second stage at 2:30, right between sets by Lush and Pearl Jam on the big one. But Jim Rose's sideshow goes on a little late, and the Boatmen don't get to go on until 3:15, right around the time Pearl Jam's beginning "Alive." The result is disastrous. There's not one single person in front of their stage—except one Kevin Lowber, twenty-six, from Lexington, Kentucky, who says kindly, gesturing toward the main arena, "Ah, I can see the video."

The Boatmen's gentle, precise music—the lovely chiming, strumming, whirring sounds of circa 1985—is being blown out of the water by the more modern distant thunder of Vedder and company. The Vulgar Boatmen deserve better, but there's a certain cruel, rough justice to their being ignored here: they really are out of time here. "We thought," says songwriter Dale Lawrence afterward, somewhat disappointedly, but as gently as he sings, "this would be the biggest crowd we ever played. Instead it was the smallest. And that's saying a lot!"

While the Boatmen's experience is not at all typical of Lollapalooza, the sideshow is a hit-or-miss operation, a prey to delays, no-shows, and rain cancellations. Booked by Ted Mico and Ted Gardner, many of its other acts, including Cypress Hill, Arson Garden, Sweaty Nipples, Seaweed, and Seam, are independent labels. The side stage is serving as a real flashpoint of criticism of Lollapalooza, especially in publications like the *Village Voice*, which allege that bands there are being exploited and not getting paid. It seemed like everybody had an axe to grind: local bands who didn't get asked to play, and ones who did, but claimed they were being ghettoized for being either female, black, underground, or just plain not big—everyone. "Why not more women or rap acts on the bill?" was a constant rallying cry against Lollapalooza—to which one has to say, "Why not more women or rap acts in rock 'n' roll in general, eh?" Except for San Francisco's Sharkbait and Archie Bell and Seattle's Jim Rose Circus, the three acts that are signed to the second stage for the entire tour, those who have appeared locally are not being paid. Some of the second-stage acts such as Boo Yaa T.R.I.B.E. have complained as well about not being provided with backstage access or food. "Ideally, further down the road, the second stage will be more together," Mico says, "promote more local and more new bands. It's starting now, but it's been kind of rushed. And it's so difficult to organize! I think we're doing a good job just keeping it on track."

Despite the beer, and despite twenty-eight arrests at the Lollapalooza in Saratoga, California, Lollapaloozas have been notably fight free, especially in comparison to the Guns N' Roses concerts taking place this summer in stadiums, like one ill-fated one in Montreal, during which crowds rioted after Guns cut their show short. At Riverport the security guards—still apparently nervous after the Guns N' Roses excitement of last July—are stunned at the goodness of the crowd. No drugs, few drunks—"Hell, Trish Yearwood played here last night and we were carrying 'em out of the front in comas," says one beefy guard backstage.

His sidekick, whose improbable name is John Bovinette, nods. "Worst crowd in the world is Hank Williams, Jr. All the rednecks come out from the country and get drunk, and after the show's over, there's just all these bodies lying on the lawn. Last year we had four o.d.s. One woman had convulsions."

Not so Lollapalooza. Except for a couple of injuries inflicted during impromptu blanket tosses on the lawn, the main reportees to the Oasis (the first-aid tent) are fainters, who keel over during Jim Rose's gory sideshow, which performs twice a day on the second stage and is fast turning into one of Lollapalooza's main attractions. A half hour before the show, Jim himself rides a bike through the crowd, hawking himself through a bullhorn, with jovial enticements such as "Human pincushion, report to the second stage," and "Medic!" By two o'clock, large crowds have gathered, awaiting the sight of hideous feats, knowledge of which seems to have arrived at each city by tom-tom. In addition to ordinary circus sideshow stunts such as sword swallowing, the Rose troupe's nauseating feats of modern primitivism include the consumption of glass shards, live maggots, and razor blades; the ritual skewering of one troupe member's cheeks and throat with a skinny metal pike; and a guy named Matt who performs "nonsurgical procedures" on himself, such as swallowing a condom and having it emerge, inflated, through his nose, and inserting seven feet of thin glass tubing into his innards via his nostril, inhaling a mixture of Coca-Cola, beer, and Pepto-Bismol, pumping his own stomach, and then drinking the results.

He's not even the main event: that honor goes to Mr. Lifto, a gentle skinhead drag queen who's unappetizing talent is for lifting heavy objects by means of hooks, which are hung through the pierced parts of his body: ears, tongue, nipples, and yes, penis.

Barsotti: "You know, Cincinnati is the home of the opposition to Mapplethorpe, and before we got here they told me that the sheriff said, 'Hey, I hear you got some weird stuff in that freak show. You got a guy who hangs weights from his penis, and you do that here in Cincinnati, we're going to arrest him.' So I told the freak show guys not to do it, and after the show the sheriff came up to me and said, 'Peter, we loved the freak show, next time they come to Cincinnati, tell 'em they can do what they want. Just don't advertise it."

Rose's enormously popular turn on the stage is important for another reason, however: it almost takes the place of a Butthole Surfers or Body Count in pushing the envelope of what is acceptable as art to the mainstream world. The show may only be, according to Rose himself, "just freaky and weird stuff," but it's also, he adds, "something live, real, raw, and dangerous. If you want to know why the people at these shows are going so crazy for us, it's because there's, like, this lost generation of kids who are *so sick* of stuff that's clean, contrived, and choreographed. I mean, a kid came up to me the other day and said, 'It's so real! It's so fun! I can't believe it's allowed!' I don't think he knew what he was saying, but it sure sounded like kids today have a real freedom problem."

Of course they do, but haven't they always? When you look out at a crowd of Lollapaloozers, you have to wonder what makes them different from punks, or hippies, or the long bland stretch of nobodies who existed in the years when nothing fun was going on.

"I think kids want to be outcasts now," comments Missy Worth, Lollapalooza's booking agent. "When I was in high school, my favorite band in the world was the New York

Dolls, but everyone else was into Crosby, Stills, and Nash, so I pretended I was too. God forbid they found out I was a freak! Now it's like kids want to be different; they want to stand out. I think they feel like they'll just disappear if they can't find some way of being individual."

Is going to Lollapalooza "being individual" anymore? Backward baseball caps and knee-length shorts, "Fuck George Bush" T-shirts, pierced noses and tattoos, even the more extreme measures of branding and bile drinking (pursuits that Ministry's Al Jourgensen professes to indulge in)—are they really as revolutionary as, say, shaving your hair into a mohawk was in 1978, or growing it long was in 1968?

I fear not. I fear it's just the current fashion. Sure, it's nice to dream that Lollapalooza is helping to educate impressionable teenagers, that the large posted signs such as "Demand Corporate Accountability" and "The Ruling Class Had Better Wise Up" are making an impression, that the kids you see at every venue are all vegans and environmentalists, nonsexist PETA volunteers all registered to vote Democrat. I think, unfortunately, there's absolutely no proof that this is so. The best that we can hope for is a world with a slightly better soundtrack; kids whose favorite song is the dangerous and suggestive "New World Order" instead of "Free Bird."

Maybe that's not such a small accomplishment. There's no question that "Smells Like Teen Spirit" is a more edifying soundtrack to 1992 than "Stairway to Heaven." Shit, even "Under the Bridge" is that! People who grew up in 1965, during the famous "Big Chill" era, have never ceased to state their allegiance to Beatles and Beach Boys and Motown songs; the sound of them has defined an entire generation's huge self-worth. Until now, though, there hasn't been a style or type of music that everyone, critics and mainstream listeners alike, could get behind, because rock 'n' roll got so polarized into a set of sexist and classist and basically vulgar popular sounds. As I watch Lollapalooza, I think hopefully that this year might be one that harks back to that type of solidarity. After all, it's been the first year that my ugly next-door neighbors have blasted songs I wanted to hear out their windows on Saturday nights. It's the first time I've seen people whose values and class don't agree with mine wearing T-shirts for bands I like. It's the first time I ever even had a smidgin of a chance of voting for a presidential candidate who might win.

OK, so a world made up of kids who have slightly better record collections than before is not necessarily one that will defeat the powers that be. But I think there's evidence to the contrary. During the Reagan and Bush administrations, popular rock music—classic rock radio, cheesy heavy metal, bimbo-laden new wave, the Black Crowes, even R.E.M.—was as backward-looking as U.S. policies. A close look at the values and beliefs of Lollapaloozers may say nothing whatsoever about the intelligence or political correctitude or individuality of new American youth. But their taste in new music does, I think, at least signify a more forward-looking mind-set.

Anthony Kiedis: "You can only be sort of brainwashed by this other bullshit for so long and then you're going to end up feeling so empty that you'll become more open-minded to new and more flagrant musical concepts. I think that the whole wave of musical consciousness of the world now is kind of reflected in the fact that people are all completely bored and unimpressed by mainstream, numb-minded, corporate-oriented, money-making music."

Ted Gardner is sitting casually at a picnic table behind the Riverbend Arena in Cuyahoga Falls, watching the awkward approach of a doofy-looking reporter from the *Cleveland Plain Dealer*. Gardner is one of those massive-looking Australians, tan and tattooed, a gray crewcut and ready grin. He began in the business as a crew member. He is now also one-third owner of Lollapalooza, Inc., the joint venture that runs this show. "I," says Ted jokingly, "am like your dream stereotypical rock 'n' roll success story; the ex-roadie turned record mogul."

The *Plain Dealer* reporter, on the other hand, is like your dream stereotypical rock critic, in badly fitting blue suit and tie. During the interview, he pompously tells Gardner how much he preferred last year's bill to this, implying (with obvious falsehood) that he throws *Rembrandt Pussyhorse* on the turntable whenever he's alone at night. (Later on, I see the same guy flee Ministry's brain-shatteringly loud set.) Gardner nods wisely. "We'll be back next year," is Ted's polite parting shot. "With the Melvins," he adds under his breath.

Gardner's promise notwithstanding, the natural cynic in me—post-Clash, post-*Warehouse Songs and Stories*—fears that over the years, Lollapalooza will become diluted, like the New Music Seminar, once a service, now a scam. It'll sell one too many T-shirts and *bam*—U.S. Festivalitis. Its parents and producers insist that this won't happen. "In a way, this is really the first Lollapalooza," says Gardner. "Last year's was just a big Jane's tour. But next year, I'd like to see us get so extreme. I'd love that. This year is going to break economic barriers, next one will be the artistic ones."

Maybe that's what will happen. This year's bill does certainly reflect the commercially grunge-laden zeitgeist of 1992, but according to Geiger, it could have included R.E.M., the Cocteau Twins, or Neil Young, who were all on the first-choice list, but who declined to consider the tour. As for next year, every band here has its own personal dream of the perfect Lollapalooza, and I wouldn't be too surprised if at least somebody's dreams come true. Anthony Kiedis wishes the Bad Brains and L7 were on the bill. (L7's inclusion was allegedly vetoed because their sound was too similar to the Seattle contingent.) Vedder's ideal bill would include Fugazi. (But supposedly they were first-round choice, till Farrell asked Henry Rollins if he thought Ian MacKaye would consider it, and Rollins reputedly answered, "You could ask him. I guarantee you he'll give one of two answers: 'No,' or 'No.' ") Lush mentions the Bulgarian Women's Choir. Jim Reid's wish list includes De La Soul and Pussy Galore. ("They broke up." "Well, Royal Trux then.") "Personally," says Soundgarden's Ben Shepherd, "I've always my whole life wanted to see Discharge open for Johnny Cash."

Won't get fooled again? Maybe. Maybe not. It kinds of depends on whether all the kids in Sub Pop shirts and backward baseball caps are vegans and environmentalists, or rednecks in disguise. Are they the new boss, same as the old boss, or are they something just a wee bit better than the thing that came before? Is Lollapalooza a Woodstock for the nineties, as papers like the *Plain Dealer* and the *Chicago Sun Times* persist in referring to it?

"I don't think so," says Kim Thayil. "If any one of these bands could draw this crowd—twenty thousand, sold out in half an hour—then yeah, I'd say maybe there'd been a change. As it is, no."

He has a good point. Then, the members of Soundgarden are the resident cynics, and with good reason. This is their third U.S. tour this year: they went out as openers for Guns N' Roses, then headlining on their own in two-thousand-seaters, and now they have the unenviable job of appearing smack in the middle of the seven-band bill, at six o'clock, when about half the audience leaves the arena for dinner and the other half to go see Jim Rose's second set, whose word of mouth off the two o'clock show has preceded him. Soundgarden aren't complaining, but in fact, theirs is a hard row. Along with Jesus and Mary Chain, whose music simply does not carry in the open air ("Ice *Cube* is more popular than us," announces Jim Reid amusedly), they are probably doing themselves the least amount of good by appearing here of anyone on the bill.

"Don't get me wrong," says Thayil. "I love seeing Ice Cube and Pearl Jam every day, and Ministry is just amazing. I'm glad we're on this bill, I'm just saying it's not that diverse. It's not challenging or underground—there's still all these bands that have yet to be given airplay. The Fluid for instance. And Tad!"

"Oh, like that's diverse?"

"OK, Love Battery and Tad!" Laughter. "No, seriously," Thayil adds. "Where's the jazz fusion? Where's the country and western? Why isn't Sonny Shorrock out there? Doesn't Cincinnati have a chamber orchestra or choir? They should be on the bill! I mean, there's a certain degree of diversity, but it's just what appeals to white kids between eighteen and twenty-four. A Madison Square Gardens Guns N' Roses show is more diverse."

"A Madison Square Gardens Guns N' Roses show," agrees Shepherd, "is like a microcosm of the whole United States. It's a lot of blue-collar workers and some college kids and some yuppies trying to relive their hard-rock high school youth. But this is just suburban kids who fancy themselves as politically right on, when they're not. They're politically oblivious. It's exactly the same age group that never votes."

Next day, Lollapalooza seems to have lost its righteous status: the skies open up and pour on twenty thousand Cleveland natives. Perhaps the gods were angry at the Boatmen's sad misfortune. Backstage all is misery, but on the field they don't seem to have a problem with it, and eventually that spirit catches on. By three in the afternoon, when Eddie takes the stage, the crowd's ripped up the turf, turning the hillside into mud. They take turns running down it and sliding, toboggan style, on their bums. It doesn't take long for the entire crowd to look like New Guinean mud people, and when they rush the front during Ministry's set, seven thousand mud people strong, it looks like nothing you ever saw on earth.

Al Jourgenson is beside himself with the appropriateness of the surroundings. "I *never* say stupid shit like this, but you guys are the best crowd I ever saw!" says Al. Ecstatic with praise from the Antichrist of rock, the blessed tear the seats off the floor and hurl them onstage in glee. By this time, the whole world had gone mad. I saw Chris Cornell climb the hill and slide it on his stomach. Miki from Lush stage-dove into the tribal rite. Soundgarden played "Body Count." Mr. Lifto danced in drag to Pearl Jam.

When it was over, damage was estimated at two hundred grand. The irony of it was that Natalie Cole—a woman who's sold many more records in just the last year than most of these acts combined—was supposed to play a gig there in less than twelve hours, but luckily she'd only sold thirty-five hundred tickets, too few for the lawn seats to matter. (Now there's a comment on modern-day concert promotion.) Also luckily, Lollapalooza's contract states that they're not responsible for any damages inflicted during the show. They'd learned their lesson on that one last year, coincidentally at the same venue, when Cleveland behaved equally outrageously during Nine Inch Nails' set.

Surveying the site at two A.M., awestruck by the destruction, I have to wonder. The huge potholes and mountains and mud glistening in the rain, the T-shirts and blankets stomped into its surface, all made it look like nothing so much as a battlefield, pitted with the explosions of a thousand land mines. It looked like Baghdad, or Serbia. I remembered what Cornell had said onstage earlier in the day: "You guys look like an army out there. Whose army are you going to be?"

EIGHTEEN

THE WORLD SET FREE

Terry Gross: "A lot of people think of punk as having ended quite a few years ago, and yet you're still playing music that comes out of that tradition."

Guy Picciotto: "Yeah, we're like Shakers. We're doing the forgotten dance."
– "Fresh Air," *NPR*, April 13, 1992

The good news was, they were all going crazy. All 120,000 of them, packed shoulder to shoulder across a flat gold plain that would have stretched into the sunset, if ever there was such a thing as a sunset in Denmark in the middle of June. They'd just gone simultaneously bonkers, roaring and rearing and bucking around, naked bodies popping up into the air like defenestrated crash test dummies, drunk, sunburned, screaming, insane. It was twelve hours into the second day of the Roskilde music festival, the largest in Europe and thus, possibly, the world, Woodstock North, Cal Jam Denmark, the U.S. Festival, and Watkins Glen all rolled into one, and the crowd simply could not be contained.

That was the good news. The bad news was, they weren't cheering for headliners and superstars Nirvana, due to take the stage as soon as the pandemonium died down. They were cheering because, against all odds, the country of Denmark had just won the 1992 European Football Championships against the much-hated, top-ranked, machinelike and seemingly invincible German team. Denmark had distinguished itself in this way even though they were only an alternative, hastily allowed into the contest when the long-suffering Yugoslavian team couldn't make it to the airport.

It was thus that the much-anticipated headlining slot of the second day of Roskilde had been suspended during play. Television screens had been rigged up all over the vast fields where the concert was taking place, and for three hours the majority of young Scandinavia, conveniently gathered together in one locale anyway, watched the proceedings in a unanimous rage of excitement. Denmark took the lead near the start of the game and from then on things got progressively more deranged in the peanut gallery. The silence that swept over the night when the game first started—it reminded me, somehow, of the eleven o'clock Armistice at the end of World War I—turned into a subdued hum, and then into a sort of hysterical buzz of breathless hope that rushed through the veins of everyone around. Near the end of the game, even those of us Americans who were using game time as an opportunity to peacefully scarf beer and food backstage suddenly began to catch the nervous tension around us. It was 2–0 in the second half when we all simultaneously realized that the country of Denmark was touchingly close to real nirvana. If they lost, we suddenly thought, the rest of the evening might be a fiasco.

As the sun slowly sank on Roskilde—it was eleven P.M. and not yet twilight—the whistle blew on the playing fields of Gothenburg, Sweden, with Denmark still ahead. And then all the Americans sitting backstage at the orange tent in Roskilde rushed up onstage to watch the revels. Somehow, almost everyone on that field had contrived to make a flag out of T-shirts, scraps; perhaps they'd brought them with them, hidden among their stuff for just this contingency. Anyway, they were waving the flags like mad, making the humongous meadow seem like a scene out of the Crusades or something. Beneath us lay a sea of faces, many of them painted bright red with lipstick, a white cross drawn on their cheeks, and their mouths, wide open, were bright red too. Someone handed us each a plastic cup and poured us champagne. Right at my elbow, I saw Pearl Jam's Eddie Vedder and Nirvana's David Grohl toast each other, and then the crowd, which was loud, became imperceptibly louder. What's louder than loudest? The world's amps turned onto eleven for a second.

Suddenly the sun sank, and the stage crew went back to work. They cleared us off the scaffolding, tightened up the drumheads one last time, shimmied back up the rigging to the lighting works, and made their way well out into the crowd to get out to the south booth. Nirvana—three skinny jerks, pale and weedy-looking in jeans and T-shirts and barely combed hair, the ultimate negative creeps of every shopping mall in America—filed on. Aberdeen, Washington, was just a dream or a nightmare; lost somewhere in the distant past, a million lights years from here. And then: "*Don't you believe it it's just my luck, don't you believe it it's just my luck, don't you believe it it's just my luck . . .*" The song stops. Two quick beats pursue our pulse rate. Duh. Duh. "*No recess! No recess. No recess!*" The dictionary defines that word as meaning "a hidden, secret or secluded part; an indentation or a cleft." The whole time I was in Europe, I couldn't help but wonder how Europeans who bothered to translate that rather idiomatic American chorus were interpreting the otherwise simple meaning of Nirvana's song "School."

No one was translating anything at that particular moment: everything was noise and confusion, an antic swarm of humanity rending up the nearly-night. Looking out at the endless field of faces, I imagined that the giant tower of speakers could blast across the whole wide hemisphere, reaching every heart and mind in the entire western world. I felt much too small to be holding so much love in my own safekeeping. As I watched Nirvana burst their guts into the universe, I felt the violent shudder of a victory so complete it made Denmark's come-from-nowhere sports one pale in comparison. For a moment, I felt as if someone had opened up all our mouths and poured pure goddamn gold down our throats.

Not so many moments later, I'd changed my mind. "Why so glum?" Those are the words that *Rolling Stone* magazine reported Kurt Cobain said backstage at a show in Amsterdam after somebody in the audience broke their face open and bled all over the stage. "Why so glum, everybody?" That's what I was thinking backstage at Roskilde, too, only I didn't mean it sarcastically, like Kurt did then. I have to admit, I was having the time of my life. I'd been the happiest of campers ever since I'd gotten backstage and then run smack into my old friend Lisa Fancher wandering around the press area. But all around me were long, long faces. Clearly, the old adage "Be careful what you wish for, it might come true" is more than a cliché.

The truth is nobody in Nirvana ever wished for anything. That's part of the burden that this band carries now: a sincerity level that's won over the entire world, and made it so much truer, so much more beloved, than all the other crappy pop bands that dominated the preceding decade. None of these bands wanted stardom. They didn't want groupies or good drugs. (Heck, you can get both those things merely by putting out a cheap seven-inch single by yourself and then selling it on Capitol Hill in Seattle.) They certainly didn't want hair weaves or houses or Mercedes Benzes or Rolex watches. They didn't want fucking anything, except to play their music in the basement and have a good old time.

This is the absolute truth. I know because I was there. When success came knocking, they shrugged and took the best offer. Why not? Corporate rock still sucks. Corporate magazines still suck. But we don't suck, so what the hell. That was the reasoning. They didn't expect anything from anyone, just to put out a record and go to sleep at the end of the day. Corruption by association? Who believes in that anymore? If we believed that, we couldn't drive a car full of gasoline. We couldn't buy food at the supermarket. We couldn't keep a checking account. We could not exist.

So they signed their contracts, they shared their music, and they changed the world. And now, after all that, they are ruined, and saddened, and spent: they feel like they've lost everything. Oh God! It should have been our finest hour. And yet there they all were, a pile of misery. The Screaming Trees and most of Pearl Jam are huddled in their respective trailers smoking hash, while Eddie Vedder wanders around looking distraught: upset over the loss of control, and the fact that he's been on the road for ten straight months without a break, he's just nixed a cover story for *Spin* and told his record company he's going home without finishing the tour. Somewhere in the fairgrounds another U.S. band called Mind Funk is facing down nobody at all: their drummer, Jason Everman, was booted from Nirvana a couple of years ago, and I can't help but wonder how he feels tonight. Like Pete Best, maybe. (Another Nirvana alumnus—former second guitarist Ben Shepherd, now bassist for Soundgarden—will show up at their Madrid gig a few nights later, having won a night off from opening for Guns N' Roses when that band suffers one of its numerous cancellations. Seems like every band in all creation is touring Europe this summer.)

Meanwhile, over in the Blue Tent, the Thin White Rope camp are equally depressed: it's their second-to-last gig ever, and they have to play it to exactly no one, since because of the soccer delay, they're going on directly opposite Nirvana. I see the members of Helmet, who have the unenviable three A.M. slot—cowering in a corner: then Kurt emerges from his dressing room, with his seven-months-pregnant wife Courtney Love, clad in a trailing, too-tight tea dress, ripped right across the rib cage, on his arm. These days they're a scary couple, so everyone keeps their distance as he escorts her up the steps to the stage, where they stand all alone, waiting for the Screaming Trees to take the stage. About three songs into the proceedings, singer Mark Lanegan drunkenly hurls every piece of equipment into the audience, while the Connor twins dutifully fistfight the bouncers. Thousands of dollars of video equipment are destroyed, and none of it in fun. Just then I reach up and feel my head: I guess in the mayhem before Nirvana's set, my K hat had fallen off, lost forever in the dusty Danish battlefield below.

Like Nirvana, even I feel no jubilation now, just a dreamlike state of discontent. I look up at the not-night sky and wonder how it could possibly be the same sky that covers England, and America, and San Francisco, and my home. It feels so small, like a blanket that's started slipping in the middle of the night, leaving parts of your flesh all cold and unsafe. The world is claustrophobic for a moment here, much, much too little.

This was supposed to be the summer of our content, not just for Nirvana, but for Pearl Jam, for the Screaming Trees, for Thin White Rope, and for me. It was the summer of success for everyone who'd ever loved punk rock and rejected the mainstream, everyone who'd ever spit in the face of corporate rock, everyone who'd been part of the American alternative underground scene. *The Year Punk Broke:* thanks to Nirvana's Christmastime victory, we'd forced the masses to their knees. We'd made them love what we loved, buy what we bought, think what we think, do what we do. We'd made them make us rich. We'd made them make us famous. We'd made them sell their fucking Michael Jackson CDs and bow down to our values and agree that we were right all along. We'd made them reject their own stupid standards and conform to our own. We'd made them kill their idols. And hadn't that been the goal all along?

Apparently not. One day, a long, long, long time ago—about ten months ago, before Nirvana had gone to number one—Eddie Vedder had said, "As the crowds grow bigger, I grow smaller." At Roskilde, where Pearl Jam went on around four to approximately seventy thousand people, I figured that Eddie Vedder felt pretty pintsized. In that case Kurt Cobain, playing to twice that, was no bigger than a gnat on the head of a Lilliputian's pin. He was so small he was almost invisible, all blond spiky hair and huge black horn-rimmed glasses, shrunk inside his tiny frame, hunched up before the microphone, motionless, defiant. He still beamed out intensity, throwing off emotion like kryptonite rays: his rough voice fraught with his own demons, his guitar barking out its agonized rumble and chime. He was like a black hole, hungrily eating up all the surrounding energy and emitting a negativity so strong that being anywhere around him was almost physically debilitating.

I love Nirvana and sympathize with their problems, but I could not stand being around them any longer. Somewhere in the vast reaches of Roskilde, I ran into this German guy I know who tells me that Fugazi—Ian MacKaye's band, the shards of Minor Threat—are playing in Berlin that Sunday night, and instantly the information takes hold. I can't escape the thought, nagging me, that that way lies salvation. Berlin, I know, is six hundred kilometers south, well away across the Baltic Sea. It's not where I'm supposed to be in Europe. But I don't care! I don't care! For the next twenty-four hours I cannot suppress certain leapings of the heart, certain secret negotiations and bargainings with my better self. In Copenhagen next morning, I accidentally go by the train station and find out schedules.

When I tell everyone my change in plans, a small, airy wave of envy passes through the ranks. In some circles, punk rock circles, K circles, old circles, these circles, just the word *Fugazi* is a green lantern-like talisman, like saying "Jahweh" in ancient Egypt, or wearing garlic next to your skin. Dave Grohl, a D.C. native, looks after me wistfully as I depart. "Say hi to them for me!" he says.

In the morning, Pearl Jam is flying back to America. In the afternoon, Nirvana's buses start off for the airport, bound for the Ruisrock Festival in Turku, Finland. In the long, long Copenhagen evening, I sit for hours outside the Tivoli Gardens watching an ugly American drill team from Ohio entertain a bunch of bewildered Danes in Hans Christian Andersen Square, waiting for my train and wondering if I am doing the right thing. Come the dawn, I am halfway to Berlin. I'm contemplating the words of Rainer Maria Rilke: "To you is left (unspeakably confused) your life, gigantic, ripening, full of fears, so that it, now hemmed in, now grasping all, is changed in you by turns to stone and stars."

Dawn, that is, such as it was on the next to longest night of the year. And at three A.M., seated on the cramped midnight train from Copenhagen to Berlin, I have a reversion of feeling. I find myself, to my dismay, doubting Fugazi.

This is a sin of the first order. But then, for hours, I've been trying to feel like Snoopy on top of his doghouse—you know, "Here's the World War I flying ace, temporarily grounded, on a secret spy mission to Berlin"—and it isn't working anymore. Locked into a smelly compartment with five snoring Germans, tired, hungry, sunburned, sick, jogging crookedly along a track through Europe in the middle of the night, it has become impossible to sustain the fantasy any longer. I realize I am not Lillian Hellman. What I am is a total mess.

The train from Copenhagen crosses the Baltic sea at Gedser, driving straight onto the tiny, East German boat's hold with a series of tedious jerks that would waken anyone except my fat German traveling companions. Being locked into the hold for the journey's duration is more than I can bear, so instead, I make my way up the steep steps to the poverty-stricken ship's poor deck, where the gray day-night—it never gets completely dark—blows a small measure of solace again into my brain.

And then I start to dream of home, where every night for the last year and a half I would get out my minitramp—because Fugazi makes we want to stomp the house down and the neighbors might not like it—and put on "The Waiting Room." "*I am a patient boy, I wait, I wait, I wait, I wait.*" Sometimes I play "Reprovisional" or "Burning Too" or "Suggestion" or "Exit Only." Or, when I'm feeling defiant or angry or just mad at the world, it's "Steady Diet of Nothing" from beginning to goddamned end. "*Out of the ashtray. In-to-the ashtray. Out of the ashtray. Because silence,*" sings Fugazi, "*is a dangerous sound. And thus we will not . . . we will not be beaten down.*"

For years before that, it was "Unsatisfied." "*Look me in the eye and tell me, that I'm satisfied. Are you satisfied?*" The question, like the Latin *num*, demanded a negative reply. "*I'm so, I'm so unsatisfied.*" Then one day, all of a sudden, my credo changed. It was right after the IPU Convention, of course, when I first saw Fugazi live. I'll always remember the lurch in the pit of my stomach, when the lights came down and the show began: Guy breathing down the mike like fucking Gene Vincent in the center of "Be-Bop-A-Lula," *"uh-huh-uh-huh-uh-huh,"* and then, as the lights came up, and the tempo and the opening notes of "Exit Only" welded themselves into one long shout of a beginning: *"Exeunt! Exeunt Exeunt!"* Leave the stage! Get down! You're done! Banishing, with that perfectly worded command, all the players who'd strutted and fretted before him, and ushering in nothing less than triumph. Nothing less than hope itself.

The first time I ever saw Fugazi was the same day the news came down that the Communist party of the Soviet Union had just been dissolved. I was with my friend Ira, a self-described Bolshevik of old, and when he heard the news on CNN he declared himself permanently heartbroken. "I'd rather," he explained, "be part of a system that's only a prey to evil than one like capitalism that's inherently evil in its very intention."

That's how I feel about Fugazi too. Like Marxism, Fugazi's ideals—their insistence on all-ages shows and a five-dollar door price, their community awareness and total indifference to signing to a major label—are probably things that, in the hands of the wrong people, would be prey to abuse. Many people already find their cant too stringent: they attack the band for supposedly being humorless and didactic, and hiss the word *ideologue* at them, as if, in this age of moral bankruptcy, that's such a bad thing to be. Some people even seem to take Fugazi as a personal affront, muttering or shouting, outraged, defensive: What's wrong with profit? What's wrong with gain? And the answer is nothing, I suppose—except that you could, in the pursuit of it, accidentally lose your very soul.

Lost amid these criticisms are two important facts. One is that Fugazi is succeeding where other bands have failed. The other is simply that Fugazi is the greatest live band playing today. What a burn on the world at large, that the best band in the entire world is the private property of youth, the scions of economic rebellion, a band that won't give a penny of its earnings to radio or MTV or advertising or the music business! And it's a burn as well that, in place of the hackneyed old rock 'n' roll values of sex and drugs and abandonment of yore, its credo is the exact opposite: asceticism, responsibility, and economic independence.

My sister says when it comes to rock, I'm a serial monogamist, completely committed to whomsoever is the band of the hour. "Remember when you were fourteen and you thought it was Bruce Springsteen forever and ever?" But I can't remember that old love; I can only remember the new ones. Only occasionally, when I'm feeling weak and sad, do I think, "What if one day I don't love Fugazi the way I do now?" And it's like picturing your parents dead. Alone on the train from Copenhagen to Berlin, horrible thoughts like these flashed continually through my frightened mind. And all the while, outside the train, the thick gold fields of Prussia flashed by. I turned back to Rilke. "Lord, it is time, the summer was too long. And on the meadows let the winds blow strong . . ."

The train pulled into the Lichtenberg station in what was once East Berlin at 6:30 A.M. It was a beautiful, hot, sunny morning in Berlin, but that didn't stop it from slowly dawning on me that I'd just made a huge error in judgment. It turned out, by light of day, that I most certainly wasn't a World War I flying ace on a secret spy mission to Berlin. No. In fact, and almost equally unbelievably, I was a cross, tired, and extremely frightened rock critic who'd just naughtily ditched my proper assignment in order to see my favorite band.

Worse luck, because it was Sunday, nothing was open—not the tourist office, nor the restaurants, nor the ticket office at the train station. I ended up having to get on the S-Bahn to Zoo Station without buying a ticket, a crime for which I felt sure they clap you in prison forever in Germany if you're ever caught, even if you're foreign and tired and palpably a moron, like me. A mean old man yelled at me for putting my feet on the seat in front of me. No one I ran into spoke English (they probably spoke a smattering of Russian, I remembered, though a lot of good that would do me), and I didn't even know where Fugazi was playing that night, much less if I could get into the show. Seldom have I felt quite as forlorn as I did when I got to the Zoo Station, with snatches of U2's song by the same name wafting unbidden through my head.

But miracles do happen, and somehow or other, it all worked out. I called a girl at home in San Francisco whom I'd met at a Fugazi show in Hawaii, and she gave me the number of her friend in Berlin, whom I'd met once at a Nirvana gig. And so it came to pass that early in the evening, Mata and I made our way through the Tiergarten to the Tempodrom, an enormous circus tent just a few steps away from the lawn of the Reichstag, where Fugazi was playing to three thousand that night.

Now, Berlin in the summer is like a quieter Paris, more stately, more realistic, and it was about ninety-five degrees out, even among the trees. From the bus I could see nude Germans frolicking on large expanses of lawn, total "déjeuner sur l'herbe" action. Gypsies were cooking gyros in the shade of the old oaks, and I felt my spirits rising as we zipped past the statue from *Wings of Desire* and approached the pretty venue. The horror of the all-night train ride had already receded in my mind as soon as I was clutching a ticket to Fugazi's show in my hand.

That's because Fugazi, as Debbie once said, is like the burning bush in the Bible. Everything about them—their music, their philosophy—is so fierce that you can't help thinking that if you touch them you'll get burned. But instead, if you have faith, you just catch fire alongside them. Engulfed by their music, no damage will be done: they just burnish your conviction, add a little rebar to your soul. Shaken by the revelations of Roskilde and the long journey to Berlin, I was lacking in self-confidence as well as in energy. Nevertheless, standing shyly in the shadows of the Tempodrom that evening, I held out what was left of my tiny wick of dreams to Fugazi. I prepared to go up in flames.

Now it's ten o'clock and Fugazi have just taken the stage. They look unusually frail tonight. Guy, his head shaved bald, is wraithlike and ill (seemingly suffering from the same complaint as Kurt Cobain, without any hint of drug-related complications). "Nice day," remarks Ian into the microphone. "It's good to see you." And suddenly I felt almost blind with fatigue. I felt as if I had walked all six hundred kilometers from Denmark. The preceding three days—hell, the preceding six months—had been so ridiculous: strange pictures from the past keep popping up to torment me, of Nirvana, of Roskilde, of Lisa and me, a mere twenty-four hours earlier, trapped in a car in some Copenhagen side street surrounded by drunken Danes who were trying to roll the vehicle in a mist of drunken joy. *What the fuck am I doing here again?* I wondered. *I must have lost my mind.*

The band begins with an instrumental before ripping into "And the Same." Then—"Exeunt! Exeunt!"—it's "Exit Only," straight into Fugazi's best-known punk rock anthem, "Merchandise," with its searing anticorporate chorus, "*You are not what you own.*" "Stop! Turnover . . ." leads right on into "Reclamation," a prochoice song, but here in Deutschland lyrics are irrelevant, their content articulated instead by that mysteriously explicit language we speak only in the throes of this peculiar kind of passion. Oh, I've always known that sheer fandom was the noblest endeavor: selfless humility and appreciation untinged with envy, the purest form of love. But now I was reaping my unlooked for reward, confidence and strength were pouring into my very being, it was like an invisible catheter was hooked into my heart. *It keeps on pumping straight to my heart.*

Fugazi had just come from a gig in sad old Poland, where it poured rain and there was some kind of protest about them being held outside the hall. They were kinda low before this concert started, but you wouldn't have known it from their performance. "Reclamation" goes into "Rend it," into "Facet

Squared," into "Latin Roots." And presently, I'm standing bolt upright, fatigue blown clean out of my system (or at least suspended, to be dealt with at a later date).

As usual, the rhythm section is going to bear the brunt of the attack, while Ian and Guy's guitars simply shriek along the top of their billowing and sinuous beats. Some people say that Fugazi is essentially a rhythm band, sharing more in common with dub bands and reggae acts than anything it has to do with the hardcore world it comes from. And it's true that their music is anchored in a slow tempo that harshens and lengthens each song to an almost unbearably tense conclusion: it stutters through its incantations, sometimes all but stopping short, sometimes whipping into an urgency and speed. But to me the important thing about Fugazi is just its sheer emotion. It's the songs themselves—bursting the seams of passion with logic, firing the synapses of sentient thought. Tonight we will be the foster children of noise, welded by wattage into some kind of inner strength. Tonight, when Ian shrieks the final line of "Suggestion," I am stunned into a moment of sudden mental clarity, as brief and profound as hitting the top of a perfect high dive, when there's a momentary gravitational pause, just before you plunge toward that inevitable rip. *We're all guilty!* I've heard the line a hundred times before, but looking out into the eyes of Germany, the words take on a bigger meaning. Beauty, after all, may not be Fugazi's province. But sometimes the truth is exactly the same thing.

And now Nirvana is long since gone, buried beneath the burden of so much money, mud and *crème brûlée*. Here in Berlin we are being torched clean, experiencing that incalculable rock 'n' roll feeling that Lester Bangs once called "an erection of the heart." The audience is a pit of flesh, swaying and jumping, red-faced, wild, and the band is matching them in sheer heart-attack abandon, bucking and rearing, possessed by the electricity that courses through their guitars and through the entire arena: building, building, building, up to *ein zwei drei repeater.*

Power permeates the arena, shaking our bodies with its electric fingers, demolishing our thoughts of fear and anger, loosening our minds from the grip of time itself.

The show is over all too soon and Guy pitches himself head first down the ramp that leads to the back of the stage. Brendan sits quietly, sweat-soaked, exhausted. Ian is hyperactive in a drained sort of way: his eyes look out at the crowd unseeing, blank with spent effort, devoid now of rage. Joe, I believe, has never turned a hair; as usual he manages to look like he just spent a day at the beach.

And me? I'm in hyperspace, lost among the stars, wandering blissfully through fields and dark forests, drinking in the beauty of this hot Berlin night. Free. And then I lean back into my beautiful life, imbued all at once with a belated revelation, struck dumb with wonder at the places I have come. The story of Nirvana might almost be over. But my life is just beginning.

NINETEEN

SAY HELLO TO HEAVEN

I heard that Dave Grohl went out to the Embassy [a club in D.C.] the other night and some guy came up to a friend of mine and said, all amazed, "Hey, isn't that the guy in Nirvana? I recognize him from MTV!" And my friend said, "Yeah, that's him." And the guy goes, "Don't you think it's weird that he's here?" And my friend thinks for a second and then he says, "No. What's weird is that he's on MTV."

– Courtney Love, March 1992

Nils Bernstein's house is full of mail. In every nook and cranny there are stacks of letters to Nirvana, addressed in green felt tip and blue ballpoint and black Sharpie pen. It feels like there are ghosts in this house, from North Carolina, from New Haven, Connecticut, from France. These are the souls of all the lonely children in the entire western world, discarded, bundled up, stifled silent, and existing, in solid form, here in this apartment on Capitol Hill in Seattle. Letters are lying around half out of the envelope on the coffee table, under a book in the bathroom, bound and gagged in giant stacks in huge cardboard boxes in the corner. They are a crushing symbol of something or other: tangible evidence of the unholy power of Nirvana's words and music. It's unlikely that all of them will ever be answered. It's unlikely they'll ever be moved. And Nils's building is currently condemned.

Except for the seemingly ectoplasmic presence of America's

youth, Nils's apartment building is much like the one portrayed in the movie *Singles*: his neighbors, Eben, Kathy, and Angela, run in and out all day. Debbie and Jenny from Sub Pop live next door, in Charles Petersen's old building; Bruce lives up the street in a newly remodeled four-story Victorian complete with a barnyard in which he keeps a pet goat. When he gives one of his all-night disco parties, he insists that everyone take off their shoes and leave them on the porch. There they stand, lined up like a shriekback song: beat-up black combat boots bound with silver duct tape, hightop Converse All-Stars with grubby broken laces, the mud of a thousand nights spent slogging down Virginia Street and up Alaskan Way to the Crocodile or the Moore or the Offramp or RCKCNDY. Clunk, clunk, clunk. "There ought to be a sign saying, 'Leave all grunge at the door,' " says Mary Ellen. "Someone should take a picture of this as the most telling sign of Seattle. There could be little signs over each shoe: Kurt, Kurt, Krist, Krist, Tad, Mark, Bruce, Jon, Kurt."

Meanwhile, Kurt and Courtney are holed up downtown at the Four Seasons in Seattle, registered under the legal names of Sid and Nancy Vicious, while Courtney finishes mixing some tracks with her band, Hole, and Kurt helps take care of the baby. He's supposed, also, to be rehearsing with Nirvana, writing new songs, and contributing the liner notes to *Incesticide*, the album of Nirvana B sides and one-offs that's due out at Christmas, but he's stalling on the latter thing pretty badly. At first glance it seems like Nirvana is now so rich and famous and powerful that their management company can't make them do anything. But then Gold Mountain probably couldn't have made Kurt do anything even if the band was bombing big time by now. One afternoon I ask Kurt if he ever wrote that piece on the Melvins my friends at *Option* had hopefully assigned him. "Well, I started it," he said all eagerly. "But you know I'm not too good with deadlines."

Then Courtney gets on the phone and we talk for a while

about things like last night's Breeders show—"Not all of us can approach Kim Dealhood," Courtney sighs—and what all our mutual friends are up to and other grrrly stuff. In the background Kurt's putting on makeup—"Courtney, do you have any eye liner?"—just to pass the time, and she keeps turning around midsentence: "I'll be off in one more minute. I'll be off in one more minute!" But the whole time they're talking to me I know she's supposed to be in the studio mixing a new single, so I'm sitting there worrying about the studio time they're pissing away. I know 7 million records buys a lot of studio time, but I also know that somewhere in Seattle right now eight or ten people—engineers, receptionists, band members, whatever—are probably waiting on Kurt and Courtney, tapping their fingers and feet, watching the clock.

Upstairs in the Four Seasons, however, time goes really fast. "And then what'd she say? You're kidding! Can you believe it! Oh God, I know just what you mean." And so on and so forth. It all sounds so normal, but deep down I feel like an emissary from the planet Earth, sending Kurt and Courtney tidings from The People. *Ground control to Major Tom, your circuit's dead, there's something wrong. Can you hear me, Major Tom?* Kurt and Courtney are just so famous now. They're just so, so famous. This week alone they've been in *Spy* and *Newsweek* and *The New Yorker* and even a *New York Times* piece on grunge entitled "Birth of a Weird Fad." When I hang up from talking with Kurt and Courtney, I feel like I have a secret: that I am a person of privilege making strange little skirmishes into an unknown country, that mysterious land of massive fame. "I really think the subtext of people's talk when they say somebody's sold out, or, like, 'They suck now,' " comments Bruce Pavitt, "is just that the band has suddenly become inaccessible. You cannot reach them. You will never communicate with them again."

Kurt and Courtney are still trying to be accessible. They're always going to shows (Beat Happening, P. J. Harvey, the Breeders) and shopping (Macy's Customer Appreciation Night) and to parties and to friends' houses and to record stores. But there's a big difference between being physically accessible and being mentally accessible. Now when a Nirvana song comes on the radio, I look at the cars driving past me, and I think how weird it is that everyone in all of them, nearly everyone I see, is probably sitting there thinking about Kurt Cobain. "Living in America is about tolerance and capitalism and mass impact," remarked Courtney, a few weeks later. "Kurt just hates what he's done," by which she means get famous, "but I think it's a beautiful, cool thing. It's just so . . . so subversive!"

And it is subversive. There are all these celebrities in the world, like Mick Jagger, whose songs and images somehow signify a particular set of values. The celebrities are not artists anymore, they're cartoon characters, each with his own stupid, set-in-stone standards to uphold. Their entire being speaks of certain archetypes, which appeal to the people who intercept them: they're either rich and arrogant, or sensitive and concerned, or they're out raising money for orphans in Bosnia and Herzegovina, or they're drinking champagne and eating bonbons while naked slave girls wave palm leaves over their flesh. I feel like I know what Mick Jagger or George Michael are doing, but *nobody* knows Kurt Cobain. The things he thinks and speaks and writes about are revealed not in language but in nuance and gesture, in the shriek of his animal voice and the rattle of his bad guitar. Behind his strange eyes there is a peculiar self-containment, a terrible privacy of purpose that has managed to intrigue everyone around him since the day he first took the stage. It's a mysterious thing, this celebrity of Kurt's: it's so unlike the celebrity of everyone who's come before him. Divorced from all the standards of American achievement, good looks or coherence or even lyrical intelligibility, Kurt stands, in a way, for the possible elevation of the ordinary man to the circles of the blessed. No wonder the mere mention of his name evokes such awe.

On any given day this fall, you never know where Kurt and Courtney will be. Some afternoons Kurt and Courtney up and go to L.A. Other days they come to San Francisco, where

Kurt's helping the Melvins record their new record for Atlantic. The Cobains assuredly do not lead normal lives, but things are going better for them than they were a few months ago. There was a really rough patch back in July and August, just before the Reading Festival and the birth of their daughter, Frances Bean, on August 18, 1992. Before that crucial date, things were looking pretty ugly indeed. At that time some people even thought that Nirvana had broken up for good.

That was right after *Nevermind* had gone ballistic, when the furor over the band was at its height. Bidding wars were beginning over bands like Helmet and Paw, with of course the most concentrated efforts being reserved specially for Courtney's band, Hole. (Kurt and Courtney got married in Hawaii on February 22, just a few days after Kurt's twenty-fifth birthday.) You could hardly get a flight up to Seattle from L.A. without being seated by some podgy A & R guy with a goatee, glasses, and a Ren and Stimpy T-shirt. *Newsweek, The New Yorker,* and *Rolling Stone* started stopping by Sub Pop (now extremely solvent thanks to the sudden influx of cash that the post-*Nevermind* sales of *Bleach* were giving them) on a regular basis, checking out bands they'd been indifferent to before.

Then Warner Brothers and Epic Records started pumping the movie *Singles,* which had previously been held for a year in postproduction. In Paris and Milan, designers like Mark Jacobs and Christian Roth began making collections of plaid shirts and baseball caps, which they called "subcouture" for the masses. The alternative world had become the mainstream and the underground was over.

From the record company's promotional standpoint, things had only just begun. Nirvana themselves were all incredulous and bummed about it: unnerved by the metal kids who were now their new fan base, worried about the underground credibility they somehow felt they'd lost. In March, Kurt told *Flipside* he wanted to find a way to continue on at club level, rather than moving up to arenas: "Somehow kids could prove that they were into Nirvana [before] with an old worn-out 'fudge packing' T-shirt or something. It would be great to do something like that but it's not very realistic. It just doesn't seem possible. We'll just have to wait until our next record comes out and bombs, and then we'll lose the audience that doesn't really matter in the first place, all the kids who just turned on to *Nevermind* in the last year, and we'll have our old fans back probably. I don't even know if that's realistic, but it's a nice thought."

At that point Nirvana was taking some time off. They had already toured off *Nevermind* for seven months straight, beginning well before its release in the United States and Europe, and then continuing over to Australia and Japan. Kurt was calling himself a walking zombie when they were, though. But those dates, booked before they became really large, were in correspondingly small arenas. And after those dates were over, the band suddenly stopped doing the things bands in that position are supposed to do—like a million interviews, in-store and radio and television appearances, meetings over covers and lyrics and money and studio time. The minute Nirvana had some leverage, they blew off doing more work. In the springtime, when *Nevermind* was blocking the top of the charts and every publication in Christendom was doing stories on the Seattle scene, the three of them sat back (in L.A., Seattle, and D.C. respectively) and watched it rise.

A lot of people thought Nirvana's skittish behavior was the result of hatred among its members, the oft-rumored drug problems of Kurt and Courtney, or even mere caprice, a kind of stubborn punk backpedaling born of discontent at their newfound position. Experts believe that if Nirvana had done a blockbuster arena tour of America in the summer of 1992, they might have sold twice as many records as they in fact did: 8 million domestically as compared to 4 million. But I do not necessarily agree. I think the band's refusal to play into the usual major-label pattern was just the obvious exercise of a power no other band had, the power to just say no. I can only applaud a group—the first group ever, that I can think of—who, in the face of total media overkill and world domination, did their best to put the brakes on things, who just said, "Enough is enough."

*

So Nirvana laid low for a few months there. But laying low didn't spare them from media scrutiny, especially since Kurt and Courtney were expecting. The entire time they were resting, the world took to speculating on their health and their wealth, while meanwhile, out in radioland, the more energetic and friendlier members of Pearl Jam took center stage by default.

In late July, all hell broke loose, when *Vanity Fair* ran an article on Courtney in which she admitted to using heroin while pregnant (which she now denies, though author Lynn Hirschberg stands by her tape). By that time the *Vanity Fair* article was causing a super stink. MTV news reported the quote, along with Kurt and Courtney's official denial. Additionally, it soon became widely known that *Vanity Fair* had ordered the image of a lit cigarette that a naked and pregnant Courtney was holding in the photo be airbrushed out, because it was too gross.

Kurt and Courtney were genuinely upset about the article—as they were about one that ran in the *New Music Express* a month later, describing the backstage scene at the Madrid show and blaming Courtney's personal obnoxiousness for the band's internal problems. But I was at that gig myself, and there certainly was an atmosphere pervading it of something getting faintly spoiled, going rotten in the Spanish sun. It felt like there was something hidden somewhere, the emotional equivalent of some really bad meat. Kurt was singing a new song called "Dumb," that goes, "*I think I'm dumb, but I can pretend. The sun is gone, can I have a light? The day is done, but I'm having fun, I think I'm dumb . . .* " He looked positively hollow, an empty vessel, ripe for refill. Troubled and troubling . . . but then, that's kind of how he always looks. That night I peered curiously out at the Spanish audience from the wings as they happily howled, "No recess!" (*A hidden or secret place or part of a whole. An indentation or cleft. A suspension of business or procedure. Rest or relaxation.*) Later people kept saying worriedly, "Did it seem like Nirvana was going to break up?" And I would say, "I don't know . . . do bands break up when they're still playing great?"

*

The *Vanity Fair* article was much more problematic, trying to be simultaneously titillating but censorious, exploiting the old "sex and drugs and rock 'n' roll" angle in a particularly ignorant, distorting manner. Since when has *Vanity Fair* run eight-page spreads on tiny independent-label bands—like Courtney's band, Hole—that only have one record out? ("Oh, I know!" exclaims Courtney disgustedly. "Who next, the Reivers?") For all the hoo-ha about it, Hole's *Pretty on the Inside* sold only sixty thousand copies worldwide (most of those in England), and everyone, including Courtney herself, admitted that the band's bucks-ridden signing to Geffen Records, artistically merited though it may well be, is based in the record biz's eyes largely on the fact that she's married to Kurt Cobain, which is so fucking sexist. It's so old-fashioned.

Courtney wants and needs Hole to put out a record that justifies all the money and media attention currently being lavished on her as Kurt's wife, and I sure hope she does. She says she's turning away from her raw interpretation of punk rock—the screaming, hellish intensity of *Pretty on the Inside*, and what she described in *Vanity Fair* as a "kinderwhore" look—toward something more accessible, more pop.

Courtney is originally from Portland and San Francisco. She moved around a lot in the mideighties, including stints in Minneapolis, New York, and Olympia, before winding up in L.A. more or less permanently. As well as attempting to maintain an acting career (which she supported in the meantime by stripping) throughout the eighties, she tried to form rock bands in all those locales. "Don't you think it's strange," Courtney has commented to me, "that every girl in the country who has tried to be in a good band knows each other?"

Some of Courtney's early band companions were Kat Bjelland of Babes in Toyland and Jennifer Finch of L7. She also played briefly, in about 1983, with an early version of Faith No More. Hole's *Pretty on the Inside*, her first record, was released on Caroline Records in 1991.

But I only met Courtney for the first time in February, on the night before her wedding to Kurt. She sought me out in a nightclub in Hawaii, and to this day I have no idea how she knew who I was (or even that I was there). There I was, happily moshing away in a pit with a bunch of others, when I felt a hand on my shoulder, whipping my face round; her gaze burning into mine. Courtney dragged me backstage, there to talk to me for the rest of the show. The noise was so loud I didn't hear a single word she said.

The last time I saw Kurt and Courtney in private was at Barajos Airport in Madrid in July. I was just standing there glumly, minding my own business, when I ran into them. My wallet had just been lifted by a creep in stone-washed denim overalls in the Metro, so, totally moneyless, I was trying to get home myself. And suddenly they appeared, as if out of nowhere: Kurt, standing by an ambulance, with Courtney, in a bright red baby doll dress, standing by his side.

As far as I'd known, she and Kurt were supposed to fly home that morning, from Bilbao to London to L.A., but apparently they'd taken a five-hour ambulance ride over the Basque mountains to get here instead. I waved, across the airport, forlornly. Their manager was over at the ticket counter, purchasing three same-day first-class seats (two of them for Courtney) on the next flight to Los Angeles. I dared not even contemplate the cost.

Just then another handler rushed up to me. "Leave them alone!" "Sure, Larry," I said puzzledly. For some reason, what popped into my head was the time I'd been driving in L.A. to the Pontiac Brothers party alone, and then a picture of myself in that train earlier on my way to Berlin. I remembered how it used to be, seeing people I barely knew in nightclubs and the hail-fellow-well-met-ness of the punk rock world of not so long ago.

All of a sudden, that ebullience was gone, and I was being smacked once and for all into a crueller reality, where nobody had ties to anybody anymore. So I was a Nirvana fan? So were millions of people across the face of this planet. In the past couple of weeks it had become an entirely meaningless distinction, entitling me to nothing, rendering me, in fact, suspect to the people I once knew.

I retreated to the airport waiting room, where I eyed the couple fearfully from afar, because I was, by now, afraid of them myself. And as the thick glass double doors of the airport closed on their wavering image, I wondered about their future.

Nirvana would play only a few more gigs in 1992: once on the MTV Awards, once in Portland, and once at the Coliseum in Seattle. In October they also played unannounced with Mudhoney at Western Washington University in Bellingham, at Castaic Lake in greater L.A., at the four-hundred-capacity Crocodile Club in Seattle, and once, in front of forty thousand people, at a stadium gig in Buenos Aires, along with Joe Cocker, Keith Richards, and Calamity Jane, an all-female band from Portland whom they forced promoters to take along with them. But that day in Madrid, I wouldn't have been surprised if you told me they would never play again. Sick at heart, I repaired, moneyless, to the snack bar, where a kind-hearted Dutch roadie for Guns N' Roses named Boom, cast off from the crew for a few days while the band sat out its cancellations, bought me a meal. He shoved a bunch of remaining pesetas in my pocket as he fled for the gate to Amsterdam. I appreciated the spare change a lot, but I couldn't help feeling, in a way, like I was taking tainted cash. I certainly never wanted to be in a situation where Guns N' Roses saved my ass. I had never thought in a million years that I would be.

Landing in Portland exactly ten weeks later was like landing on the set of "Twin Peaks." The toilets in the airport flushed whenever you got near them. Then the car radio announced, before bursting cheerily into "Achy Breaky Heart," that two bodies had been found on the slopes of Mount Rainier. The woods encroaching the highway's sides, all brown and damp, smelled faintly of coffee, and wood smoke, and some kind of fish. It was three o'clock on a rainy afternoon and I tooled up

Interstate 205 on autoscan till I was electrified into action by a randomly heard announcement: "We're here at Portland Meadows, where the Nirvana show's about to start . . ." and immediately I stepped on the gas.

When I got to my friend Dan's house, however, it turned out there was no hurry: instead everyone was sitting around smoking cigarettes and drinking brandy, ostensibly waiting for the first few of four opening acts to be over with. The walls of Dan's house are painted black and the color of flesh; the tables are purple and appliquéd with fake jewels. It was a bit like stepping into the cover of *Ritual De Lo Habitual*, only nobody was naked. Someone was giving somebody else a tattoo, and Dan obligingly flipped the futon mattress over to exhibit an enormous bloody mark in the shape of an elaborate dragon for my perusal. The last houseguest had slept on his back there right after getting stained.

Presently we all piled in the car and went to the Portland racetracks, where the show was being held. Eyeing a parking lot packed with teenagers and coolers, Dan said he was getting nervous. "I hate things like this," he said gloomily. Dan and his friends live such a subterranean life, unclouded by the taint of commerce. They don't poke their heads up into the real world for even a second, and they certainly weren't prepared to hear rednecks in Slayer T-shirts and itty-bitty baby mustaches singing "Been a Son" word perfect in the beer line. "What could they possibly think this song is about?" Dan wondered aloud, as the crackers around us bellowed, *"She should have stood out in a crowd, she should have made her mother proud, she should have borne another stance, she should have had another chance"* into the darkness. I shrugged. When worlds collide, you know? What did it matter what they thought about the words, as long as they were singing them? It was just like Emile Coué: "Every day, and in every way, I am becoming better and better." And anyway, where had Dan been all year? Nirvana had, after all, played the MTV Awards show the night before, sandwiched between acts like the Black Crowes and Eric Clapton, Elton John and Guns N' Roses.

Of course, anything on cable – heck, anything on television – is just a giant question mark to Dan. He couldn't hum any Guns N' Roses song if you paid him. It's partly why I love him so. The last time they saw Nirvana, Dan's best friend, Chanda, recalls, was when a friend's band called Earth came to play Portland. "There were, like, eighteen people in the audience, and two of them were Kurt and Dave, and they were slamming each other silly against the stage."

"They stayed at our house once," added Dan. "Kurt slept the whole time."

As the fairgrounds filled up, Dan and company kept glancing around nervously. Eventually, we got locked into the so-called "Beer Garden" (actually a bit of field corralled by a few yards of storm fencing) with a Red Hook in each hand. Far off in the distance we could hear Helmet playing, but we decided we didn't like them. "It sounds," someone said with a flash of rare genius, "like they're playing all the bass parts of *Bleach* twice as fast and on guitar." Everybody chortled. Then, as the moon rose slowly over the meadow, we made our way to the front of the field.

This was Nirvana's first concert in America since the one in Hawaii last February, and it happened to be a benefit for Oregon's anti-Proposition 9 forces. Proposition 9 would, among other things, allow discrimination against gay employees. So Kurt began with a public service announcement. "Did you know I'm gay?" The crowd cheered. "I married a transsexual recently, but I like to butt-fuck," he added. "It feels really good."

Then the band went into almost everything from *Bleach* and *Nevermind* and the yet to be released *Incesticide*, not excluding their Vaselines covers, "Molly's Lips" and "Son of a Gun," and three new songs, including "Dumb," "Rape Me," and a song whose chorus goes, "*What else could I be? My apologies.*" They did a version of "Lithium" in which, it seemed to me, there was a reversal of meaning: "*I'm so happy 'cause today I found my friends. They're in my head*" was no longer a bitter comment on loneliness, but a suggestion of solace, a measure of peace. Nirvana were flying through their back catalog, but what had just a few weeks ago seemed tarnished and totally sloppy had turned into a triumph of will.

Then they did "About a Girl" and "Love Buzz," and a Wipers cover called "L7," and the audience blended itself into a kind of whole. There was no yakking, no brawling, just one slow-mo mosh, an interlude of unity, a brief hint at the joys of a possible sedition.

But then, suddenly, there occurred one of the weirdest unrehearsed midconcert interludes I've ever seen: a passage that patently illustrates the difference between Nirvana and any other band of their stature. Around midset, Kurt started telling the audience about the fight he and his wife, Courtney, got into with Axl Rose at the MTV Awards the night before. According to Kurt, while she was sitting in front of their trailer backstage nursing their new baby, Frances, Courtney had yelled repeatedly over to Axl as he walked past, "Hey, Axl, will you be the godfather of our child?" Finally Axl turned to Kurt and said, "Hey, Cobain, if you don't get your wife to stop flipping me shit, I'm gonna take you down to the pavement!"

Krist interrupted. "Can you imagine? He had a three-week-old child in his arms!"

Kurt, sarcastically: "So I turned to Courtney and said, 'Shut up, bitch!' "

Suddenly, a kid leapt onstage, grabbed the mike, and said, "Dude! I'm not defending Axl, but . . ."

And Krist, stationed on the other side of the stage at another mike, says, "Good, 'cause you can't. How can you defend a homophobic, sexist asshole?"

"No, no, let him speak," interrupted Kurt from his side of the stage. "This is a good forum."

Kid: "Thanks, man! 'Cause the thing is, metal music, alternative music, they're both totally valid!"

There was kind of this silence in the crowd, as we all took in that statement, and I wondered whether it was indeed true. Valid? If I didn't believe that Nirvana—their music, their actions, their behavior backstage at concerts, their whole demeanor—is more valid than heavy-metal music, if I didn't think we were making progress here, I don't think I'd be writing this book. I thought for a second about my generous friend Boom, and Duff from the Fastbacks, who's been in Guns N' Roses since 1983. And then I thought of the Concrete Marketing Convention, and the big-breasted girls who are encouraged to lift their tops to the video cameras at all Guns N' Roses concerts, and about the essential personality differences between Axl Rose and Kurt Cobain. I thought about the IPU Convention. I thought about Fugazi.

Finally: thought about something Gerard Cosloy once said regarding Nirvana, that he had more respect for them as a big famous band in a huge arena than he did for them when they were sharing the stage with Railroad Jerk. "I think as public figures they're funnier and a lot more honest than Sammy Hagar or Madonna . . . They've done a great job with getting their point across in front of thousands, whereas in front of a couple of hundred people in a club, it didn't really matter."

And then, as if to end the argument, Kurt looked over at Krist and commanded him to come to his side of the stage. "Come over here, man."

Krist loped over, puzzledly.

"Krist," said Kurt. "I love you, man." And the two of them went into this deep French kiss, tongues and all, while behind them Dave beat up the intro of "Stay Away" and the show drew to its beauteously anarchic finish. There was no encore, and incidentally, no destruction of their instruments: Nirvana doesn't do that when all's right with the world. Afterward, moshed to near pulphood, the beads of my best necklace crushed into Oregonian earth, I crept behind the stage to retrieve my souvenir T-shirt from its hiding place under a riser. Off in the distance, a crowd of backstage revelers were waiting to receive the conquering heroes of the hour, but there in the shadows I glimpsed Kurt and Krist and Dave in a postshow huddle, arms round one another's necks, laughing, high-fiving, three big huge beams splatted across their faces. Healed. You know what they say in baseball: it ain't over till it's over.

TWENTY

HEARTS AND MINDS

At the end the singer observes, "The animals I've trapped have all become my pets," and when you hear that you will either turn the music up or off. Forgetting the pain again that you never wanted to remember in the first place, returning to your life of functions, you may opt for off. But sooner or later, there will be no more forgetting, the remembering will be irrevocable. And then off is just another function. Up is a direction.

– Steve Erickson on *Nevermind*, *L.A. Weekly*, October 1991

When I was a little girl my aunt and uncle lived in a town near London called Harrow-on-the-Hill. Their house had a badminton court and a fish pond at the bottom of the garden, and once my cousin Andrew pinned me to the lawn by hooking the croquet hoops over my arms and legs and neck and left me there to stew for what seemed to a six-year-old like almost overnight.

Then we all grew up and moved away and I never went back until four nights after the Fugazi show in Berlin, when I wound up on the station platform there by accident on my way to the Bruce Springsteen concert at Wembley Arena. It was one of those rare days in England, all sweet blue sky and sunshine, a golden evening like out of history, like they say they used to have there every summer before World War I, and for a moment I wished desperately that we could go out of the station and up Harrow Road and see the old house, and the ways that the haunts of my youth had changed. But we didn't have time, so instead I just stood there, breathing in the green and thinking all about the past. After all, nothing is as pertinent as the past is, when you're on your way to see Bruce Springsteen.

I should have known that Bruce would be bad. But worse than John Cougar Mellencamp, or even Bryan Adams? Bruce's band was boring, and he himself was awkward and stagy. All the new songs were at best mediocre, and the old ones filled with unconvincing cant, and between songs he said dumb stuff about how yucky success is and how great his kids are, and when his wife, Patti Scialfa, came on like Linda McCartney everybody was supposed to clap. I liked hearing "Badlands" and "The River" and "Darkness" – those were the table scraps we were supposed to suffice on within an endless string of bad new material. But even they were pretty perfunctory, and everything else seemed like ashes and dust. Long before it was over I saw Sting and his wife get up and leave.

The first set finally drew to a close with an interminably long version of "Roll of the Dice," replete with false endings and fakoid line dancing and cavorting on the part of his incredibly contrived-looking band. And as I watched the smarmy faux Motown and gospel stuff, I thought of the shows I'd just seen by Nirvana and Fugazi, and I thought how completely unbelievable it now seems that once upon a time, I felt about Bruce Springsteen the way I now feel about them. I ought, I thought, to go out and buy a gun. It would save us all a lot of heartache later on.

I'm just kidding, of course. I'd never shoot Fugazi, because they'll never, ever falter. As for Nirvana, there's little doubt that, like the Sex Pistols before them, they'll take matters like that into their own hands well before there's even any need to. Besides, it's Nirvana themselves who've made Bruce so meaningless that his records are dropping right off the charts. I mean, think of "Smells Like Teen Spirit" in comparison to "Better Days." It's not just that the first-named song has (like the Velvet Underground, like the Pistols, like Grandmaster Flash and the Furious Five) rendered all that came before it entirely dated and old-fashioned. It's that what Nirvana expresses – their nihilism and alienation, their world-weary resignation – is exactly what 1992 is all about. Sure, it's negative. But there's nothing more positive than to think, "Yeah, that's *exactly* what I think."

Of course, this is the same sensation I had when I heard Bruce in 1978, only he was saying positive things, post-Watergate things, like "dreams come true" and "don't look back." Well, maybe those were the right things to hear then. But now the world's all mini-malls and fascists. Now downtown San Francisco looks like Calcutta. And meantime Bruce is saying all this stuff about working hard and loving your fellow man and retaining your family fucking values – shades of Dan Quayle, for God's sake!—and it's pretty thin shit. It's like the man's turned into his very own dad.

There's nothing wrong with that in itself. I'm sure Bruce's dad is a very nice man. (Like Paul Westerberg said, circa 1981: '*I hate my dad. Someday I won't.*") But it's just not rock 'n' roll. It is the opposite of rock 'n' roll. I mean, when you and I successfully find the life of our dads—reach safety, as it were; get into home port—then we simply won't need rock 'n' roll anymore. We'll need other things, like a mortgage and a Volvo and earplugs.

And when that happens, it might turn out, as Nirvana has recently discovered, that a dream is just as much of a lie when it does come true as when it doesn't.

I worry that when people look back on the late twentieth century, they'll see so much surface stuff: stupid sound bites of infotainment and MTV; crack houses and mini-malls; dope, guns, and fucking in the streets. They'll visualize this era as stunted and shallow, and they'll point to the tunes of Whitney Houston and Madonna and Phil Collins and Bruce to prove it, instead of knowing the beautiful truth: how, deep in the heart of our very own small towns, we took the tools of our culture and hewed them into our very own road.

Punk rock dreamed of a world where the line between

audience and rock stars had blurred, where you could be your own hero, where economic independence existed, where money and power changed hands at the top. Nirvana has started to make that dream real, but they made it to the top only with the help of a major label: for all the money the band is making, Geffen Records is still making more. Thus our victory is not yet complete: "It's not like," says Kurt, "if we were the Melvins or Jesus Lizard. If they were to sell as many records as we did then that really would be a phenomenon."

Now I dream of the day when an indie from our world gets to where Nirvana is under its very own steam. Why shouldn't it? If Run D.M.C. and Ice Cube can do it that way, hitting two million sales on a five-thousand-dollar promo budget, why not Fugazi next? Nirvana will always be glad to give them a leg up. Hell, knowing them, they're probably already poised, hands clasped at knee level, preparing to give them or someone like them that crucial boost.

Nirvana's music hasn't caused people to think differently, but its success with the masses is symbolic of the change of heart within the very fabric of youth. Because my world, the independent world of the eighties, for all its supposed liberality, was essentially apolitical: it was white, it was sexist, and it was cruel. Yes, it rebelled against conformity and greed, but it also reflected the whole era's selfishness in its ultimate dismissal of responsibility and kindness. The subsequent success of campaigns like Rock the Vote and Rock for Choice, and the eventual election of President Clinton, are proof that the generation following mine has changed some of its focus: I do not know what it means, but I know it is no accident that all the events described herein occurred during the years that the Republicans held office. As Simon Frith once said about the economic contradictions inherent to subcultures and the dominant majority, "The issue is not how to live outside capitalism, but how to live within it."

The drama of Nirvana won't be viewed in the telling of its

economic triumph or the hearing of their artistic subversion or even in the honest expressions of their personal dismay. It's not in the sight of the repoliticization of America that their world domination has ultimately been proved. No, the drama of Nirvana is going to be in its quiescence; in watching the fallout of the things it has symbolized, the injection of fuel into the moribund music industry, and the infusion of teen spirit into the hearts and minds of American youth. Nirvana has dragged us all up along with them, and now here we stand, looking down at the past, at a mental map of our traversal of the route that brought this all to pass.

There really was a Route 666, you know: as clearly marked as any place on the atlas, as historically significant as the Appian Way. You could have gotten on it anywhere—in Palo Alto or Madrid, a stick slung over your shoulder, with your toothbrush tied up in a bandana—and it would have led you to all the same places I went, to Maxwell's and Merlyn's and the 7th Street Entry, Austin and Boston and Minneapolis and Seattle. Nowadays, if you can only find its on-ramp, it will lead you to other places – perhaps to San Diego or the Maritime Provinces, perhaps to the future, perhaps to freedom, or perhaps it will lead you all the way home. It's there for everyone, a toll-free road, just waiting for a new generation to bend it to its will.

If only Nirvana could have known in their hearts exactly how liberating their music was for us: if they could see the blossom here next spring. Henry Rollins once said that music exists to put furniture in your mind "because life is so cruel and TV is so mean." When I think of the precious pieces with which punk rock has furnished my brain, of the enormous gift it has given to my life, I cannot be too grateful. Because I grew up thinking that everything had already happened, and it turned out I was wrong.

Because of Nirvana, everything's different now, the bands and the industry and the history of rock 'n' roll. But that doesn't mean that our revels are now ending: sleep, I hope, is still not on the cards. For the moment, at least, the future and the past must live together in my imagination, like Nirvana's music and my uncle's old house out on Harrow Road, unsullied by time and grief and disillusion, still shining in the evening sun. It's not necessary for me to find out just how much the garden's shrunk; I think instead I'll just stand here at the station. Presently another train will come by and I will get back on board again. You see, I haven't quite reached nirvana yet, but it's coming along now, getting nearer . . . I know it's out there somewhere. It's around the next bend.

All Pan Books are available at your local bookshop or newsagent, or can be ordered direct from the publisher. Indicate the number of copies required and fill in the form below.

Send to:	Macmillan General Books C.S. Book Service By Post PO Box 29, Douglas I-O-M IM99 1BQ
or phone:	01624 675137, quoting title, author and credit card number.
or fax:	01624 670923, quoting title, author, and credit card number.
or Internet:	http://www.bookpost.co.uk

Please enclose a remittance* to the value of the cover price plus 75 pence per book for post and packing. Overseas customers please allow £1.00 per copy for post and packing.

*Payment may be made in sterling by UK personal cheque, Eurocheque, postal order, sterling draft or international money order, made payable to Book Service By Post.

Alternatively by Access/Visa/MasterCard

Card No. ☐☐☐☐☐☐☐☐☐☐☐☐☐☐☐☐

Expiry Date ☐☐☐☐☐☐☐☐☐☐☐☐☐☐☐☐

Signature ____________________

Applicable only in the UK and BFPO addresses.

While every effort is made to keep prices low, it is sometimes necessary to increase prices at short notice. Pan Books reserve the right to show on covers and charge new retail prices which may differ from those advertised in the text or elsewhere.

NAME AND ADDRESS IN BLOCK CAPITAL LETTERS PLEASE

Name ____________________

Address ____________________

____

____

____

8/95

Please allow 28 days for delivery.
Please tick box if you do not wish to receive any additional information. ☐